Eileen

Memories of a Working-Class Girl in Depression and War

1919-1945

by

Eileen Baker

Published by
Robin and Gwyn Campbell

Published in 2006 by
Robin Campbell, 390 Heol Ganol,
Gendros, Abertawe/Swansea, SA5 8EN

A CIP catalogue record for this book is
available from the British Library.

ISBN 0-9542980-1-2
9780954298012

Printed and bound in Wales by
Dinefwr Press Ltd.
Rawlings Road, Llandybie
Carmarthenshire, SA18 3YD

*This book is dedicated
to the memory
of my husband Jack
and daughter Ruth*

CONTENTS

LIST OF ILLUSTRATIONS

COLOURED PHOTOGRAPHS
(between pages 144 & 145)

These oil paintings by Eileen illustrate some of her childhood memories:

At home in the Gurnos Cottages. Eileen can be seen reaching for her favourite toy, Sunny Jim, while Ronnie and her father busy themselves with the 'Cat's Whisker' listening set.

Eileen's memories of her mother coming home after scavenging for coke on the 'Patches' during the General Strike. The tin works and the Darren are in the background.

Jackie Jones (later Jackie Campbell and Eileen's husband) aged about three, sitting on the step of his house in Ystalyfera.

Towyn Farm where Eileen's grandparents were tenant farmers. Her grandmother is standing at the corner of the longhouse, while her grandfather is working in the field.

A train steaming into Ystalyfera Station where Eileen's father worked as a signalman.

FOREWORD

When Ruth, our eldest child and only daughter, died from cancer at the age of 39, the whole family was grief-stricken. While my husband Jack immersed himself in the Book of Job, I found myself remembering my early childhood and the wonderful love of my parents. The memories flooded back with such clarity that I felt as though I was a child again and I was inspired to put pen to paper. Jack encouraged me – and as he was, for a time, part of these memories, the whole experience helped us enormously. By the time Chapter Ten was completed, it was Christmas 1984, eight months after Ruth's death and I felt that it was time to stop. Little did I know that Jack would die suddenly in May 1985. Some time later I found that he had kept all my letters to him between 1936 and 1944, an invaluable resource for writing about those years. The first part of my autobiography was published as *Yan Boogie* in 1992. The years up to 1944 have now been added to complete this particular volume. I hope that you will enjoy reading the story of an ordinary working-class girl who lived through some extraordinary times.

My thanks goes to my immediate family, David, Gwyn, Robin and Huw, as well as my close friend Muriel, for their encouragement and help in producing the book. Also to Ken Dickinson who patiently reproduced many of my photographs.

Finally, a word to those generations of my family that will follow me. I hope that by reading this story, it will give you a better understanding of your roots and help enable you to appreciate what is good in life.

Eileen Campbell,
Swansea.
June 2006.

Chapter One

HOME

Eileen Baker
Pen-y-Gurnos Cottages
Lower Cwmtwrch
Swansea Valley
South Wales
Great Britain
Europe
The World

This is the long scrawl of an address I found the other day. It was written in childish handwriting in a yellowing copy book. Children today write similar addresses, but would add 'The Universe', 'Space', 'Outer Space' and goodness knows what else ! Yet that old address has special personal significance, for my brother Ronnie and myself spent our childhood in the Gurnos Cottages.

There were three attached cottages. Ours, the smallest, lay on the north side. These were 'Railway Cottages'. They had originally belonged to the Midland Railway, but as the latter had been incorporated by the L.M.S. (London, Midland and Scottish Railway) as early as 1921, we children considered the cottages and ourselves as 'belonging' to the L.M.S., and we were proud of the fact. Our line ran from St. Thomas' station, close to Swansea Docks, up the Tawe valley to Ystalyfera, before branching left up the Twrch valley as far as Brynamman. The L.M.S. in 1921 had also swallowed up the L.N.W.R. (London and North-Western Railway) whose Central Wales line, running from Swansea to Shrewsbury, could be reached by a short stretch of G.W.R. (Great Western Railway) line between Brynamman and Pantyffynnon. On free passes, we 'railway children' were granted access via this line to the wider world, even to Scotland. However, our allegiance was to the Valley and to the Gurnos Cottages. We first moved there late in 1919 after my father was appointed a signalman at Ystalyfera station. Ronnie was two years and nine months old at the time, and I was only six months. We remained in those cottages from 1919 until 1932, years of hardship, deprivation and poverty for the majority of ordinary people.

Memory sketch of Gunno's Cottage. Eileen Campbell

The Gurnos Cottages have now been pulled down and, on reflection, I have to admit that they were not really suitable for habitation. Ours was 'one up, one down', while the two larger adjoining cottages possessed two additional rooms, a parlour and a bedroom. From a wide path that passed by the cottages, two steps led down to a shorter pathway that, skirting a tiny square of garden, ran to our front door. This, in turn, opened almost immediately onto a steep flight of stairs. On the ground floor my father had constructed a thin partition with a door, that separated the living room from the front entrance and the stairs. In similar fashion, he had divided the upstairs into two bedrooms, a small one at the front for Ronnie and me and a larger one at the back for my parents. However, the total space was so small that the underside of my parents' bed was clearly visible as you climbed the stairs.

Our home was sacred and our neighbours felt the same about their houses. If something needed to be talked over with next door, or if we wished to play with other children, it was done on neutral ground – outside. Only on exceptional occasions did we enter one another's houses. This unwritten law did not stem from a wish to protect private property, but from the need we all felt for a place, no matter how small or humble, that we could call our own and where we could enjoy some privacy. Perhaps it was a reflection of this that outside the house Ronnie and I referred to our parents as 'mother' and 'father', whereas inside our home, as in our thoughts, they were always 'mammy' and 'daddy'.

My mother kept the cottage as clean as a new pin. Everything in the living room shone as a result of 'elbow grease'. The stone floor was covered with linoleum on top of which my mother laid a number of home-made rag mats. In the evenings, after the oil lamp had been lit, she would bring out her pile of mending and, when that was done, would resume work on her latest rag mat. She always sat in a low rocking chair in the corner opposite my father's chair, close to the banked-up fire. Beside her she would lay her assortment of cloth for sewing, mending, crocheting and mat making. She worked fluently on the mats with a special needle, rhythmically stitching strips of rag through the sugar sack which she had already slit open and washed. The glow of the fire played across her face and busy fingers. If his shift did not finish too late, my father would also be home, completing the family. And whatever the company, the big black kettle straddling the hob and fire sang constantly in the background.

The fireplace was the focal point of the living room. It was also my mother's kitchen. She would polish even the back of it with black lead. To one side lay the singing kettle and on the other, the square iron door of the oven. All her cooking was done either on top of the fire or in the oven – and she spent much of her time preparing food. There was always bread rising in the large earthenware bowl set before the fire, or delicious-smelling cakes and tarts cooking in the oven. Like most women of her time, my mother was an ingenious cook,

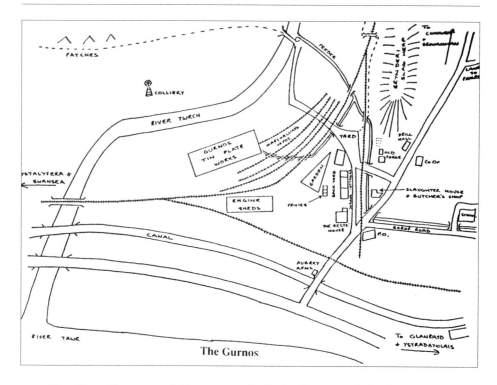

The Gurnos

capable of creating a meal from morsels. This she was obliged to do, for my father earned little and responsibility for the household budget rested upon her shoulders. For years, Ronnie used to carry a carefully prepared shopping list to a small grocer's shop in Ystalyfera, just across the Twrch bridge, where my mother did most of her shopping. She also bought through the nearby Co-op, both because of the 'divs' (dividends) and because it was Labour affiliated, while for minor purchases she used a local store that sold mainly clothes, boots and shoes, although some food was also for sale. One of my errands was to run to one of the shops on Gurnos Cross to buy fresh yeast, little bits of which I used to nibble on the return journey.

On Sundays, we enjoyed the traditional joint of prime beef, roast potatoes, Yorkshire pudding and gravy, but for the remainder of the week we lived on left-overs – soups or toast with dripping. The latter was delicious. Crouched before the evening fire toasting my mother's home-made bread was a treat in itself. We would smother the toast with beef dripping, sprinkle it with salt, then eat it slowly, savouring each mouthful as the dripping soaked into the thick toasted bread. It was a feast fit for a king ! I would also eagerly anticipate Monday's meal of 'bubble and squeak' which comprised a meat and vegetable fry-up of the remnants of Sunday's dinner. It was cooked in a large heavy frying pan over the fire until the underside had turned a crisp golden-brown. When it was ready, my mother would gently turn the frying pan upside down, expertly flipping its savoury contents onto a large hot plate. She would then slice it into portions for us. This was without doubt my favourite dinner of the week.

Except in summer, we always ate porridge for breakfast. We were not allowed fresh milk with it, but were given the choice of a teaspoonful of either Nestlé Milk or Demerara sugar – either way it tasted wonderful – administered by my mother. I was fascinated by the patterns created as they melted over the porridge. In the summer months, our breakfast regime changed as a cereal called 'Force' replaced porridge. Much later, after other cereals like 'Post Toasties' and 'Shredded Wheat' came onto the market, the latter became Ronnie's favourite, although I continued to prefer 'Force'. We were also given one orange a week.

Our Weekly Diet			
Weekday	*Breakfast*	*Dinner*	*Tea*
Monday	Cereal (summer) Porridge (winter)	Bubble and Squeak; Pudding (usually suet 'Roly-Poly'); Tea or water	Home-made cake with tea; Bread and butter or Dripping; (bedtime) cocoa with a little milk and boiling water
Tuesday	ditto	Minced Meat Pie with Potatoes top	ditto
Wednesday	ditto	Liver and bacon, tripe and onions; Cawl (winter); Pudding	ditto
Thursday	ditto	Soup with suet dumplings; Pudding	ditto
Friday	ditto	Fish (often in pie) with potatoes	ditto
Saturday	ditto	Bacon; Laver Bread; (Occasionally) Egg and chips	ditto
Sunday	ditto	Full Roast Beef and roast potatoes; Yorkshire Pudding, gravy and vegetables; Rice pudding or (for a treat) tinned fruit and custard; Tea or water	ditto

We ate well until 1932 mainly because:

1. Our mothers were good managers and wasted nothing – they could make a meal out of practically anything.
2. Meat, especially prime beef, was cheap – as were its products; suet, bones, lard (used for cooking and pastry).
3. Butter was also fairly cheap, although we used it sparingly. We looked down on margarine.

Monday was not only 'bubble and squeak' day, it was also 'wash day'. Indeed, washing the clothes took all day. All available floor space was used to sort the clothes into great piles which gradually diminished until every garment had been cleaned. Through a latched wooden door, opposite the cupboard under the stairs, one step led up into a 'lean-to' cold scullery. This housed a deep sink, a wooden draining board, and some shelves. Cold water was laid on, so the washing of clothes and dishes was done there. My mother boiled white clothes in a large iron cauldron on top of the fire, prodding them from time to time with a bleached-white rod of wood. Really dirty garments she would scrub with rough red blocks of 'Lifebuoy' soap on a ribbed board in the outside sink. She used the same brand of soap to scrub us with, and to this day Ronnie still buys 'Lifebuoy'. I love the clean smell of it. Occasionally, we used a brand of soap called 'Sunlight'. One of my tasks was washing-up, and here again 'Lifebuoy' was used. One of my earliest memories is being hoisted onto a chair next to the sink in order that I might wash the dishes. I thoroughly enjoyed the experience, though I must have taken hours and used up plenty of soap. I delighted in creating surface bubbles which I poured from dish to cup and back again, fascinated by their swaying forms and rainbow colours. Often I would pause to cup my hands and blow bubbles of my own. Invariably, I would end up soaking wet although my mother took the precaution of wrapping me in an ample apron and rolling my sleeves well up.

"Sunny Jim".

Back in those early days, my mother saved sufficient 'Force' packet coupons to exchange for the 'Force' mascot – a stuffed man-doll with a curiously firm pigtail projecting from the back of his head. He wore a hat and trousers, and sported a red waistcoat. His name was 'Sunny Jim' and we adored him. Every time our toy cupboard, high up at the side of the fireplace, was opened, he was the first to fall out, and invariably he was the last toy to be packed away.

Indeed, it was a joy just to open that cupboard. A thrill of anticipation would run through me whenever its door swung open, for pasted on its inner side by my mother were pictures the mere sight of which would transport me into a world of fantasy. We possessed few toys, for money was scarce. Ronnie's favourite was Meccano which he collected little by little over the years until he amassed enough pieces to enable him to construct some remarkable models. Once, with the aid of my father's tools, he built a working model grass-cutter. In similar fashion, he built up quite a collection of Hornby trains.

Then there was the radio. This started as my father's hobby, but Ronnie quickly grew to share his enthusiasm. They commenced with a 'Cat's Whisker' listening set. I was more enthralled with the name, which I would repeat endlessly to myself, than with the set itself. The two of them would listen intently on headphones while my father carefully adjusted the controls to improve reception. Together they would pour over the latest 'blue-print' spread over the kitchen table. My father once constructed a set with a backward sloping panel, knobs on the outside and valves hidden inside. I copied it in cardboard, making several miniature sets which I took to school and gave to the poorest children. As poverty was widespread, this meant those dressed literally in rags. In pursuit of the perfect radio, my father and Ronnie would travel down to Swansea for spare parts. Whenever they did this, they always brought an inexpensive present back for my mother and me. Quite often, I would get a tiny celluloid doll. I collected miniature dolls which my imagination would transform into real people, tiny adults or children, according to my fancy. One time they might be school children and I would teach them, distributing minute books to my class. Other times, they would be customers in my draper's shop. From scraps of my mother's material, I would fashion sets of tiny garments and stack them in neat piles, as in a shop. I used to make up identical sets of diminutive pyjama trousers and tops, dresses and coats, as well as having rolls of material which could be bought by the 'yard'. These would be placed on wooden struts, to the back of the downstairs partition, that formed the shop 'shelves'. The kitchen table was the 'counter' and I knelt on the sofa between to serve my customers. One day, Ronnie constructed for me a Meccano cable that carried the shop takings overhead to an imaginary chief cashier, just as happened in the big Swansea stores. Another time, my father bought me minute shiny bone-china animals. Later still, he brought home boxes of crayons: The first were made of wax, but were soon replaced by lovely subtle-coloured Reeves' pastels, which have remained favourites of mine down the years. On one memorable occasion, my father arrived home with a cylindrical box full of rainbow-coloured pencils. They had newly arrived in Woolworths which boasted 'Nothing in this store over 6d' !

Brother Ronnie aged about 5 and Eileen, aged about 3.

That long leather-bound sofa of ours was a boon. Apart from constituting a major prop for our fantasies, it was functional in a house possessing few chairs. For special occasions, like birthday parties, it could seat up to six children and was once used as a downstairs bed, when I contracted Scarlet Fever. That was the only time that I remember my grandmother from Pontardawe coming to visit us in the Gurnos. Around her neck she wore a fur at which our cat arched his back and hissed. It was after I had recovered somewhat, and was playing in my favourite corner on the floor, that 'Whooper-in' knocked at the front door. 'Whooper-in' was the nickname we children gave him. He was in fact the 'Whipper-in', the official truant catcher appointed by the School Board. He questioned me briefly, hinting that as I was sufficiently well to be playing,

I should be back at school. However, my mother gave him short shrift and he did not stay long.

In addition to the lean-to scullery, my father had built a shed at the back of the cottage in which he stacked wooden blocks that he had sawn from discarded but well-preserved railway sleepers. Next to these were heaps of coal and coal dust, and a mound of clay. Finally, the shed contained all his implements, including gardening tools. My father's back garden was triangular in shape and, stretching beyond the three privies that served our cottages, was sandwiched between the main railway line and the tin plate works branch of the 'feeders'. On returning home from his eight hour shift, my father would rest briefly before entering the garden, where he stayed for as long as he could. He grew as many vegetables as possible on his plot, succeeding in keeping us supplied with one variety or another for most of the year.

Those privies, on reflection, were primitive – mere holes in the ground! Later, just before we moved from the Gurnos, and mainly due to repeated representations by my father, they were replaced by water closets which, in comparison, were luxurious. Even so, the tank water always froze in winter – and so did we. I used to suffer agonies there in the morning having to sit and wait as the 8.45 train whistled, signalling the last possible departure time for us if we were to reach school on time.

To the front and rear of the cottage we had both 'feeders' and railway lines. The former tapped the river Twrch; one 'feeder' ran through a deep gully beside my father's plot before disappearing under the railway track, while a second 'feeder', in which water flowed like a stream, passed the front of the cottage, following the shunter rails that ran down to Gurnos Cross and beyond to the neighbourhood tin works and collieries. It was into this water that the slaughter house waste was jettisoned. The smell lured the rats who swarmed from their holes in the side of the 'feeder' stream. We children often stood in silence on the banks watching them. But we possessed a wonderful cat. Coloured black, save for a fleck of white under his chin, he was adored by all except my father who merely tolerated him. His name was 'Tiddles' and, as I cannot remember a time when he was not with us, he must have arrived in the household as a kitten. And what a ratter he was! Seldom content with one trophy, his usual catch was three rats. He would carry them to the front door and lay them there. More often than not this occurred before dawn, my mother discovering the bodies when she first opened the front door. Her praise was nectar to that cat. I can see him now when, as a reward, my mother poured him a saucer full of milk – proud and purring, he wrapped himself so tightly around my mother's legs as to almost trip her.

Chapter Two

FAMILY

The cat could not have been happier than Ronnie and myself in that cottage and its immediate neighbourhood – our personal patch of territory. Our home contained all that a child could wish for and our parents' love enveloped us in a warm blanket of happiness and security. I was always my father's girl, and Ronnie my mother's boy. Not that such distinctions materially affected the love we felt for each other as family. But I would love to clamber up onto my father's knees and cuddle up close. There I would play with his watch and chain which, formed by links won in the annual Railway Ambulance competition, increased in length each year. My favourite place in the house was in the corner behind my father's upright wooden chair. There, on one of my mother's rag mats, I spent many a happy hour. I can remember, way back, crawling over and under the bar beneath my father's chair, emerging unexpectedly between his feet to startle him. In return, he would surprise Ronnie and me by coming home occasionally as if empty-handed. He would stand there searching his pockets, first on the outside, then on the inside of his jacket until, as if by chance, he discovered something for both of us.

Just to know that my father was at home gave us a warm feeling – even if we were playing outside. On one such occasion, someone came running down the slope from the slaughter house shouting that a bull had escaped and was on the loose. What a commotion! All the children quickly scampered indoors. As soon as Ronnie and I had reached the safety of home, my father locked the gate, the front door, and the two front windows. Then we rushed upstairs to watch events from the window. It was true. The poor beast, head lowered and bellowing, came running down the incline towards our cottages. He was closely pursued by a score of stick brandishing men with ropes. Gates were hurriedly secured at the crossing, shunting track and the path which skirted Brynderi tips. Cornered, the bull was quickly captured and dragged mercilessly back up the hill. Following that incident, the weekly flush of blood from the slaughter house lost its fascination for me. Another time when my father was at home embedded itself in my memory. A number of us were playing, jumping to and fro across the 'stream' in front of the house when I happened to look up at the bedroom window. My mother stood there, watching us. We waved to her happily. She looked lovely framed in that window, in her white petticoat and her long brown hair hanging freely over her shoulders. We turned back to our game. A small boy, making his way up the valley, joined us. He jumped, but not far enough, and fell awkwardly into the water. My mother, who had witnessed the incident, rushed from the cottage with her long hair and white petticoat flowing. At the stream she reached down, gathered the little boy up in her arms, and carried him back to the cottage where she laid him on the sofa. There, my father examined him for broken bones, but found that he was only slightly hurt. Soon, his clothes were dry, his cuts and grazes treated, and he was on his way home. That was the only time I saw my mother both wearing a petticoat and with her hair down. It is a vision I treasure.

Although I used to enjoy the times we as a family spent indoors, I would keenly look forward to the Spring and Summer holidays and the occasional family outing. These were necessarily rare because of the long hours and shift

Ronnie and Eileen, Gurnos Cottages, c.1925.

nature of my father's work. Outside his holidays the furthest we managed to go together was the Mumbles and, more frequently, Swansea. Inevitably, Swansea with my father turned into a shopping trip, with Woolworths the main depository for our burning coppers. My earliest recollection of the town is being hoisted by my father onto the window sill of a building – possibly a bank – at the bottom of Wind Street, in order that a street photographer might take my picture.

Nearer home, he would sometimes accompany us on picnics up the Palleg. This foothill of the Black Mountains was bare, supporting only a few farmers who rode horseback to round up their scattered sheep. The hills could be treacherous if mists descended, and storms could rapidly fill the narrow, steep sided Twrch valley. To reach the Palleg we took the main Cwmtwrch to Bryn-amman road as far as the Welfare Grounds, before turning off onto the mountain track as far as the Gwys river. There, the flat riverside grassland, shaded by bushes, formed the perfect picnic spot. There were plenty of dry twigs to light a fire for our tin kettle, and we overlooked the clear Gwys water as it flowed around boulders and splashed the edges of a small pebbled beach.

It was somewhere up on the Palleg that 'Benny the Milk' had his farm. A bilingual Welshman, he was the only milkman in our area. Every morning, with a handsome horse, and a trap sturdy enough to carry the heavy milk churns he packed into it, he descended into the valley to do his round. From the side of the trap and from the churns hung by their handles a variety of metal measures that he used to ladle out precisely the volume of milk each of his customers wanted. Benny was a great character, always willing to joke with us children. Ronnie and I used to wait for him in the summer months when occasionally my mother would permit us to invite him in for a cup of tea. However, she rarely bought milk from him, preferring to use Nestlé because it was cheaper. Sometimes, we accompanied my mother on visits to my father's signal box at Ystalyfera Station. To reach him, we had to pass through the station building itself, walk the length of the platform, cross the lines, and then climb up the wooden steps leading to his box. On the way,

Father in his Signal Box, Ystalyfera Station, 17th October 1940.

we invariably met and greeted some of his colleagues. We only went there in the company of my mother on special occasions, and it was a real treat for us to see my father at work. We would watch as he wrapped a cloth around his hand in order to grasp the signal levers, as he exchanged 'tablets' with the drivers of passing engines, or as he conversed by telephone with the next signalman up or down line – giving and receiving information about passenger and freight traffic which would afterwards be noted in meticulous detail. When things were quiet, he would smilingly respond to our torrent of questions. The place was full of unique signal box smells, and strange, fascinating objects – many, like the levers, made of gleaming brass. There was also his signalling lamp and, stretched along one wall, an oblong map displaying the rail and points complex for which father was responsible. During his break, he would seize the opportunity to brew up on his spotless stove. Unlike my mother, he would pour the tea before adding milk. The two of them would always engage in gentle banter as to which of them made the better tasting tea. We children enjoyed it simply because we were happy to be there.

Our parents were soft spoken and cross words were rare. In all the years we lived in the Gurnos, I recall but one occasion when my father really lost his temper. It was a dark wintry evening when he was out, either at work or attending a meeting. My mother had banked up the fire with anthracite and 'pele' (small balls of coal and clay) to make the room extra warm in preparation for giving us a bath. It must have been a Friday. The tin bath, with its high curving back to ward off draughts, was ready in front of the fire. I was first in, and my mother had just knelt down to scrub my back when there was a knock at the door. "That can't be daddy", my mother exclaimed, "he's got his key." She rose and quickly went to the door. It was a travelling salesman who came round periodically, his suitcase crammed with wares. It was an odd time to call, but my mother felt obliged to ask him in to avoid losing all the heat. My back was already feeling the cold. My mother ordered me to stand up – I felt acutely embarrassed in front of the stranger – and hurriedly wrapped a warm towel around me. Simultaneously, she asked the intruder to leave and return another day at a more suitable daylight hour. Ignoring her, the man placed his case on the table and proceeded to unpack its contents, at the same time maintaining a smooth sales patter which was accompanied by familiar glances at my mother. He even announced that he had presents for Ronnie and me, producing two fish hooks complete with a tiny feather. I wondered what use they could be as the only fishing we did was in the stream outside where we trapped tiddlers in jam jars. It was at that moment that my father returned home. He summed up the situation immediately. I had never before seen my father angry. That salesman was out of the front door before he had time to push everything back into his case. He never did come back.

25

How cosy it was in that little cottage of an evening, when all four of us were present. In the winter months especially, it seemed sometimes that we were completely cut off from the world, secure in a familial cocoon. We had no difficulty keeping ourselves happily occupied. Frequently, the nights would pass in studied silence as we busied ourselves with our respective hobbies. My mother kept an old scrapbook that bulged with cuttings. Apart from mundane pastings like recipes, household hints, and patterns, it also contained some delightfully illustrated verse, and anything else that took my mother's fancy. She allowed us to flip through it sometimes, but one day someone borrowed the scrapbook and it was never returned, much to my mother's grief. The borrower denied all knowledge of the book and my mother felt she could do nothing further to retrieve it.

My father, too, possessed a special book. It was large, thick, and full of coloured plates of railway engines and carriages, with their company arms displayed. He had had the volume bound and, whenever we were permitted to look through it, Ronnie and I handled it with the greatest care. How I wish I knew where that book is now. I hope against hope that it will turn up some day. I was also fascinated by another of my father's treasured books – an illustrated anatomy textbook. As an 'ambulance' man, he was already proficient in 'First Aid', but wished to expand his knowledge as much as he could. It was an

Winning the Shield. The St. John's Ambulance Team with George Baker
standing at the far right of the picture (1940s).

unusual book in that it had transparent sheets between the layered coloured plates of the human anatomy. The volume opened to display a naked torso. As each transparency was lifted, first the skin, then other parts of the body were progressively peeled to show muscles and ligaments, followed by internal organs, and finishing with the skeleton. It was a marvellous teaching aid. Then there were the books we obtained in exchange for tokens in the *Daily Herald*. They had on offer the Everyman series of books on a wide variety of topics – we obtained from them *Everyman's Guide to Home Medicine* and a complete set of Dickens. These, my father read avidly, but I found them too difficult at the time.

The *Daily Herald* also carried a children's corner which attracted both Ronnie and me. Its characters, Bobby Gear, Maisie Mouse and Ruby Rabbit, rapidly became intimate friends of ours. If possible, our parents would send off for the *Bobbie Bear Annual* as a joint Christmas present for us. Ronnie and I also had a particular book of nursery rhymes in which I delighted. One of the rhymes went:

> What are little boys made of?
> What are little boys made of?
> Slugs and snails and puppy dogs' tails
> That's what little boys are made of.

Little girls, of course, were 'sugar and spice and all things nice'! I teased Ronnie so much about those verses that he became quite upset and rubbed away at the print until nothing remained of that part of the rhyme but a hole. Besides, he had his own back in another way whenever my mother quoted the line of another rhyme which went, 'Good enough and tidy new'. I was 'Good enough', and Ronnie 'Tidy new'. I do not know where she learnt that line, but whenever I did something in a slip-shod manner, my mother would say, "There goes 'Good Enough' again"! Reading soon became a consuming passion with Ronnie and me. Besides books and comics, our parents bought for us *Arthur Mee's Encyclopaedia*. The final and largest volume was called 'A Hundred and One Wonderful Things'. It was an absolute treasure house of short stories, puzzles, instructions for making models, and a host of other interesting items. I also loved reading *Mill on the Floss*, *Lorna Doone* and *Tess of the Durbervilles*.

We often played family games of an evening. The oil lamp, set in the centre of the table around which we would seat ourselves, had a broad yet delicate china shade which suffused a beautiful light throughout the small room while also vividly illuminating the table top. My parents were excellent card players and taught us many games. These included whist, rummy and 'Strip Jack Naked', while patience, of course, filled many an odd minute. Then there was

Father standing at our front gate, Gurnos Cottages, c.1925. Behind him, on the left, can be seen a much larger house belonging to a miner.

Ludo, draughts, dominoes and 'Snakes and Ladders'. In addition, we possessed a horse racing game which I loved for the life-like cardboard models of horses which were set firmly in wooden bases.

Occasionally, my father would play records. I can faintly recall an old horn gramophone which was replaced by a large square 'His Masters Voice' one, which had a lid, a hole in the side for the handle, and the famous picture of a dog on the front. Only my father was allowed to touch that gramophone and the records. He handled them with great caution, taking care never to over wind the handle, brushing the records free of dust before placing them on the turntable, and using each needle once only. Due to these precautions, he eventually built up a fine library of records in good condition and of great variety – song and ballad as well as light and classical music. Any money he was able to put by for himself, my father would spend on buying records or improving his radio. He grew to appreciate classical music mostly through Ronnie's love of it, and we were early introduced to great composers like Wagner, Beethoven and Mozart. Of the singers, Harry Lauder was a favourite with us, my father being particularly fond of him singing 'Keep right on to the end of the road'. We also liked John McCormack and Gracie Fields. When I was very young, I loved a record called 'The Dance of the Elephants', though I have never heard it since, nor have I been able to discover the name of the composer. My favourite record of all, and possibly the first one I can remember, was called 'Mignon'. It was a short, lively piece which, in those early days, was played frequently. When Ronnie was very young – I was a few years younger than him – he used a language of his own. When the tune 'Mignon' was played, Ronnie put his own words to it, skipping round singing, "Oh Yan Boogie, you is nice, oo oo oo oo oo oo oooo !", 'Yan Boogie' being me. From my earliest days, that was his pet name for me and I loved it.

Snatches of song come to mind as I think back, but I cannot tell whether I picked them up from the records or from my mother who used to sing to us often. I remember songs like 'Little Dolly Daydream, Pride of Idaho', 'I don't want to play in your yard, I don't love you any more'. 'She's the Lily of Laguna – She's my Lily, she's my Rose', 'Hold out your hand, you naughty boy !', 'In the twi-twi twi-light', 'She sells sea shells on the sea shore' and many others. My mother also had a repertoire of 1914-18 war songs like 'It's a long way to Tipperary', 'Let the Great Big World Keep Turning', 'Keep the home fires burning' and 'Good bye-ee'. The Great War was a recent and meaningful event for my parents. My father had joined the Royal Navy, but was quickly invalided out with chest trouble and spent some time in Plymouth Naval Hospital. However, for Ronnie and me, the Great War was already part of history. In our very early childhood, my mother used to play her violin. But after the 'Cat's Whisker' arrived, her playing diminished for my father tolerated no other noise when he was tuning his radio. However, she would bring it out before the 'English Cong' chapel competitions when, with infinite patience, she would teach me the set piece, instructing me where to breathe and pause, and how to master the most intricate phrases. On reflection, it is a great pity that she eventually forsook the violin altogether.

Every night at bedtime, after we had hugged and kissed our father, my mother would take us upstairs. She would tuck us in and hear us recite our prayers, singing with us the final one:

> Jesus, Tender Shepherd, hear me,
> Bless Thy little lamb tonight,
> Through the darkness, be Thou near me,
> Keep me safe 'till morning light.
>
> Amen

Sometimes, my father would then play records. It was lovely to lie in bed lulled by the music drifting up through the floorboards. As one record finished, we would call for another until we succumbed and fell asleep. When I was young I always felt thirsty after going to bed, so I used to cry out for water. There was in vogue at the time a gramophone record of a small child calling out to his parents in just the same way – and my parents bought it! Someone recently told me that the song was *Mommy, Gimme a Drinka Water* by Danny Kaye.

Once asleep, I used to have two recurrent nightmares. In the first, I dreamt that I was falling into a pit, swirling round in ever decreasing circles in the darkness until, as I was about to hit the bottom of the shaft, I would wake up screaming. In the second nightmare, the canal burst its banks at Ynyscedwyn, near Ystradgynlais, flooding the surrounding area and sweeping back up the valley to the Gurnos, where we lived. I often used to gaze up at the embankment, wondering if it was sufficiently strong to contain the water. But I never spoke of this to anyone, and I suppose it was my suppressed fears which re-emerged in my dream. As with the first nightmare, I would wake up screaming until my parents came. They would take me into their bed where I would soon sink into a secure sleep. Those occasions must have tried their patience, but they never displayed any anger or annoyance.

Chapter Three

MY MOTHER'S SIDE

My mother, Charlotte Jones, had a typical Welsh complexion, and rich brown eyes, set wide apart, to match her hair. Like most adults, she wore false teeth, having lost the originals due to pyorrhoea of the gums when she was a teenager. She was brought up in Clydach, Neath and Pontardawe. Her family was Welsh and when my father started courting my mother, he was not made welcome in their home. Even on the morning of their wedding at St. Peter's Parish Church in Pontardawe, my grandparents forced my mother to complete her usual chore of scrubbing down the steps from their kitchen door to the outside path. And this ill-feeling continued after they married. Grandfather Jones never came to visit us in the Gurnos, and my grandmother rarely.

The relatives on my mother's side with whom we were most friendly were the family of her youngest sister, our Auntie Edith. Like my mother she had married an Englishman – Uncle Jim came from Radnorshire. With their son Harry they lived in the tiny village of Rhydyfro, about eight miles from the Gurnos and two miles up a steep valley road from Pontardawe. When we visited them in the early days, we travelled to Pontardawe by train and the rest of the way on foot. We found it quite a climb from my grandparents' house. It was a notoriously dangerous road, especially the first stage up Gelli-gron hill. As we walked, my mother would warn us to keep well away from the low wall that separated the narrow pavement from the deep ravine below. "People have been known to fall and kill themselves" she would tell us repeatedly. Later, buses came to the valley, running from Neath to Pontardawe and Gwaun-cae-gurwen.

What a welcome we used to receive in Rhydyfro, both from our relations and from their neighbours ! Auntie Edith's family lived in the first of a row of about ten small terraced houses positioned on a sharp bend on the main road. After motorised vehicles came into use, that immediate locality became dangerous. When we first arrived at her house, Auntie Edith would let us in the 'front' way. This caused a real commotion for a long chenille curtain, which hung on the inside of the front door to keep out the draught, had to be carefully drawn back before the door could be opened. Thereafter, we used the side door and, in addition, had to wipe our feet !

Eileen's mother in her early 40s with Ronnie, c.1934.

After arriving in Rhydyfro, an early visit to Mrs Arnold's General Shop, across the road from Auntie Edith's house, was high on our list of priorities. As soon as initial greetings were over, Ronnie, cousin Harry and I were given coppers, let out of the side door, and scooted across the road to her shop. There, arrayed both in rows of bottles lining the front of the counter and stacked in nearby boxes, were amongst the most mouth-watering sweets we children had ever seen. Mrs Arnold always welcomed us as if we were long lost friends, although she knew from experience that she was in for a lengthy wait as we deliberated how we could obtain the most for our money – quantity and not quality being our chief criterion. So, big woman that she was, she settled her weight onto an upturned cask and knitted. I used to peep at her between sweet bottles for she had a moustache and a few bristly hairs projecting from her chin. Not that her looks worried her – she was one of the jolliest women I ever knew. Moreover, she was boss in her house, possessing a husband who was rarely to be seen. She possessed a booming voice and would roar out "Mrs Reynolds" from across the road whenever she wanted to see Auntie Edith. The fact that the entire row could hear Mrs Arnold's summons would greatly embarrass Auntie Edith who was prim and proper, but there was absolutely nothing she could do about it.

During the summer holidays, Mrs Arnold used to organise picnics on the nearby Gellionen Mountain. On one or two occasions we joined her party, and how we enjoyed ourselves ! Although we never started out until after dinner, it seemed that the mountain would claim us for an entire day. Armed with food and 'pop', we set off in crocodile fashion up the main road to the end of the village. There, we forked left onto the track that ascended the mountain. Mrs Arnold was the undisputed leader of the expedition. She joked and sang all the way up, as well as on the return trip, and soon had everyone joining in music hall favourites like 'Come, come, come and make eyes at me, down at the old Bull and Bush', 'Knees up Mother Brown', 'It's a long way to Tipperary', and 'Pack up your troubles in your old kit bag'. On reaching the picnic spot, we children were free to roam while the group of mothers were busily occupied chatting and laying out tablecloths. We had been told that ancient monuments existed somewhere on the mountain and we set off in search of them. Indeed, we were convinced that we found traces of them. Once the voices of our mothers had died away in the distance it was all so quiet. The air was pure and only a ripple of breeze or the occasional call of a bird disturbed the silence. It was almost as if time stood still – that is until the booming voice of Mrs Arnold summoned us to the feast.

Back in Rhydyfro, Auntie Edith was always very fussy about her home. There was never a speck of dust to be seen and everything was in its proper place – china ornaments abounded and everywhere brass shone like burnished gold. She became quite upset if anything disturbed her order of things so that I would be afraid even to sit down until given directions. However, Auntie Edith possessed such an amiable nature overall that we accepted her fussiness. Next to the living room fire was the usual oven, though she used it for little more than boiling the kettle as she possessed a gas stove in the back kitchen which she used for cooking. Surrounding the fireplace were many of her gleaming brass ornaments. Although the living room was small and the stairs ascended directly from it to the first floor, it was charming. Auntie Edith loved aesthetic furniture and materials, although it was my mother who did most of the needlework for her.

When my mother was seriously ill and had been taken to my grandparents in Pontardawe, I stayed for a short time with Auntie Edith. I remember attending the tiny village school and one day accompanying our teacher to collect black-berry bush twigs. We chose with care, for they had to possess both leaves and fruit. On returning to the school, we had great fun drawing the twigs with their foliage and berries – we rarely had drawing lessons in the Gurnos school. Also, during school holidays, or at weekends, we sometimes stayed at Rhydyfro. I vividly recall the sound of men arriving in the dead of night, or so it seemed to me, to empty the latrine buckets. Firstly, I would hear the clip-clop of horse and cart grow steadily closer and louder until it stopped outside my auntie's house. Then, the faint light from a lantern flickered on the bedroom wall and I heard the muffled voices of men. In a strange way, their presence was simultaneously eerie and comforting. For some considerable time they came to and fro, for they were obliged to use Auntie Edith's side entrance to gain access to the privies which stood at the top of the gardens of the row of houses.

Uncle Jim was a pleasant, unassuming man who worked as a road-man on the steep valley route from Pontardawe up past Rhydyfro and towards Gwaun-cae-gurwen. He had the reputation of being the finest road-man for miles around and he was also an excellent gardener. It was a real joy to visit his garden which was reached from the back of the house by climbing five or six steep stone steps and then, at roof level, turning sharp right through a little wooden gate. Like my father's plot in the Gurnos, Uncle Jim's garden was triangular in shape, but was prettier than ours which was surrounded by railway lines, gullies, the privies of neighbours and a large black corrugated-iron shed. One side of Uncle Jim's garden was separated from the main road by a thick privet hedge which was sufficiently high to prevent us children from looking over. This was just as well as the hedge was perched on the edge of a walled embankment which dropped steeply to the narrow pavement and road beneath. The widest section of the garden ran from the corner of the hedge nearest the front of the house and along the side of the house. It then extended about fifty yards from the back of the house, eventually tapering to a point. A network of narrow paths divided the garden into a number of plots, in which grew flowers as well as sufficient vegetables for Uncle Jim, like my father, to provide for his family's needs.

Somehow the food at Auntie Edith's always tasted better than at home. Being the smallest, I was always made to sit for meals in the recess under the stairs where the table was normally stored. This was quite a novelty and I enjoyed scrutinising the underside of the stairs. Auntie Edith made a lot of apple tarts which we ate with custard. The pastry was much whiter and softer than that cooked by my mother – an effect, I later discovered, that was achieved by using more than the normal volume of water and by undercooking – and we considered it delicious. We likewise relished my auntie's herbal beer that she brewed in a number of cloth-covered stone jars in the large scullery adjoining her living room. Two of the jars always contained beer ready for consumption. Auntie Edith's house was considerably larger than our cottage in the Gurnos, which on winter evenings gave us more scope for amusing ourselves than by simply playing cards. Auntie Edith allowed us children into the scullery, and it was there that Ronnie and Harry would put on Magic Lantern shows and where the three of us would perform surprise plays which the adults would bear with true stoicism. The memory of one of our productions still gives me a certain satisfaction. It was 'The Crucifixion', and I was chosen to play the part of Christ. Ronnie and Harry toiled all day to make a cross which, at the hour of the performance, they laid upon the scullery floor. I was then fastened securely to it by my wrists and ankles, and raised into the air before the shocked gaze of our audience. I remember my unsupported belly flopping forward. We were most proud of this one-off production, despite the numerous hitches that occurred.

As an only child, Harry possessed his own bedroom, over the scullery. He had long wanted wallpaper with animal motifs, but it took a long while before my mother and Auntie Edith eventually found something they considered to be appropriate – a wide frieze covered with animal scenes. I saw it and thought that it was lovely. So one Saturday, unbeknown to Harry, they pasted white paper onto his four bedroom walls, and then the frieze as a border all around the top. When they had finished, Auntie Edith called Harry up, with Ronnie and I following in his wake. I was delighted by the effect, but not so Harry. He had anticipated finding animal scenes completely covering the walls, and burst out crying.

For years, Ronnie, Harry and myself were equals, inseparable in play. Then one day the inevitable happened. The two boys had spent the day constructing a trolley while I watched. It comprised a four-wheeled frame onto which were nailed four pieces of wood, two on top to form seats, and two beneath to act as foot rests. They then fitted it with a swivel handle attached to a length of rope by which to steer. When they had finished, they took the two-man trolley several miles into the hills behind Rhydyfro for a trial run on the steepest slopes. For the first time, our threesome was broken as I was left behind anxiously awaiting their return. They eventually reappeared, but from that day something in our association had snapped irrevocably – things were never to be the same again.

Ronnie and I saw our other cousins from time to time. Uncle Ellis, Auntie Nellie and their four children lived in Trebanos. They too were a lovely family – quiet and gentle. Uncle Ellis, who was very tall and broad of shoulder, but thin, formed a stark contrast to Auntie Nelly who was short and plump. Of our cousins, Connie was the eldest, followed by the two boys, and finally the youngest, Betty, who owned the darkest, flashing eyes I have ever seen. I wish that we had had more opportunity to meet them all. Occasionally, we would visit our cousin Lydia, the only child of Auntie Mary Anna and Uncle Ivor. Auntie Mary Anna who, like Uncle Ellis of Trebanos, possessed a high, flute-like voice, had so fragile and delicate a body that I felt a breath of wind would have blown her away. Only once did they visit us in the Gurnos, an occasion which was to prove a disaster for poor Lydia. Ronnie and I took her up to the Welfare Ground to play on the swings, slide, roundabout, and on the metal horse from which she fell heavily on her face, cracking one of her front teeth diagonally in half. In those days, nothing was done in such cases and poor Lydia carried that broken tooth for years, a souvenir of her visit to us.

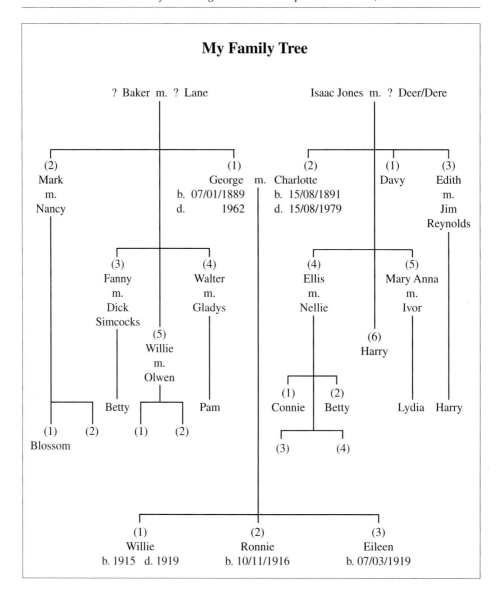

My Family Tree

Other relatives of my mother we met even more rarely. Her eldest brother, Uncle Davy – I cannot recall the name of his wife – was so much older than her that we never met his children who had already grown up and moved away. I can also just remember her youngest brother who, like Auntie Edith's son, was called Harry. He was the last to leave home, and I recall visiting my grandparents' house in Pontardawe when he still lived with them. He was six foot tall and a keen middle-weight boxer. I once told him that I did not like the thought of him hitting anyone, or of someone else knocking him about. He burst out laughing and, picking me up, thrust me high above his head. My mother was very fond of Uncle Harry, treasuring a photograph she possessed of him posing in boxing shorts and gloves. He joined the Indian Army but, unfortunately, Tunney's defeat of Jack Dempsey in America, on the very day he left, eclipsed the drama of his departure. He must have gone on to be a champion boxer in India for when, years later, he returned home, he brought with him many silver trophies.

Not long after Uncle Harry left for India, my mother became ill. Unable to care for her at home, my father took her to my grandparents in Pontardawe. They fetched in a young doctor who lived in the same street as them, and he diagnosed that she had 'Sugar Diabetes'. He used white cards to write out what food and drink she could and could not consume. She was permitted soda water, and I recall my astonishment when my father immediately went out and bought a 'soda water syphon'. I had never seen anything like it in my life before, but was destined to see many more before my mother recuperated. While she was ill, I stayed for some time with Auntie Edith, but for all that I loved Rhyd-yfro, it was wonderful when my mother had sufficiently recovered to return home, and we were all together once more in our little cottage in the Gurnos. Soon, everything was back to normal, but we never again took my mother for granted. We helped her in every way we could, and I remember taking upon myself the responsibility for her welfare. For a long time, I kept checking to ensure that she was still with us, and that she looked well.

We all felt grateful to our grandparents for taking my mother in and caring for her, but I never enjoyed visiting them in Pontardawe. My grandmother suffered from a chronically weak chest so, every other Saturday morning, my mother and Auntie Edith took turns to do some housework for her. When it was my mother's 'turn', she, Ronnie and I would catch an early train from Ystaly-fera to Pontardawe Station, from where we walked to 15 Quarr Road. After exchanging greetings, my mother would unload a basket of goodies for grand-mother. Then, without more ado, she would don her apron and start work. I had my part to play too, and I dreaded it. I was despatched to my grandparents' bed-room upstairs to complete two sickening tasks. Firstly, I had to empty the chamber pot. This entailed crawling underneath the great double bed, dragging the full chamber pot out, and then carrying it to the lavatory across the landing. The stench alone made me feel unwell but, even worse, the pot was always so full that, try as I might, I could neither avoid getting my thumbs wet nor spilling it. Once the chamber pot had been emptied, I had to clamber underneath the bed once more to dust the floor. I was used to helping my mother dust at home in the Gurnos, but this was different. Under my grandparents' bed there was invariably so much whitish fluff mixed with dust that the duster quickly filled and I was obliged to do several trips. I would stand on a chair to shake the dust out of the bedroom window but some of the hated stuff would inevitably stick to my clothes. The memory of this, as well as of the stench of the chamber pot, remains with me.

I would always want to leave for home as soon as possible, but we usually waited in order to see my grandfather. Between the table, laid for one, and the kitchen fire, stood his empty chair. Waiting on the hob, over a saucepan of hot water, lay a covered plate on which had been stacked a huge meal of beef, vegetables, and potatoes. As the time of his arrival approached, my grandmother would grow more anxious, flitting about the room and sighing heavily. We could tell his measured step the moment he turned off the road onto the side path leading to the kitchen. He was very tall and gaunt, possessing fine facial bones over which his shiny skin was tightly drawn. His eyes, sunk deep in their sockets, were so laden with fatigue that we rarely glimpsed them properly, but when we did, they pierced us like bores. I was terrified of him, but Ronnie did not share my fear and got on well with him.

My mother once told me that when she was a child in Neath, my grand-parents were well respected as they not only owned the house they lived in, but also possessed a shop. My mother would sit in the front window of the shop demonstrating what was then a new machine for making socks and stockings, while passers-by would gather to watch. In those days, their family were regular Baptists, and my grandfather was as ardent a teetotaller as he was a chapel-goer. However, as my grandfather's employer was an Anglican and insisted that his workmen attend his church, the entire family was obliged to sit through the service at the Church of England before going to chapel. My mother did not mind particularly, except for the fact that when marching into church they were obliged to follow the pauper boys from the Workhouse !

My grandparents moved from Neath to Clydach, then to Pontardawe. It was when my grandfather took a job in the new tin plate works there that he took to drink, which in turn proved the ruin of him. On pay day, he would fritter away his weekly wages in the various public houses that lined the route home. No wonder my grandmother sighed as she did. Yet, for all that, they had salvaged something, for their house in Quarr Road was paid for. Moreover, my grand-father was a man of some culture. He was very well read and their house, though dismal, was full of reading matter; the cupboards bulged with books, and maga-zines lay in piles on the middle room floor. He started to buy monthly editions of *Harmsworth's Encyclopaedia* before the First World War. In those days he had them bound, but when I knew him, he would merely stack them on the floor. He must have thought a lot of Ronnie because, when my brother passed the scholarship into Maesydderwen School, he gave him his entire collection of Harmsworth – a treasure house of information from which I also benefited. We were further informed by my mother that her father was what is commonly referred to as a 'Quack Doctor', although he was actually skilled in the use of herbal medicines, which he kept secure in a triangular cupboard high up in the kitchen. He was particularly renowned for his success in treating leg ulcers. He was also a staunch Liberal, and had an enormous sepia photograph of Gladstone hung on one of the kitchen walls.

Yet my abiding memory is of the oppressive smells, sounds and sights in their dismal house; of the rank chamber pot, my grandmother's eternal sighing, and the stench of drink on my grandfather. I could not get out of that house quickly enough! This feeling was reinforced when, one particularly hot summer, a nasty incident occurred involving my mother and grandmother. I must have been ten years old for it was the summer after we had been informed that we could not sit again for the school scholarship. As usual, Ronnie and I turned nut-brown under the summer sun, but so hot was this summer that the sun had turned part of my fringe blonde. The following Saturday, when we turned up as usual at Quarr Road, my grandmother took one look at me and turned angrily to my mother, exclaiming in Welsh that by peroxiding my hair she was allowing me to grow up like a slut! She adamantly refused to believe the truth. From that day, I resolved to stop visiting my grandparents and, using school work as a legitimate excuse, Ronnie and I accompanied my mother less and less frequently on her trips to Pontardawe.

Chapter Four

MY FATHER'S SIDE

My father, who had a slight stoop, was a kind man, with warm blue eyes and a gentle Dorset lilt to his voice. He was a good listener though, as an intelligent man, he was himself worth listening to. He often spoke about his upbringing in Uplyme, Devon, where his parents worked as farm labourers for the local squire. As the eldest of the family, he too was required to work on the land, and in consequence missed much schooling. Often, he was despatched into a ploughed field to act as a human scarecrow. He resented this, he said, as he also hated the obligation to raise his hat to both squire and vicar whenever they passed him. He disliked the Church of England thereafter, describing it as an institution to foster boy recruits for the army.

When still young, he determined to leave home to seek work in the highly industrialised and prosperous South Wales. On his arrival, he found work on the railways, first in Neath, where he met my mother, then in Hereford. When I was very young, in the Gurnos, my mother would constantly talk about those early days, and especially about 'Little Willy'. As I got older, I gathered that Ronnie and I had had an elder brother – our parents' first born. My mother told me that Little Willy had never had a day's illness until, at the age of three, he was struck down by the influenza brought back by the troops at the end of the First World War. We were told that no family escaped the epidemic. The influenza that hit Willy turned to meningitis, and he died on Palm Sunday 1919, when I was a baby a few months old.

My father, who had recently been demobbed from the navy, was at the time working on the old Midland Railway at Credenhill, near Hereford. Apparently, we lived in a sweet little country cottage, but my mother could not bear to remain after Little Willy's death, and we all moved back to Wales, to Lower Cwmtwrch, to the Gurnos Cottages. Little Willy was buried in the graveyard of St. Peter's Church, Pontardawe – the same church in which my parents were married in 1914. I can only imagine what a sad blow his death must have dealt them. The way my mother described him, he must have been a lovely little boy. In the early days, she spoke of him so frequently that we grew up feeling his presence, but as the years passed, his memory became less poignant to her, and his name was not mentioned as often.

*Eileen's father George standing at the back to the right of the picture
at his sister's wedding during the Great War.*

Great Aunt Fan – my father's aunt – in Uplyme, near Lyme Regis.

My father's reports home of life and opportunity in South Wales must have been glowing, for soon the entire family uprooted and moved to Pembrey, where they farmed a small holding on the burrows and, at the same time, worked long hours for the owner of the large Towyn Farm nearby. There were eight of them in all – my father's parents, his sister Fanny, her husband Dick and daughter Betty, Uncle Walter and his wife Auntie Gladys, and my father's youngest brother, Willy. We used to stay with them at Pembrey for one week every summer. We travelled down by rail, but instead of the usual ride down the valley from Ystalyfera, we would travel up the valley to Brynamman, passing the back of our cottages en route. At Brynamman, we simply got off one train, crossed the road, and climbed aboard another. This took us through Ammanford and Panty-ffynnon to the estuary and Llanelli, a town thick with industrial works, their tall chimneys belching fire and smoke. The next halt was Burry Port, after which we soon began to recognise the familiar landmarks of Pembrey Burrows.

Pembrey halt comprised a tiny sandy platform. Once outside the fence, we climbed up onto the bridge which crossed the railway, and started off down the road leading to the burrows. We then took a right fork off the road and struck out along the path leading to my grandparents' house. It was a long haul, partic-ularly once we had passed the old munitions building, when the depth of sand beneath our feet began to slow us down but Ronnie and I did not mind at all. For us it was an adventure into the land of sand dunes, rabbits, mysterious copses, and the long straggling dew-berry plant. We danced along, counting rabbits,

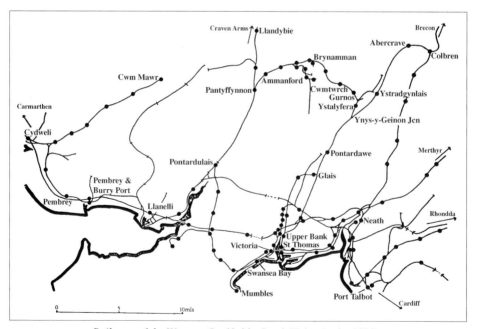

Railways of the Western Coalfields, South Wales, in the 1920s.

peering deep into the dark shadows under fir trees and, delightedly, plucked berries from the way to present to our mother and father who were following steadily in our wake.

However, even we tired, and were glad when the trek came to an end. We would top the last of the high-crested dunes to see before us the land flatten out into the treacherous waters of Gwendraeth inlet. As Ronnie and I glimpsed the house, we would let out a whoop of joy to alert our parents, before tumbling on down, shrieking and calling out to our grandma, a darling little woman of soft lilting speech, who would appear tiny in the far distance, waiting with arms open to enfold us.

Most of the family lived together in a Welsh long house. We passed through the porch into the living room, where the farmyard smells that we had brought with us mixed with the interior odours of the ancient thick stone walls, of pine burning in the grate, of food cooking, and the sweet smell of my grandma's dairy. The long house was divided into three distinct sections. The central section, or living room, ran the width of the house of which it formed the focal centre. Whenever we visited Pembrey, that was where we slept, and it is the portion of the house I became most familiar with. I recall one evening in that room, when a huge pine log fire was roaring and my mother was preparing to go to bed, that my father and grandfather were debating some legal issue – my father was looked up to by his family who often sought his advice, notably on legal matters. The argument was good natured, but my grandmother would not have them disagree, and brought their discussion to an abrupt end by saying, "Listen to them what knows, won't ye !"

Adjoining the living room were a number of other rooms secured by latched doors. Immediately on our left as we entered the house was the storeroom where Uncle Willy used to sleep. We never saw much of him. From the living room wall next to the storeroom hung a picture portraying a large tent and entitled the 'Ark of the Tabernacle'. A door, on the other side of the picture, opened into a cool flagged area from which two steps led up into the dairy. There, my grandma made sufficient butter to satisfy the family's requirements for the week. The butter was coloured a vivid yellow and oozed minute droplets of saltwater – I drool even now at the thought of it spread on fresh home-made bread. Grandma produced butter, surplus to household needs, which she would take by horse and trap to sell in Cydweli market. Once, when I was accompanying her, one of the wheels dropped into a ditch as we were cantering up to the level crossing. We took a bit of a tumble, but no-one was hurt. Half way across the back of the long house living room was a deep window set deep into the wall. During the heat of summer it was left open, and frequently one of the shire horses, or my grandmother's little mare, would stick its head through for a friendly nuzzle or a lump of sugar. Also positioned against that back wall was a

Grandfather Baker, Towyn Farm, Pembrey.

table on which stood a glass case containing a stuffed fox – although it looked almost alive to me. Further along, behind the high-backed wooden settle which bordered the fire, was another latched door which led into the second main section of the long house. Inside the door was a single step which led down into my grandparents' bedroom. Adjoining their room was a spare room where my parents would sleep, and beyond that again, near the front of the house, was the room where we children slept. Over each of our beds, which were draped with heavy pure cotton coverlets, hung a long narrow-framed angel to guard us. We always slept well in that house. No rattling trains or piercing hooters disturbed our nights – only the occasional shuffle of an animal.

Each morning, we woke to the heavy tread of grandfather and Uncle Willy going off to work, and to the smell of Welsh bacon filtering under the latched door. Soon we were up, dressed, and washed in the cold water outside. The farm's sole water sources were the great butts positioned around the house to catch rain from the roof. The one next to the porch was reserved for drinking purposes. My father worried about the water's purity, but it tasted fine and we never came to any harm. Other casks, hidden in the front portion of the long house, contained home-made cider, which the men drank. My grandfather once gave some to Ronnie and me, then tested whether we could walk the straight line between the flag stones outside. I cannot remember if we succeeded, but it was great fun.

Breakfast at my grandparents was enormous, comprising crisp fat bacon, egg, fried bread and, on the morning after Cydweli market, the additional joy of laver bread. To my child's mind, it seemed never to rain at Pembrey, and after breakfast we would scurry out of the house to spend the entire day in the open air. Immediately outside was a path, consisting of two broad lines of flag stones, which ran the length of the long house. A wall the far side of the path separated the house from the barn and meadow. It was in the meadow that the privy was located. I detested using it both because of the thick growth of nettles that stung my legs on the path down and because, once seated on the privy, I became plagued by the fear that someone else might come along to use it. Still, that was a small price to pay for the marvels of Pembrey. We would explore the farm buildings, play on the long swing in the barn, and visit grandma's garden which lay a short distance from the house in the direction of the burrows. She possessed green fingers, for plants abounded both within and outside the house. In her garden, which was redolent with the scent of sweet peas, she grew magnificent gladioli, a huge cluster of which she would always present to us before we left for home. We would also venture deep into the woods, returning triumphantly laden with basketfuls of dried pine and cones for the fire, and would launch dewberry picking expeditions. Or we might pluck the mushrooms which grew in a profusion of rings around the farm, and eat them fried in salty bacon fat. Sometimes my grandfather would take us to see a new born lamb or kid. I remember one kid which was born very weak. They named it after me, and did all they could to heal her, but she died while we were still there.

The reason we did not see much of Uncle Willy was that he was courting. It was not long before he and Olwen were married, and the front storeroom cleared for them to live in. Whenever we entered their room, I was struck by how bare it was. They had two little girls, born so close together in time – the second was born during one of our stays – that when they were toddlers they could have been mistaken for twins. Ronnie and I felt old enough to be uncle and auntie to them. They were still very young when Uncle Willy, driving a farm machine pulled by shire horses, fell backwards onto its cylindrical spikes and was killed. We were in the Gurnos at the time and only our father attended the funeral. The following summer, when we visited Auntie Olwen, she seemed very sad. Shortly afterwards she returned to her mother's to live, and we never saw her or her daughters again.

One afternoon during the week we spent in Pembrey we were invited to tea by my father's sister Fanny, who had also accompanied her parents to South Wales. She married a Mr Simcocks, and they occupied the third major section of the long house. She was jolly, but we never took to Uncle Dick, or to cousin Betty who preferred to spend her time with the two little girls at Towyn Farm than play with us. Still, we used to enjoy having tea with them – until Betty commenced piano lessons. Auntie Fanny would proudly usher us into their parlour to listen, but it proved an ordeal for we had been spoiled by the fine music we had heard from father's gramophone, and from my mother and father with their violin and mouth organ. By comparison, Betty's clumsy key-bashing on an ill-tuned piano was a travesty. So although Auntie Fanny and Uncle Dick were all smiles at their child prodigy, it was as much as we could do to wait politely for her performance to end. Another afternoon would be spent visiting Uncle Walter who lived closer to the railway, two miles from the long house, near the one road that led to Pembrey. I cannot remember the time before he was married to Auntie Gladys, who wore a glass eye following an accident in the munitions works during the war. Their little girl, Pam, was younger than me. As a baby she was a real dumpling, with rosy cheeks, beautiful blue eyes and a head of fair curls.

The only member of the family not to live in the Pembrey region was Mark, my grandparents' next eldest son, who, when the family left Dorset, went to work on a farm near Ledbury. We visited his family on a few rare occasions. In looks and character Uncle Mark was very like my father, and they thoroughly enjoyed each other's company. Auntie Nancy possessed the dark complexion

Uncle Mark.

*Eileen, on the left, enjoying the hop-picking season
at Ledbury with cousin Blossom.*

and flashing good looks of a Bohemian gypsy, and they had a daughter called
Blossom who was about my age. When I was about twelve years old they
invited me up for the hop-picking season. Floods of gypsies came to take part,
and a special type of camaraderie developed between us. I took the fancy of the
farmer's son who demonstrated to me each stage of the of the hop-picking
process, from the actual picking to the piling of the hops into the kiln. During
the final evening's ritual, which involved pitching each picker into his or her
last canvas of hops, that young farmer tossed me more frequently than was
warranted. He subsequently asked Auntie Nancy to let me stay on, but she in
her wisdom refused. I did not visit them again at Ledbury. In later years, after
Auntie Gladys had given birth to a boy, they moved to a farm near Stourport.
We once paid them a brief visit, but never again saw them. Indeed, from about
the time I was twelve, our visits to Pembrey also became less and less frequent.

Chapter Five

THE NEIGHBOURHOOD

The Jones family, our immediate neighbours, occupied the middle of the three railway cottages. It was a slightly larger house than ours, but the Jones' were more numerous than us, and so had a harder life. Mr Jones augmented his income by chicken rearing, while most of the girls were encouraged to find work in local shops. Aileen, the eldest, helped with the management of the house. She was engaged to 'Williams the Boot', a crippled cobbler who had been left a widower with a small son about the age of Arthur, the Jones' youngest. Williams the Boot would sometimes drive to visit Aileen from Ystalyfera on his motor bike, with his son in the pillion seat. They remained engaged for some time, eventually marrying at the English Congregational Church in Ystalyfera. The next eldest to Aileen was Ena who, whenever possible, helped out in Bests' shop in our lane. It was in her spare moments there that she taught me to knit. Something was clearly wrong with Tilly, the third girl, who was both obese and very slow witted. I never knew her to attend school and, when she was about fourteen, she had a baby which her family cared for. The baby appeared fine mentally, but also grew up to be obese – so much so that she could scarcely walk. Poor Tilly just carried on oblivious. By contrast, Ida, next to Tilly in age, was an intelligent girl. My mother said that she was bright enough to have attended the County School, but when she was fourteen she left to enter 'service' away from home, and we never again saw her.

Between Ida and Arthur there was a gap of several years in which Mrs Jones became pregnant again, but the child was stillborn. I vividly recollect my mother taking me next door to visit mother and baby. When it came to viewing the still-born child, I hung back with apprehension. As my mother lifted me up to see it laid out on top of a tall chest of drawers, its tiny ashen face like wax, framed in a white bonnet, I willed with all my heart to be released to run home. I was still very young when I became aware of the high infant mortality rate in the locality – of babies stillborn or dying shortly after birth. News of such events was gained in a patchy way from conversations overheard between my mother and Mrs Jones in the back yard – there were no dividing walls. Quite often when they were gossiping I would be hanging around and, although I generally paid little attention, my ears would prick up if anything of real interest cropped up. This usually happened when they switched from English, in which language they invariably commenced their conversation, to Welsh – a change prompted by the mistaken belief that I would not understand. I do not know why I could comprehend but not speak the language, but it certainly gave me the advantage at such conspiratorial moments. I distinctly remember one occasion when their voices dropped as they switched into Welsh. I crept closer to my mother and strained to catch every word. They were talking about dead babies, and how Mrs Jones had seen yet another that very morning. It was the time of the General Strike, when our mothers left home early in the morning to search for pickings from the tin furnace and coal tips. Mrs Jones had looked down from the colliery tip to see the tiny corpse – a miscarriage or abortion – floating downriver. Higher up the valley the mountains closed in, pushing the houses to the very verge of the river Twrch, and it must have been from one of these that the pathetic object had been jettisoned. What tales of heartbreak that river must have carried in those desperate days. I was disturbed by such stories and felt a sense of pity, though for whom or what I could never quite work out. My mother had a miscarriage once too – I saw it in her chamber pot – but she made no fuss.

Whenever we were ill, we went to see Dr Walsh. My mother had looked after the children of Dr and Mrs Walsh for some years before she and my father were married. She often talked of those days – of her fondness for their children, and of how well the doctor and his wife treated her. She spoke too of their tragedy. While she was with them, one of their sons went out on his new bicycle – he was just old enough to have been given a two-wheeler. He lost control after rounding the corner by the canal and, careering down the steep hill, he swerved, crashed into the wall bordering the road, and was killed. His parents were heart broken, and remained so for a long time afterwards.

The Walsh family were very fond of my mother. Before she was married, they permitted my father to visit her at their house, which was fortunate for them as my father, an Englishman, was not welcome at my mother's parents' home in Pontardawe. My father called my mother 'Lottie', but the Walsh family referred to her affectionately as 'Lotts'. We were also always made welcome at their house, but on one social visit I witnessed Mrs Walsh's infamous temper. I remember her leading us into a large red-flagged kitchen to have some tea. The room was bare save for a long scrubbed wooden table surrounded by chairs, on one of which sat a shabbily dressed tramp, slouched over a plate of food which he was hungrily devouring. Around his feet scampered a number of poms, animals Mrs Walsh bred and to which she was devoted. Being nervous of dogs I stuck close to my mother. The tramp rose as we entered, accidentally knocking his chair into one of the poms. The dog, reacting as if his life was being threatened, started yapping ferociously at the 'assailant', and was the next moment joined by Mrs Walsh whose fury had the poor man cowering before she ban-

Eileen, Mammy and Ronnie. Daddy took the photograph. The wall is the back of the three new privies. We are standing in my father's garden, facing the Swansea to Brynamman railway line.

ished him from the house. She subsequently examined the dog for non-existent injuries and, in stark contrast to her mood of a few moments before, started cooing softly to it. On our return home my mother explained that Mrs Walsh's tempers abated as suddenly as they arose and that she was in fact extremely generous to people. Anyone who called asking for food she would invite in, ensuring that they were given a square meal. Unfortunately, the tramp did not have the time to appreciate her true nature.

Dr Walsh was a big strong man with a rich Irish accent and a sense of humour. There were only three occasions when we were too ill to walk to his surgery and he was obliged to call at the cottage; twice for me – once when I contracted scarlet fever, and again when my gum would not stop bleeding following the extraction of a tooth – and the third time after Ronnie had to be stitched up following an accident at school. He never charged us for treatment because my mother had once worked for him. For minor ailments, we walked up to the surgery which was located in a huge empty barn adjoining the stables behind their house. Patients sat in a queue on a long hard bench which ran the length of one wall of the barn. Straw lay strewn across the floor and fixed high on the opposite wall was a shelf, lined with coloured bottles. The place was pungent with the smell of disinfectant. Dr Walsh always rose in welcome, immediately putting us at our ease, whenever our turn came to enter his room which, although large, was heated and comfortable.

But to return to our immediate neighbours. I remember most Arthur Jones because he was much the same age as me. His four elder sisters were much older and spoiled him. The Jones family would refer to Arthur and me as 'The Bisto Kids', which vexed me greatly for it implied that we were so fond of each other as to be virtually inseparable. Nothing could have been further from the truth, at least as far as I was concerned. We were the only two children in the neighbourhood of approximately the same age, and Arthur did constantly hang around me, but he would often want to play or do things I did not like, and if he could not have his own way he would become disagreeable or pout. One of my earliest recollections of him was when my mother was looking after him while a spiritualist séance was being held in his house. He said something at the time which has stuck in my mind ever since – "The silly budders! They hold hands and the table starts to rise up."

Arthur stole from me once. My father always brought home presents after his 'Railway' team had travelled away to participate in the annual St. John's Ambulance competition. That particular year, the competition had been held in either Swindon or Crewe, and the gifts for Ronnie and me reflected this, for they were perfect working models of a dynamo. I was proud of the fact that my father considered me worthy enough to warrant having the same present as Ronnie. The technical details of the dynamo were lost on me, but I loved the look of it, the way it gleamed, and how it sparked when mobile. Shortly after this, I was sitting at the side of the 'stream', enjoying the feel of it in my hands, when Arthur Jones suddenly appeared and sat beside me. He was inquisitive about the dynamo, but I maintained a firm grasp on it. Then something took my attention, and I placed it on the ground between us, with my hand resting lightly on top of it. The next moment, he had seized it and disappeared into his house. I could have choked with grief, and was laden with the thought that I would never lay eyes on that dynamo again. My mother confronted Mrs Jones, but when Arthur denied all knowledge of it his family closed ranks around him. Thereafter, my mother got nowhere, but Ronnie had different ideas. At the first opportunity, he collared Arthur Jones and literally smothered him all over with truck grease. Mrs Jones raised the incident with my mother, but with little conviction, and Ronnie was not rebuked. I was most proud of my brother, although I remained upset for a long time afterwards because I felt myself to have been responsible for the affair. I made certain that Arthur Jones never again stole from me.

One day, Arthur persuaded me to accompany him to their chicken run on the far side of the 'stream'. Inside it stank and was slippery with chicken droppings. In my bones I felt that my mother would be very cross if she knew where I had gone. Arthur climbed up into one of the hutches and summoned me to follow. As soon as I had entered, he dropped the wooden latch, shutting us in. The hen house was minute, its atmosphere close and warm. Arthur then asked me "to take my knickers down" and let him "see"! I cannot recall how, but I was out of that hen house in a flash, leaving him flat on his back and wailing with the beating that I had given him. When I reached home, one whiff betrayed where I had been. My mother scolded me, hauled me to the tap at the back of the cottage, and scrubbed me from head to toe. Yet I was so upset that I could hardly speak for sobbing, and her attitude soon softened. From that day, I kept as clear of Arthur Jones as I possibly could.

If Arthur Jones was the bane, Kenny Cornelius was the joy of my life. Slightly older than me, he was the youngest of the Cornelius family who occupied the other end cottage in the Gurnos. His hair was cropped like a convict's, his eyes rolled up behind metal-rimmed spectacles, and he was a cripple, his legs in irons, jointed at the knees. Yet I loved that boy. I felt very protective of him, and for as long as we lived in the Gurnos, helped him to walk, willing that his condition improve. Kenny was a pleasure to be with, laughing at everything and everybody – except our cousin. Whenever we were visited by Auntie Edith and Harry, the latter derived great satisfaction from tormenting Kenny. He would corner the poor boy and shout, "Get out of my house, Kennimore !", until I screamed at him to stop. This behaviour was uncharacteristic of my cousin who was normally gentle and considerate – so much so that at one stage I decided that it would be pointless searching further afield and would marry him when we grew up.

I only saw Mrs Cornelius once. I cannot recall why I was taken inside their cottage to meet her. Ill, possibly paralysed, she sat enthroned in a leather padded armchair in the corner of their parlour. To me, she was every bit a queen – her hair pushed up high, and around her throat a delicate ruffle of lace, to the front of which was pinned an oval gold brooch. It was a brief visit and I never saw her again, although I often saw her big large-hearted husband. I only possess faint memories of their two eldest boys, who left home shortly after we moved to the Gurnos, but I knew the other children well. Violet was their eldest child. I remember her caring for me when I was very young, pushing me around in a wooden-framed push chair. For some reason, I admired the dark rings which lay under her eyes and hoped some day to be similarly blessed. However, Violet suffered increasingly severe bouts of asthma and died when still a young woman. Her sister, Ethel, was considered 'wild', but I liked her boisterous nature. Tall, with short fair hair, Ethel was forever romanticising about the future. Like Ida Jones, she quit school at the age of fourteen and we heard no more of her. Most local girls left home for domestic service in England, or became nurses. After Ethel came two boys, Alan and Edie, though I do not know which was the elder. Alan was fostered out, and on his regular visits home would initially cause havoc, spoiling for a fight with the other boys. However, his aggressiveness never lasted very long and he soon became one of the Gurnos Cottages 'railway children' again, distinct from the other children of the locality who were sons and daughters of miners and tin workers. We were always sorry to lose Alan when the time came for him to return to his foster parents.

Because they were so different from us railway people, we found the Bests to be interesting neighbours. To me they appeared enormously wealthy, living down the lane from us in a large house they owned. They also rented out a tiny cottage, adjacent to the house, and owned a small shop and a garage, located next to the cottage and back a little from the lane. There were six in the family; Mr and Mrs Best, a very stout couple, Aunt Selina, who was Mrs Best's maiden sister, and three sons. George, the eldest boy, was as stout as his father with whom he laboured in the local tin plate works. Davy, the middle boy, who was tall and slight, seemed to have no job and just pottered about all day. He would tease us younger children in a gentle fashion, and was always ready for a laugh. We found him such fun that whenever we caught sight of him, we would run up to see what he was 'up to'. One of the mad things he did was to let us ride on the chassis of his car – a seemingly sound vehicle which he stripped down until only the engine and steel frame remained. It was on this frame that we children would sit, clinging on for dear life and legs dangling free, while he raced up and down the lane, turning in the space in front of the shop and garage. Ronnie fell off once but, miraculously, was unhurt. Ronald, the youngest son, who was a little older than me, was quite obese. Aunt Selina, who acted as his nurse, spoiled him silly and, until he was six or seven years of age, dressed him in frilly white petticoats and dresses – we would stare at him with unabashed curiosity. When he was eventually pushed into trousers and wanted to play with us, he was given a rough time. As the price for our 'friendship', he accepted the nick name 'Fatty Arbuckle'. We still gave him as wide a berth as possible, but he nonetheless invited all of us to his birthday party which we attended not so much for his sake as for the mouth watering goodies that were always laid out to eat. However, Ronald Best got his revenge after tea, for it was he who chose what games were to be played. I cannot speak for the other girls, but I dreaded Postman's Knock. Seemingly, I could never avoid my fate for no matter how well hidden I was, that fat boy would hunt me down and administer a slobbering kiss. But I reckoned then that Ronnie Best and I were quits, and I would make for home.

The children of our neighbourhood played mostly in the vicinity of the Gurnos Cottages. However, the amount of spare time we had depended on our mothers who determined what tasks we first had to complete. All of us were expected to help out at home in one way or another – and we really did not mind. We did housework, ran errands, watched out for the milkman, rag and bone man, the fish man, and other passing tradesmen. The rag and bone man was our favourite because, if we collected sufficient scraps of cloth for him, we would receive a goldfish in return – although the poor creatures would never last long.

We played the same games year in, year out, but all in their proper season – marbles, hopscotch, spinning tops, skipping, tin and string stilts, conkers and many more. They formed a natural rhythm to which we unthinkingly adhered. As for creative play, that centred on the network of local railway lines; most ran along the back of the cottages where were located a number of marshalling yards and the main L.M.S. passenger and goods line linking Brynamman to Swansea. Immediately in front of the house, between the main path and the 'feeder' stream, lay a single set of lines used for shunting. Wagons and trucks were constantly being pushed along them so that we children never knew from one day to the next what we would find parked there. Once the last engine had left the shunting area, and the entrance gates were locked, it was quite safe for us to play there.

Away from the immediate area, we exploited any wooded land, seeking trees for climbing, swinging and jumping. This could be quite dangerous when jumping from one branch, hoping to land on, or swing from, another! We quickly became familiar with those trucks and vans that we clambered over, crawled beneath, squeezed between and, wherever possible, probed inside. We grew to know their every nut and bolt, chain and coupling, wheel and bumper. Attached to the side of each vehicle were wooden boxes with sloping, hinged lids, filled with a thick grease, meant for the wheels but which the boys used for ammunition during fights. The vans had sliding doors which were frequently left unlocked, giving us the opportunity to use them as a stage for spontaneous theatre – the doors forming rolling curtains between acts. We required no audience to sustain us.

Adjacent to our cottage, on the northern, valley side, stood a forbidding, black, corrugated iron building. I would try to examine it from our front garden, but the wall surrounding it proved to be too high. Scaling the wall and then finding a peephole in the side of the building appeared to be the only way to discover what lay within. However, even that plan faltered. Ronnie and some of the bigger boys managed to clamber over the wall from time to time, on the pretext of retrieving balls shied from their improvised cricket pitch in the yard outside, but the building was securely locked and no peepholes were discovered. We were therefore left guessing as to precisely what lay inside, although we discovered the origins of the dreadful stench, the impact of which varied according to climatic conditions, that emanated from the building. The odour was of animal gut and waste which at night was brought by cart from the nearby slaughter house and dumped outside the building, beside the level crossing. This brings me to the one event not even our mothers could hold us back from – the weekly slaughter of animals in the large corrugated iron building the far side of our 'stream'. It formed one of the highlights of our week. Alerted by the high pitched squeals or bellows of condemned beasts, we bolted as one to a spot opposite the hole in the slaughter house wall from which the torrent of blood would shortly gush. We would stand there, hypnotised and strangely excited, as the rich red fluid emerged and flowed like lava to the crystal stream below. At once the water sucked it in, pulling at it, separating it into long circling strands, diluting its strength. Fascinated, we would scramble and stumble along the bank, endeavouring to follow the paling mass as it was carried downstream, until it vanished under the roadway at Gurnos Cross. Only then did we return to our tasks, scuffing our feet slowly back up the lane, thinking of the treat in store for us the following week.

Beside the slaughter house, our greatest amusement was the cinema. Mothers never accompanied us to see the silent films shown at the 'Collie', and only years later did they venture out to sample the 'movies'. The Collie, or Coliseum Cinema, built in 1908, was, besides the chapel, the most important centre of social life for us children. Ronnie and I would eagerly anticipate the matinees there which we attended almost every Saturday afternoon, except during the summer months. As we Gurnos children had further to walk than our friends from Heol-y-Varteg, we would leave home early in the hope of securing a good seat. Once past the Aubrey Arms we struck along the canal bank that provided a short cut to Ystalyfera Railway Station, from where we would trot the remaining 'stone's throw' to join our friends outside the Collie. When the doors finally opened, we rushed forward, rife with anticipation, to enter a different world, dimly lit, rank and flea ridden. Marching past the more elevated tiers at the back, we would make our way to the front of the cinema, there to select our seats with caution, for some were badly damaged. Having chosen, we pulled down the seats and wriggled onto them, struggling all the time against the counter pull of the seat hinge. Once settled, however, it was sheer luxury on that sprung mounting and we would spread out our arms and lie back for the rest of the afternoon, relishing the thought that we were monopolising space designed for an adult. Before us hung railed curtains that hid the piano, while high above our heads swung the long faded drapes concealing the screen. When the pianist appeared beside the screen curtains to start his descent to the piano, the paper throwing and shouting ceased as if by magic. The last stragglers struggled into their seats as a few dramatic bars from the piano heralded the hesitant unfurling of the screen covers. Then, to the whirr of the projector, a few odd characters flickered onto the screen, and the entire audience was immediately captivated. The credits appeared first, followed by the title of the first film and the pianist was forgotten as the action, music and captions fused into timeless drama. The afternoon's entertainment climaxed with the serial, which always ended with the hero or heroine yet again on the verge of a gruesome death.

The show over, we shuffled out, blinking as we re-emerged into the harsh light of day. Outside, groups of friends would cluster in animated speculation as to the fate of our screen heroes, and to relive the highlights of the programme.

When we finally drifted apart, we would confirm a rendezvous the next morning in chapel. In the weekdays between shows, we would re-enact and embellish scenes from the previous Saturday's cinema. Being the only girl of playing age in the immediate vicinity of the Gurnos Cottages, I was privileged to always play the role of the heroine – who for many years was Pearl White. For the boys, there were a multitude of heroes from whom to choose; Tom Mix the cowboy, or comics like Harold Lloyd, Fatty Arbuckle, Buster Keaton and Charlie Chaplin – although the last named once brought tears of sadness to my eyes in a film played with Jackie Coogan.

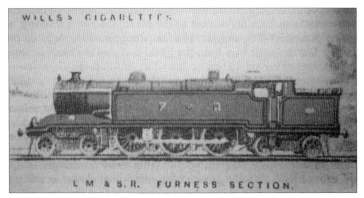

No. 6 of a set of 50 Railway Engines issued by W.D. & W.O. Wills (Cigarettes) of Bristol, January 1924.

Saturday afternoon at the Collie also provided us with the opportunity to swap cigarette cards which every child in the area collected. Apart from cinema screen favourites, there were enchanting series of wild flowers, kings and queens of England and medallions, as well as sets comprising, amongst others, cricketers, footballers and household hints. As railway children, we were keen to collect sets of railway engines, particularly those of the L.M.S., for which our fathers worked, although the series depicting L.N.W.R. engines came a close second. We swapped with the intention of building up complete sets, but here our companions from Ystalyfera had the advantage for en-route to and from Wern School, they passed Williams the Boot. The cobbler was an avid collector of cigarette cards, which he displayed in his shop and tiny workroom, and was prepared to exchange his swaps which were always in mint condition. As my father repaired all our footwear at home on a couple of lasts, it was only on the rare occasions when he required further supplies of leather, or steel tips for making studs, that we had the chance to visit Williams the Boot and exchange cards. Despite this we fared reasonably well. From discarded cigarette packets we scavenged cards that, because of the sliver paper lining the boxes, had been protected from the elements and were often in perfect condition.

Chapter Six

THE RAILWAY PEOPLE

Community

The railway people were quite distinct from other working communities in the valley. Firstly, our fathers worked on the railways and were therefore different from the coal and metal workers around them. Secondly, we lived in close proximity and stuck together socially. We in the Gurnos cottages constantly exchanged visits with the larger railway community in Heol-y-Varteg, which lay along the river bank at the foot of Darren mountain. Indeed, it was as if we were neighbours. Down in the Varteg we would call on the Thorpe, Stallard, Starr, Evans and Mathias families, whilst through chapel and elsewhere we became fast friends with other railway families like the Cookes, Crawfords, Jenkins and Jones. My father's surname was Baker, but he was known by all as George. As the surnames indicate, many railwaymen were, like my father, English.

My parents were most friendly with the Evans family, the Stallards, the Thorpes and the Starrs. Mrs Ben Evans was one of my mother's closest friends. I distinctly recall once when she called for, amongst other things, it was the only time my mother hit me. She arrived at the Gurnos early in the afternoon of the children's' 'Summer Competition', to be held in the Drill Hall, just up the slope on the main road opposite the Co-op. I had entered for the brass ornament competition for under eights. Competitors, carrying Brasso and rags, had to clamber up onto the stage and polish up a given brass ornament. I was determined to rub and polish so hard that I would bring home the prize. It was time to make the final preparations for the competition when a worried looking Mrs Ben Evans appeared at the front door. My mother sat her down and soon the two were engrossed in a serious but whispered conversation. Time passed and I feared that my mother had forgotten all about the competition. In the end I decided to act and, despite having been taught never to interrupt grown-ups, gently reminded my mother about the competition. Once more I was ignored, so I determined to keep nagging until I was listened to. Eventually my mother did take notice; she became so furious at my repeated interruptions that she hauled me into the back yard, pulled down my knickers, and gave me the hardest smacking I have ever received. Smarting with pain and an acute sense of injustice, I refused

Ystalyfera viewed from the Darren. Heol-y-Varteg is in the foreground at the foot of the hill.

to go back into the house. Soon afterwards, my mother reappeared armed with Brasso and rags and fairly dragged me up the slope onto the main road, and into the Drill Hall. We arrived in time for the competition, but my heart was no longer in it. I put no effort into the polishing and, immediately it was finished, ran home, miserable and dejected. I could sense that my mother felt sorry for what had happened. I, too, regretted having upset her, but I still felt aggrieved. Then she quietly explained the nature of Mrs Ben Evans' problem. I was aware that one of her boys, Fred, had a disease of the bones, but what I did not know was that Mr Evans had a brain tumour which caused him to become increasingly and unpredictably violent to his wife and sons. When he died soon afterwards, I felt very sad for him, and for Mrs Evans and the children. However, we saw much more of the Evans' boys following the funeral and Mrs Evans gradually started to look healthier, aided undoubtedly by Fred receiving a course of treatment which led to his full recovery.

The Stallard children were quite grown up, so we never got to know them well, although Ronnie and I frequently met their father because he was a clerk in Ystalyfera Station. He had lost an arm in the Great War, and had his empty sleeve pinned back to his shoulder, but was always cheerful and appeared to do his job and care for his garden as competently as the next man. The Thorpe children also were considerably older than Ronnie and me, but I remember them being active in chapel. Gazing at them on Sundays, I used to think that Miss Thorpe, who was engaged to a young railway man lodging in the area, was very pretty. We all attended the wedding at the 'English Cong', at which she looked radiant in her bridal veil and gown. The Starr's, who were like uncle and aunt to us, were childless. Mr Starr, who was a skilled carpenter and did a lot of fret work, used to construct jig saws as Christmas presents for Ronnie and me – my favourite showing the head and shoulders of a smiling, rosy cheeked girl wearing a woolly cap with a tassel and a woolly scarf, set against a background of snow. The wood of the jig saws never broke but the paper would peel off and my mother would use a flour and water mix to paste it back.

The local Railway Ambulance Team, of which my father was the instructor, constituted his closest social group. Amongst my father's best friends were Mr Cooke and Mr Crawford whom I would meet whenever I accompanied my father to the Friendly Society Hall, close to Ystalyfera Station, where weekly benefit payments were made and where the 'team' met. The final group of railway people with whom we formed a close friendship were the Jenkins family who moved up the valley from Swansea about the year 1929. Mr Jenkins was a maintenance worker, ensuring that signals, points and other equipment on the Swansea to Brynamman line functioned efficiently. We would sometimes meet him in Ystalyfera signal box, when he stopped to share a pot of tea with my father. Other times, when we saw him working on the section of track opposite the Gurnos, we would run over to climb the crossing gates and pass the time of day. At first the Jenkins lived in Alltygrug Road, in Ystalyfera, but then, just as we were moving out of the Gurnos Cottages to Glanrhyd, they also moved, to a house in Lower Cwmtwrch. They had two daughters with whom we became, and remained, fast friends; Eunice was Ronnie's age, while Muriel was a little younger than me. Muriel and I paired off from the start. She was a quiet girl and could be serious, though she also possessed an elfish sense of humour and had the most infectious laugh I had ever known; it would commence as a subdued giggle, but progressively grew into a full blooded laugh. In no time she would have me rolling about helplessly, though mostly we had no idea what we were laughing about. We would eventually stop, only to recommence, until finally we were quite exhausted.

Of the Heol-y-Varteg folk, those we children loved most were the Mathias family, comprising Mr and Mrs Mathias and their two sons, Victor and Bert. Vic was Ronnie's age and Bert was slightly my junior. Like my parents, Mr and Mrs Mathias had lost a child in the 1919 flu epidemic – a pretty faced girl, judging by the sepia photograph of her that hung from their living room wall. The atmosphere in their home was nevertheless richly infused with a sense of domestic contentment, whilst Mrs Mathias' grace and her husband's contagious good humour, worked wonders on their company. Mrs Mathias possessed striking good looks, and it was obvious that her short, broad shouldered husband worshipped the ground she trod. Ronnie and I frequently went to tea there and, although I did not play with the boys much, Mr and Mrs Mathias would spoil me to the extent that I would feel like a princess. They must have paid return visits, although I cannot recall any. Their house always seemed full of their sons' playmates, chief of whom was Jackie Jones, a great pal of Bert's. Jackie

Mrs Mathias surrounded by children, c.1929. Her son Bert is in front of her with his boyhood sweetheart – he joined the RAF as a pilot and was killed in action in the Second World War. Jackie Jones had left for England.

could not have been more than four years old when he arrived in the valley from Bristol with his widowed mother, who was a native of London. She set up as housekeeper to Mr Dan Jones, whom she subsequently married. Although Jackie was the odd man out in the gang, for his father was Welsh and a miner, he was quickly accepted by us railway children because he came from 'away', his mother spoke English, they attended the 'English Cong' and they lived in the midst of the railway community of Heol-y-Varteg. He became one of our closest and lasting friends. Wherever we railway children went, so did he – to chapel, the Mathias', birthday parties and, of course, the Collie matinees. The only event from which he was excluded was the free railway excursion.

Chapel

The issues of language, nationality and religion compounded the occupational and social differences between the railwaymen and the rest of the valley community. Some of the railway workers, and many railway wives, like my mother, were of Welsh parentage, but they chose to speak English. In a Welsh-speaking valley, this marked the railway community apart. More significantly, the Ystalyfera railway 'contingent' all worshipped at the English Congregational Chapel in town, whereas the real valley people flocked to the many Welsh chapels in the district. Often, when passing one of the huge Welsh chapels, we could tell from the singing that one of the 'Cyrddau Mawr' was in session. We would stop to listen, but never dreamed of going inside. Also, while playing outside the Gurnos Cottages, we frequently caught the strains of Welsh hymns drifting down from Beulah Chapel, a mile up valley. If the tone was melancholy, we knew that it was yet another funeral and Ronnie and I would run up the slope to listen – but again would never venture in. The Welsh custom was for all the men, sometimes accompanied by the women, to follow their dead to the graveside where they would sing their final farewell. The scene would lure Ronnie and me like magnets to the thick yew hedges that bordered the cemetery, and from where we would watch in fascination. I was drawn by more than mere curiosity, for that open air singing would move me strangely, until I would yearn to join in. I recall, when I was about seven, being so affected by the music as to feel distinctly a divine presence to which, turning my gaze to the heavens, I presented my soul. It was an experience I was to have again one balmy summer's night after our move from the Gurnos to Glanrhyd.

However, to a man it was to the 'English Cong' that we railway people went. This tie to a particular chapel was strong; for example, whenever one of the railway men wanted his hair cut, he would patronise Mr Schauss, a popular member of the chapel. Shift work obviously affected the regularity with which the men could attend chapel, but not so our mothers, who ensured that we children accompanied them. On Sunday, weather permitting, my mother would walk Ronnie and me to chapel three times – and we would think nothing of it ! From the Gurnos Cottages we followed the shortest route, through the back of the 'Patches' and across the river Twrch, before climbing over the tips of worked-out collieries to the rear of the chapel round which we would make our way to join our friends in the forecourt. During the summer, following the evening service, it was a universal custom for chapel folk, both Welsh and English, to stroll up and down the main valley road between Ystalyfera and Glanrhyd. It was a leisurely, communal affair, during which social intercourse for all ages and 'conditions of heart' was legitimate. Most of the railway families from the Gurnos and Heol-y-Varteg extended their walk into a circular trip, strolling from the chapel down the steep hill to the foot of Varteg mountain, then along the river bank to Glanrhyd where the river was crossed and the route turned back up Wind Road to Gough Corner. There, the Gurnos Cottages people branched right for home. Some railway people who lived down river did the circuit the other way, which was great fun for us children as we kept meeting

The English "Cong".
(Photograph courtesy Bernant Hughes).

friends coming in the opposite direction. If we encountered them along the riverside path there was always time to stop, for the adults to chat and we children to play.

The 'Cong' was busy throughout the year. In the flourishing Sunday School, the children competed for the annual attendance prize, well bound works of reputable authors. As the afternoon prize giving ceremony approached, the excitement was intense. I can still see those beautiful new books stacked in piles, one for each class, on the large table in front of us. On the day, we sat in rows, each class accompanied by its teacher, while Mr Feltham, the Sunday School superintendent, conducted a brief service. At its conclusion, he and his assistant, Mr Peters, would distribute the prizes – first presenting the youngest scholars. Few were disappointed, for almost all children had full or almost complete attendance records. Ronnie and I received some marvellous novels which we read and re-read until they eventually became worn, some to the point of disintegration. The other main prize giving ceremony in Sunday School followed the opening of the Missionary Boxes. We did not fare as well on these occasions because neither our family nor, when we tried collecting, most local people, had any spare cash. The prizes comprised for the most part slim-volumed missionary biographies, some of which would be read on the spot and then swapped for another. Through them we learnt of legendary figures like Mary Jones with her Bible, and of missionaries to Madagascar and other far off places, South Seas missions being the boys' favourite.

Chapel also marked the passing of the seasons. To me, it appeared that summer arrived precisely at Whitsuntide. On Whit Sunday, all females dressed chapel and church in white finery, though the Welsh girls and women would form a vast unified parade of white, which we would watch stream past. The 'English Cong' competitions were was also held in summer, we children being entered according to our talents – Ronnie would recite, while I would sing. The adjudicator of each competition would launch into a detailed analysis of the merits and defects of every performance. The chapel women made the prizes, small exquisite bags, enclosing a coin, which were hung with a ribbon or tape around our necks. As, year in, year out, Jackie Jones and myself would stand on the stage to receive the prizes for the boy's and girl's solo respectively, I collected a good few such prizes. My favourite was a frilled, delicate cream silk pouch which took pride of place in my treasure box until, eventually, the silk threads split and the bag became hopelessly frayed. Only one pouch survived; it was diamond shaped, of a deep orange-velvet hue, and lined with tiny beads embroidered to form the initials E.C.C. – English Congregational Church – in the heart of the diamond. Although a cluster of beads eventually dropped from the bottom corner and broke, the bag itself remained intact, and keeps turning up from time to time.

Autumn signalled the start of serious choir practice in the chapel under our conductor Dan Jones, a true Welshman. As we practised cantatas through Tonic Solfa, which I never managed to read, I learnt the pieces by listening to the conductor and committing to memory the words and music. Mr Dan Jones was a perfectionist, insisting on practising phrases many times over until we sang them flawlessly. He was fortunate in having in the chapel congregation famous singers like Mr Ross Richards, of the Carl Rosa Opera, Mr Richards' wife – also an excellent pianist – and his sister, who could be called upon for major solo parts. I vividly recall one occasion when Mr Dan Jones was rehearsing an aria with us lesser mortals in preparation for a Spring rendering of the 'Messiah'. He was dissatisfied with our singing of the phrase "All we like sheep, have gone astray". He made us practice it repeatedly until, in a fit of exasperation, he sang the phrase as he wanted us to interpret it – his English was so poor that he thought the plural of sheep should be sheeps. To his amazement, our next rendering of the phrase was perfect. The incident was a major talking point for a long time, the choir's subsequent success being ascribed by many to its adoption of 'sheeps' for 'sheep' !

Although Jackie, Mr Dan Jones' son, and I were only seven or eight years old, our voices were considered sufficiently good for us to be included in the choir for the concert. It was a memorable night. Specially for the occasion, my mother made me a blue dress, trimmed with rosebud braid at the neck and bottom as well as round the edges of the puff sleeves. But the dress was forgotten as the concert started. We sang our hearts out and at the close of the oratorio the packed chapel rose to its feet and applauded for what seemed an eternity. Jackie and I felt so elated standing to the front with people in the audience smiling and nodding at us. It took some time for the realisation to sink in that it was all over. Whenever I now think of the chapel, it is that concert I most remember.

Chapel going was not always a pleasurable experience. The sermons I found tedious and impenetrable, and often during the evening service I would fall asleep against my mother, waking every time she stood for a hymn. Being obliged to remain for the communion service was the last straw to a tired, bored and by then irritable child. Occasionally, in order to keep me from fidgeting, my mother would let me taste a sip of her communion wine. The only other relief was when the organ ran out of air ! Ronnie and Jackie Jones were responsible for working the long wooden handle behind the pulpit which pumped air into the organ, but sometimes they would forget, with disastrous musical consequences. Whenever this happened, Mr Philips, the minister, would swivel around and glare down at them from the pulpit. I would want to giggle, but a rap on my knees from my mother would stop that. Also, my mother would sometimes oblige me to accompany her to the women's midweek meetings, which were well attended – for they provided women with one of the few regular opportunities they had to escape from their homes. They would look forward to such gatherings with relish, and would achieve much good work in aid of the chapel, but for us children they proved wearisome affairs from which we were only too glad to escape.

Chapter Seven

THE GENERAL STRIKE

When the 1926 strike started, the railway workers came out with everyone else. We would listen out for the colliery hooters which, for the duration of the strike, sounded at the same time every evening. For a time, it seemed as if they would sound forever. Among those little affected by the strike were the Best family, even though Mr Best and his eldest boy joined their colleagues and did not return to the tin plate works until the strike had been called off. With their large house, cottage, shop and garage, the Best family seemed to me to enjoy enormous wealth. For us, however, life, which was tough when times were normal, was particularly difficult during this period. Ronnie and I were raised to be industrious and thrifty – "Whatever you can't afford, you must wait for", was one of the many maxims my mother drummed into us, as was "Watch the pennies and the pounds will look after themselves". It was not that my parents were mean; they taught us by example to work hard, but also to be generous, to help and respect others, and not to carry tales.

During, and for some time after the 1926-7 strike, my mother would rise extra early. She first cleared the grate, lit the fire, and cleaned the living room. Then she called on our neighbour, Mrs Jones, and the two of them, wearing men's' caps back to front on their heads, and with one empty coal bag over a shoulder and another under an arm, would go in search of lumps of coke or clinker at the tin plate furnace on the far side of the railway. Sometimes they might venture further to pick coal at the colliery tip close to the river. They were not alone, for many families were poor and their women too would scavenge for fuel. While my mother and Mrs Jones were away on these sorties, Ronnie and I used to lay the breakfast table before leaving the cottage to await them at the level crossing gate. As soon as they arrived, we would open the gate on our side of the crossing and give them a hand the short distance to the cottages. My mother would devote the remainder of the morning to cooking and other household chores, then washed and changed so that when evening arrived she would be sweet smelling and tidily dressed. During the Strike a well meaning friend suggested to my mother that selling tea might provide an additional income for us. Ronnie and I helped fill flat packets with the tea, which would arrive in chests lined with tin foil. We then had the humiliating task of going round houses distributing the packets to our customers, most of whom were fellow chapel members. How I detested that job as, I guess, did Ronnie. I also know that my mother considered the tea to be cheap, and that she did not wholeheartedly approve of the venture. Fortunately, it did not last long and for our troubles we ended up with precious little bar a few tea chests.

The railwaymen soon decided to end their participation in the strike and return to work. They simply had no money left to live on. Even before the strike a railwayman's wages were barely sufficient to keep body and soul together, with very little that could be saved for a rainy day. By comparison, the miners and tin workers earned reasonably high wages from which, if they so chose, they could save. In our neighbourhood they certainly lived in larger and more comfortable houses, and generally enjoyed a higher standard of living. Nevertheless, when the railwaymen stopped striking, a degree of animosity developed towards the railway community which affected us children both in and outside school. It reached such a pitch that my mother became afraid to let us venture out of doors unaccompanied after dark, for ruffian gangs started roaming Cwmtwrch. We would hear them approaching our cottages along the lane from Gurnos Cross, and would sigh with relief when they had safely passed us by and their clamour receded up the valley. One such gang formed in Lower Cwmtwrch, and they plagued me. Many of its members were of school age, and their ring leader would often wait to taunt me on the way home from school. One afternoon, when I was walking home from school along the Gurnos road, I became aware of someone rushing me from behind – a heavy coat was pulled over me and, the next moment, a blow to the head sent me reeling to the ground. It was that same gang leader. Somehow I staggered home, where my appearance shocked my mother into anger. She made me recount the incident in detail and, although my parents never normally interfered at school, the following morning she took me to see the headmaster.

The interview changed little, for I was attacked again shortly afterwards. I was sitting atop Bryn-Deri tip, examining my new doll. Years before, I had possessed a malleable life-like doll with dark hair and brown eyes that I adored. When I was about four or five years old, I remember my father's mother, on one of her visits, asking if she could cut the doll's hair for me. Together, we sat the doll on the mat before the fire and, taking great pains, my grandmother proceeded to cut, until my doll finished up with a short but smart hairstyle, with a fringe. I was delighted and from that moment loved both doll and grandmother with greater intensity. The doll was my constant companion until eventually, through wear and tear, it literally disintegrated. By that time I was older and more interested in other pursuits like painting, reading and making models, but my parents must have thought that I missed the doll for they scrimped and saved to buy another one for my birthday. Although I did not say so, I really did not like the new doll which was like almost every other doll in the neighbour-hood – big, blonde, blue-eyed, and stiff to handle – quite unlike my erstwhile brown-eyed beauty. I nevertheless let my mother dig out my old wooden push chair, with a tapestry seat and back, and sat the doll in it. I felt silly as I set off down the lane and hoped I would not meet anyone. However, I bumped into Aunt Selina, Ronnie Best's auntie, just outside their house. She looked down at the doll, then smiled at me and asked "And how is your little baby today ?" The question made me cringe inside, and I felt so embarrassed that I wheeled the push chair straight home, ditched it, and carried the doll to the tip. I wanted to get right away from everyone and think things out. I had just sat down when the thug who had hit me before appeared on the path that skirted the bottom of the tip. When I realised that he too had seen me, I became paralysed with fear. Up he climbed, relentlessly towards me. As he reached me, he snatched the doll from my grasp and hurled it to the bottom of the tip where it shattered. I waited for him to throw me, but he turned away laughing, and shouting something I could not make out. I made my way down to where the doll lay, and collected the pieces. I returned home with mixed emotions; a black loathing for my per-secutor, pity for my parents whose precious money had been wasted, and a personal relief that I need no longer pretend to like the doll. Certainly, I was determined that my parents should never buy me a replacement.

The miners continued the strike alone, enduring great hardship, until they too gave in. Groups of them would frequently meet locally, as well as trudge miles to attend gatherings further afield. We would watch as great streams of them passed by the Gurnos on their way up or down the valley, conversing excitedly, changing fluently from Welsh to English and back again. I had little idea of what they were saying, but Ronnie informed me that they were discussing the 1917 Revolution in Russia, and how they would remain out until a socialist revolution was effected in Britain. Those from Upper Cwmtwrch and Cwmllyn-fell considered themselves to be the elite of miners and were the most united and adamant in their demands. When the strike ultimately collapsed, their feelings of bitterness ran as deep as their former resolve to win. Ronnie re-members them muttering "We lost, we lost" as they made their way home from the last great meeting to the east. Their anger then was not directed against the railwaymen but against their fellow miners elsewhere, mainly in England, who they believed to have betrayed the revolution.

One evening shortly after that last big gathering the hooters remained silent, and we knew that the strike was over. The collieries and tin works became active again and it appeared that conditions might improve for the valley community. Certainly, things initially went well for us. However, there was no work for many miners, and the standard of living for all gradually deteriorated. Following the Great Strike, the character of the Capitol Cinema also changed

The Ystalyfera Kitchen Workers during the 1926 General Strike, and those who received their mid-day meal at this centre. Jackie Jones (later Jackie Campbell, who became Eileen's husband) can be seen as a little boy sitting at the front, second to the right of the placard. Mrs Mathias, distinguished by her white hair, can be seen sitting to the left of the placard.
(Photograph courtesy Bernant Hughes).

as, with the advent of talking movies, the era of silent films passed. We heard of new cinemas with names like the 'Plaza' and 'Astoria' springing up in Swansea, but the entire valley had sunk into depression, and few from our area could afford to see films there. All around were men out of work and down at heel, huddled in corners, many of them ill and with grating coughs. They would form long queues outside the Capitol to buy tickets for the cheapest seats and a brief respite, a temporary escape from harsh reality. They and their families were suffering in a cruel and unjust world. Hardship hit Jackie's family more than it did most railway people. Mr Dan Jones had come out in 1926 with his fellow miners and, like everyone else, they managed as best they could. Jackie went picking coke or coal from nearby tips, while his mother cooked pasties which she and Jackie would carry round, trying to sell to neighbours. They would also queue up outside the soup kitchen for miners, which would be set up at the end of their road in Heol-y-Varteg. Following the strike, Mr Dan Jones could not find work locally and, in the company of others, would tramp miles from valley to valley looking for an opening. Jackie would often accompany him. However, Mr Dan Jones was unsuccessful, and the long trips only served to aggravate his miner's chest. Eventually, in 1927 or 1928, he left his family to search for work in the Midlands, and in 1929 summoned them to join him in Kidderminster, where he had obtained a position in a carpet factory. Jackie was only ten years old and the future at last looked rosier for them. Then, in 1931, news arrived that Mr Dan Jones was dead.

By 1930, when I was nine years old, the railway people were also feeling the pinch. They started a mutual aid scheme whereby members paid into a Friendly Society through which I received a parcel of clothes from a Swansea based engine driver and his wife, who had a daughter the same age as me. I well remember the contents; a silk hyacinth-blue dress, which fitted me perfectly, and a pair of brown shoes, which did not. However, times were so bad that I knew my mother could not afford shoes for me, so I lied and told her that they fitted. Despite the constant pain, I never let on to my parents, and wore them for a long time. They turned my big toes in, and the other toes back and up, and I have ever since been plagued with feet problems. The mutual aid scheme was just one reflection of the close co-operation that existed within the ranks of the railway community which formed a second, wider family for Ronnie and me. The adults always had time for us, fostering our sense of belonging. Looking back, I consider it a privilege to have known such a group of kind, considerate men and women.

Chapter Eight

SCHOOLDAYS

We did not have far to walk to school. Turning left at Gurnos Cross, towards Ystradgynlais, we followed the 'stream' for two hundred yards, then crossed it over a small hump-backed bridge, and finally climbed a slight incline to the school. The school grounds were divided into two distinct parts, the Infant classrooms positioned on the crest of the hill, and the Junior and Senior sections clustered at its base. Between, lay their respective playgrounds, separated from one another by a high retaining wall. The 'senior' yard was restricted to boys, the one above it to girls and infants.

On our way to school, we would pass Anna Jo's sweet shop. It was not a proper shop, consisting only of the tiny front room of her house, yet it held much more attraction for us children than the large general store set square beside it on Gurnos Cross. It appeared to be open at all hours, a candle lighting the window at night. Hard against the pane, fogged with neglect, lay bare wooden boards upon which, in her higgledy-piggledy fashion, Anna Jo would arrange all the sweets likely to attract our attention. We would peer in at them for some considerable time before entering the shop. If we were judicious, we could purchase quite a variety of sweets for our half-penny piece, or farthing. We would also examine the cavity beneath the window boards for corpses, as embalmed in this miniature morgue lay a multitude of insects, the most prized of which were the larger flies. The prospect of finding a dead bluebottle, a rare event, formed an integral part of the attraction of Anna Jo's. Further on, beyond Gurnos Cross, and on the same side of the road as the shop, were a few cottages from which, as we passed, spilled school-bound children like ourselves. Opposite these cottages, set back from the road in their own grounds, stood several large houses, though they were scarcely visible behind the screen of shrubs and trees that lined the driveway leading up to their solid front doors. If people lived behind the iron gates that guarded entrance to those grounds, we never saw them.

The Infants' School comprised three classrooms, separated by sliding partitions that were pulled back for morning prayers, but it possessed only one outside door. How congested that entrance became as we children scrambled into the school. It opened into a cloakroom that possessed two coat pegs and a

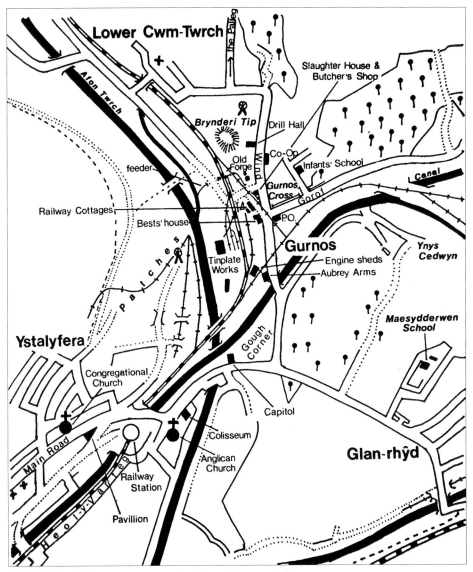

The Upper Swansea Valley.

peculiar 'cloakroom' odour that I can still recall. Very few children went home at dinner time and, as that room was our only shelter, we would, packed tightly together, eat our sandwiches there on rain-sodden, or freezing days. When thirsty, we cupped our hands under the cloakroom taps for water. On fine days, I would seek out my little 'cwtsh', the corner at the bottom of the infants' playground where the dividing wall met the edge of the Senior School building. There I would eat, sheltered from all but the warm south wind. One morning, I could barely wait for break time for I had brought a sticky pear drop with me to school. When the bell sounded, I skipped merrily down to my cwtsh, slid my back down the sun-soaked wall, and carefully extracted the sweet. I opened my mouth and started to gently suck, but somehow it got firmly lodged in my throat. I could not move it hurt so much and, frightened, I longed for my mother's comforting presence. After what seemed an age, it started to move, slowly and painfully, down my throat. The bell rang, and I walked stiffly back to class. It took most of the remainder of the morning for the triangular shaped object to complete its progress to my stomach, leaving me with an extremely sore throat and a resolve never again to buy a pear drop.

Most of the girls in the Infants' School came from Welsh homes and, though we were friendly enough, and often played together, I possessed no special friend until I reached the top class. Marjorie Reeves' family moved to our valley from Cornwall, where her father had worked in the mines. As they lived in Glanrhyd, they had the choice of sending Marjorie to school in either Ynyscedwyn or the Gurnos. I was very glad they selected the Gurnos because from the day she started school, Marjorie and I became close friends. We had much in common, being English-speaking, the same age, and possessing roughly the same academic ability – though in character and appearance we were like chalk and cheese. Marjorie was, in fact, completely different from any girl I had ever met. She had a mass of frizzy black hair, a pale plain round face, and a short stocky body. Come summer or winter, school or holiday, she wore the same kind of clothes; long thick black stockings inside buttoned boots, and a long-sleeved black or dark navy serge dress, with a high neck, over which lay a striped and bibbed apron. Some of the girls used to mock her for the way she dressed, which I confess used to puzzle me – I wish that she could sometimes have worn pretty clothes. My mother constantly praised the benefits of sunshine to us and, even in winter, we bared part of our legs to the elements, wearing thick socks only up to the knees. Ronnie and I both wore boots, and our mother used to knit or crochet caps and scarves for us. For some years, I treasured a warm red coat, with a matching beret, that she crocheted. She cut from the best cloth of my father's discarded railway uniforms to fashion clothes for Ronnie, who never looked out of place in them. In summer we dressed as freely as possible, Ronnie in short-sleeved, open-necked shirts, and shorts, and myself in dresses that had the hem turned right up. Our skin, ruddy in winter, turned bronze in summer. By contrast, Marjorie wore the same dull clothes, and remained pallid and wan.

Our friendship consolidated with time, and we were soon permitted to visit each other at home. It was a real novelty for me to have a girl as a close and constant companion, as in the Gurnos there were only boys to play with. Although I thoroughly enjoyed the rough and tumble of their games, having Marjorie around was special, for her ladylike demeanour – she was very quiet and sedate

– was a revelation to me. I agree with my mother's assessment that Marjorie possessed "an old head on young shoulders". Marjorie lived with her parents and Walter, her younger brother, in an end-of-terrace house in Glanrhyd. I would always enter through the kitchen, at the back of the house, which was reached via the side gate in the fence that surrounded their small, flag-stoned, back yard. The clothes line in the back yard appeared never to be used, and the kitchen was always full of damp clothes, drying on a wooden rack worked by pulleys, that hung low enough to brush my hair as I passed into the living room. This, too, was cluttered; it was so full of furniture that there was scarcely room enough to negotiate the dining table and even finding sufficient space to sit down for tea proved difficult. Dominating the living room was an American organ, that took up so much space that the dining table had to be jammed right up against it. An open hymn book rested on the keyboard stand and, on top of the organ, lay a large family Bible. Marjorie's father was a lay preacher who, when at home, would demonstrate his abundant preaching skills. He was a tall, very powerfully built man who, from his great height, would talk down to us children, at some length and with great solemnity, of the Lord and the importance of salvation. So strict were he and his wife that the atmosphere in their house was oppressive, and if it had not been for my regard for Marjorie, I would never have gone there. However, I kept my feelings secret, as I am sure did Marjorie her impressions of our home.

To return to school, we had a morning half-day holiday for Empire Day, when we would wave little Union Jacks, but the finest celebration was March 1st, St. David's Day, when no school work was done. Although nearly all of us pinned either leeks or daffodils to our chests, many Welsh girls arrived in school in traditional costume; dainty ebony shoes, white stockings, and full flannel skirts in scarlet, red and black stripe, or check. The crispest of white frilled aprons hung from their waists above which they wore white blouses overlaid with black and white check shawls. Finally, on their heads, were tall black hats, brims pleated with white lace. How I envied them! I faintly recall my first St. David's Day in the Infants' School, six days before my fourth birthday. A little boy and myself recited and simultaneously acted out a Welsh poem. Later, in the Senior School, the headmaster, Mr Edwards, would make us rehearse for weeks for an afternoon concert with which to celebrate the national day. The medium of teaching in the school was English, but for the concert he would tutor us in Welsh folk songs, and in 'Penillion', a style of singing unique to Wales. The school possessed a harp, but only Mr Edwards was permitted to touch it. I made the school choir which, although I had to stand at the back, was a privilege because I was English-speaking and had to learn the words and techniques of Welsh singing – something which came naturally to the Welsh children. During one rehearsal, Mr Edwards abruptly stopped the choir, pointed at me, and forcibly told me not to hop up and down like a monkey. After that, I always stood quite still. Over the weeks, I grew to love the music, and came to understand a little both of the beauty and sadness of the Welsh language. It created in me an enduring love of the country and a pride that, on my mother's side, I too was of Welsh ancestry.

I was very happy in Gurnos School, and found learning easy and enjoyable. In September 1927, Marjorie and I skipped a class to Mrs Thomas in Standard Three, a form considered sufficiently advanced to try for the scholarship. Pinned to the class wall before us was a huge map of the British Isles, which to me assumed the shape of three animals; the first was a pig, of which Wales constituted the head, and southern and western England the trunk and legs, the second was a stag, comprising Scotland and the Midlands, which sat astride the pig, while Ireland formed the third animal, a bear seated on its cuddly backside, gazing out across the Atlantic Ocean.

By the time we reached Standard Three, Ronnie had entered Maesydderwen County School. He was not quite ten years old. Not long after he had started there, I remember arriving home from school to find my mother at the door. It was unusual for her to meet me like that, and from her pale and worried expression I knew that something was amiss before she informed me that Ronnie had had an accident at school and was upstairs in bed. Without waiting for her to finish the explanation, I rushed up the stairs, full of apprehension at what I might find. I was very relieved, on turning the corner at the head of the stairs, to see Ronnie propped up on one elbow, grinning from ear to ear. He was, however, making light of a serious injury. He related what had happened. As the Maesydderwen School playing field was being extended at the Glanrhyd end, the boundary railings there had been torn up and stacked on the ground. These railings were of iron and had spiked heads, which tempted some of the senior boys to use them as javelins. Ronnie was playing with a group of lads his own age well away from the older boys, but when running to retrieve a ball, he ran directly into the flight of one of these 'javelins'. It plunged into his groin, and had it not been for the immediate attention of Dr Walsh, and the subsequent nursing of my mother, he could have sustained permanent damage. Dr Walsh cleared and stitched the wound, which my mother afterwards kept scrupulously clean with Lysol – the house was for weeks filled with the pungent odour of antiseptic. Ronnie made a surprisingly quick recovery – we all cheered when he first managed to hobble downstairs – and he was soon back in school and as physically active as before the accident.

In the September of 1928, Marjorie and I moved into Standard Five in preparation for sitting the scholarship paper the following summer. About eight pupils from the area won scholarships to Maesydderwen each year. Miss Jones, our form teacher, worked us hard, but we rose to the occasion. For her, the 'three Rs' were of paramount importance. In mathematics, she assumed that we had already mastered the 'twelve times table', and so concentrated on mental arithmetic, every morning session commencing with a verbal bombardment of problems, the answers to which we were soon throwing back almost before she had completed the questions. We were also given written problems to solve, in arithmetic, algebra and geometry – all of which we thoroughly enjoyed. Our spelling was meticulously checked in all subjects, but especially in English where a very high standard of written work was expected. Mr Edwards ran a lending library which we were encouraged to use. I would borrow from it regularly, my passion for books growing so great that I recall my father warning me lest I damage my eyes by so much candlelight reading.

By May 1929, we were confident that Miss Jones had fully prepared us for the approaching examination and a considerable excitement of anticipation had built up in the class. Then, quite unexpectedly, we were informed that the scholarship age had been raised, so that we younger candidates would have to wait an additional year before sitting the examination. Such a sense of betrayal, frustration, and anger swept over me at this apparently arbitrary ruling that I felt physically sick. Looking back, I consider that that decision altered the course of my life, for it drained me of my enthusiasm and ambition. We did attend cookery classes at Ynyscedwyn, but most of the additional year was spent monotonously re-working familiar exercises. Moreover that extra year in Standard Five was clouded by an unhappy incident, for Marjorie was accused of stealing sixpence. Marjorie was no thief, and there must have been a good reason for her possessing the money, but the attitude of Miss Jones, and the rest of the class, was condemnatory. The affair was further confounded by a mis-understanding, which threatened the friendship between Marjorie and myself. I was by nature a bit of a dreamer, and in that idle year I spent so much time gazing out of the window next to the double desk we shared, that Miss Jones started calling me the 'Day Dreamer'. Not only would I stare past Marjorie into space, I would also compose and silently mouth nonsense rhymes. One such time, shortly after the alleged theft, I was brought sharply back to reality by Miss Jones' voice saying, "Eileen Baker, I know that you despise Marjorie Reeves for being a thief, but there is no need for you to keep pulling faces at her". Those were her exact words ! I felt hot with embarrassment and confusion, hoping desperately that Marjorie understood, and hating the girls who were tittering behind their hands. I think Marjorie did understand, but even today I wish that I had been seated on the window side of her. We eventually sat and passed the scholarship in 1930, but I know that I would have achieved a far higher grade had I sat the examination the previous year.

Moving to the new school in Maesydderwen reversed the distances that Marjorie and I had to cover each morning, for she now lived nearer school whereas I had to walk a couple of miles to reach it. Maesydderwen School was an old converted mansion which instilled in all who attended it a great sense of pride. Set in lovely grounds, it was approached by two drives, one from the direction of Ynyscedwyn, while the other, from Glanrhyd, ran past the care-taker's cottage and an enclosed orchard where, in season, we could buy apples – mainly russets. As it neared the school, the drive passed a huge monkey tree, the first any of us had ever seen. At Maesydderwen we had for the first time to wear a school uniform, an obligation that proved traumatic for my parents who did not possess the money to buy either a shop made uniform or the proper material to make one up. The gym slip, which school requirements specified should possess three deep pleats to both back and front, proved to be the most problematic garment for my mother, who had to skimp on cloth. In the end, she managed to provide the slip with token pleats. I distinctly recall my first day at school – autumn was in the air. Provided I remained erect, my sham pleats remained unnoticed, so I started the morning walking stiffly around, beret pulled firmly over my head, gym slip pleats falling neatly beneath my Co-op blazer, and my Co-op satchel stretched tightly across my chest. However, my resolve to maintain appearances did not last; in no time, the beret had been stuffed into the blazer pocket, the slash had slipped up from my hips to hang loosely around my waist, the pleats on my gym slip had virtually disintegrated, and my satchel swung nonchalantly from one shoulder. By contrast, Marjorie, who still sat next to me, although in a separate desk, was transformed by the uniform for she wore a gym slip of quality material, and neither sash nor beret ever strayed from position. However, true to character, she thought nothing of it, from the outset concentrating her attention on academic work.

From conversations between Ronnie and his school mates, I already knew a considerable amount about the Maesydderwen teaching staff. I had learnt their nicknames, the forms and subjects they taught, and their various foibles. Mr Rees, the headmaster, was nicknamed 'Cochyn' ('Red One') because, when he became incensed, the colour of his face would match that of his hair. He was also head of mathematics, which he taught mainly to the fifth form, although he took us in the subject for the entire four years we remained at Maesydderwen. We innocently awaited our first mathematics lesson, nothing Ronnie had related having prepared me for his appearance. In my entire life, I have never been so terrified of one man, and my fear was shared by all my class mates, including some very tough boys. We all dreaded each subsequent lesson with him, the sound of his approaching footsteps being sufficient to have us shaking with fright. Thankfully, mathematics came easily to me, but woe betide those who performed badly in the subject. Any child failing to answer a question, written or oral, was liable to be hauled to the front of the classroom, boys by the ear, while girls were either pulled by their hair or pushed. I felt desperately sorry for them. None of the girls in my form had long hair, but a girl in another class was regularly dragged out by her plaits which she would unsuccessfully attempt to hide down the back of her blouse. At the close of each lesson with him, we had all added something to our store of mathematical knowledge, but were so limp with nervous exhaustion that we cared not. All we longed for was the sight of his gown-clad back in retreat down the corridor. He succeeded in getting every one of us through the mathematics section of the C.W.B. School-Leaving Certificate, but at what mental cost to his pupils! He cast a dark cloud over what might otherwise have been for me a happy four years at school.

Paradoxically, in view of the manner in which the headmaster terrorised pupils in class, he once displayed uncharacteristic kindness to me, though the memory of it does not surface easily. I was twelve years old, in the second form at Maesydderwen, and had woken one wintry morning with temples throbbing – the first of the migraines from which I was regularly to suffer in subsequent years. At school, the pain grew steadily worse and I was grateful when, finally, the bell ended the morning session and I could slip out to the girls' lavatories. Feeling quite light headed, I sat down on the toilet seat cover, but my head and eyes ached so much that I felt physically sick and was soon alternately vomiting and sitting. The retching was so painful that I became increasingly faint and eventually, in search of an empty classroom where I might lay down my head and rest, started slowly and unsteadily down a corridor. I had just reached a doorway, and was about to grope my way through the entrance, when strong hands lifted me off my feet and carried me into a room buzzing with adult conversation. I was lowered gently into a large leather chair warm from the heat of an open fire. Only then, through eyes half closed with pain, did I recognise before me Mr Rees. My incredulity turned to acute embarrassment as I realised that I was sitting in the heart of the staff room, a 'Holy of Holies' no pupil normally dared even to approach.

Physically incapable of obeying the instinct to flee, I looked up again to see the headmaster talking to a group of teachers, from which Miss Thomas 'Brec' (short for Brecon – used to distinguish her from Miss Thomas 'Llan' – i.e. Llanelli) presently detached herself. She approached me, and said she would drive me home – being one of the handful of staff who ran a car – a small black one. A plump but pretty and popular teacher of biology, she was particularly kind to me that afternoon, thankfully not attempting a conversation. We quickly reached Gurnos Cross where she asked for directions, whereon I guided her up the main Cwmtwrch road, past the butcher's which fronted the slaughter house, as far as the ironmonger's, where we turned left down a short incline onto the narrow bridge over our 'stream', then across the railway siding in front of the cottages. My mother, wearing a sack apron, was taken by surprise when she answered Miss Thomas' rap on the door. After the brief explanation as to why I had been brought home, my mother politely thanked Miss Thomas, who left, then shut the front door and helped me upstairs. I sank with relief into bed and a sleep which lasted until evening. As I woke, I heard my father's voice softly enquiring how I was. It turned out that he had been sitting beside my bedside since he had got in from work, ensuring that the cloth covering my temple was kept cool and moist. That instant, an intense surge of love for my parents swept over me. The headache, dizziness and nausea had passed, and the following morning I was back in school, much to the surprise of my teachers. Mr Rees continued to be as brutal as ever, but that incident ensured that I never again feared him.

On the timetable, Mr Rees' lessons were followed by English or Geography, heavenly subjects compared to what had preceded them. I suspect that the masters who taught them, knowing of Mr Rees' reputation, put themselves out to be kind to us. As we relaxed, our nervous tension evaporated, with the result that we both enjoyed and did well in these subjects.

However, throughout secondary school, we were afflicted by fortnightly tests in each subject, the marks for which counted towards the end of term examination results. We were also plagued by 'lines', liberally doled out as a form of punishment by many of the staff, but notably by Miss Thomas Llan who thought nothing of handing out 1,000 lines for a minor misdemeanour. She once gave me as many in order to teach me "to be a lady", although to this day I cannot imagine what unladylike activity I might have been engaged in. That punishment had three consequences: It gave me cramp, a permanent dislike of Miss Thomas Llan, and a distaste for history, which was a shame as I had enjoyed the subject in the Gurnos School. Miss Thomas Llan also numbered amongst those teachers who could set unreasonable amounts of homework. Indeed, homework grew so onerous that, when I also had 'lines' to do, my 'free time' at home was completely whittled away. Often, I had to remain up until 10 o'clock in the evening to complete schoolwork and, as we would inevitably postpone the writing of weekend essays until the last moment, chapel attendance became infrequent. All this worried my parents, who were concerned that my workload was becoming too great, but felt they could not complain to the school authorities because we had been fortunate enough to have gained places at Maesydderwen.

One teacher suffered alone for the sins of her colleagues. Miss Pugh, nicknamed Pug, taught Welsh, a subject only two members of the class took at all seriously. One was a Welsh speaker who carried off many Eisteddfod prizes, and whom we labelled 'Teacher's Pet', and the other was my friend, Marjorie. The reason we, and the vast majority of school children in South Wales at that time rejected Welsh was because scorn was heaped upon the language from all quarters. We were everywhere discouraged from considering Welsh to be a serious academic option, being told that the subject would lead up a blind alley, and that to get on in life we should concentrate upon the English language. The prevalence of this attitude amongst adults affected us children to such a degree that Miss Pugh's lessons invariably degenerated quickly into a shambles. Miss Pugh would react to our contempt for the subject in two ways: Firstly, as the lesson progressed, more and more pupils would be sent to stand facing the wall. To my shame, I admit that I was as bad as the rest of my class mates. Outside school, I could both understand and converse in vernacular Welsh, but inside the classroom I simply made no effort. On the occasions that Miss Pugh attempted to teach us the Lord's Prayer in Welsh, I was soon despatched to the wall, for I could never memorise more than the first two lines. Secondly, when Miss Pugh could tolerate us no more, she would break down and, in a flood of tears, flee the classroom. In the fortnightly Welsh tests, I would regularly come near the bottom, whereas Marjorie, who could neither understand nor speak the language, would always come second. Latin was another subject derided by the majority of pupils. It was termed a dead language, and only those with a premature religious calling, or those possessing more enlightened minds, would continue studying it beyond the first two compulsory years. I had no compunction about dropping both Welsh and Latin at the earliest opportunity.

Life at Maesydderwen was enlivened by the arrival in my class of two Spaniards and a Portuguese, from Abercrave and Colbren. I forget the name of the Portuguese lad, but the others were a boy called Lalo Macho and a girl named Eusebia Estaban. All three displayed a remarkable intelligence and, more importantly to us, possessed striking good looks. Eusebia was particularly beautiful, and grew increasingly so as each school year passed. She would attract both boys and girls, give them a heavenly time for a short while, then drop them like hot cakes. I, too, developed a crush on her, but it was of short duration and was not too painful.

When Ronnie was in the fourth form at Maesydderwen, he performed well enough in the School Leaving Certificate to qualify for matriculation, despite being only fourteen years old at the time. However, the Higher Certificate course at Maesydderwen, which took an additional two years, catered only for Arts students, and Ronnie's specialities were the Sciences. Consequently, he left school and started to attend an Unemployment Training Centre at Ammanford. With Vic Mathias from Ystalyfera, he would travel there daily, on a free bus pass, to learn wood and metal work skills. Later, he worked a bakery round for a time. However, my mother was determined that Ronnie should enter university, whatever the cost, a sentiment with which I was in full accord for Ronnie was a brilliant scholar – so much so that in school I was dogged by his reputation, teachers often quipping, "You're not as bright as your brother, are you ?" As the 1931-2 academic year commenced, Ronnie was still travelling to the

Unemployment Training Centre at Ammanford, but unbeknown to either of us, a friend of my parents was helping him to achieve his dream of attending university. This friend was a County Councillor from Lower Cwmtwrch who, at a distance, had watched our progress from the moment we started in Gurnos Infants, and who advised my parents about the possibility of obtaining a loan from Breconshire Education Authority to enable Ronnie to go to university. With his support, my mother made several trips to Brecon to plead Ronnie's case and was eventually summoned before their Education Board. As a result, Ronnie was awarded a grant to study at Swansea University, which accepted him to start at intermediate level in October 1932, a month before his sixteenth birthday. My mother's 'cup' was full at this success, while my father and I were delighted and immensely proud of the two of them.

1932 was a leap year – I had to pay attention as my birthday was early in March – and the year that the school burnt down, after rats in the cellars had gnawed into electric wires. Ronnie and I woke unusually early on Monday 29th February, which would normally have been St. David's Day. We were used to the odours emitted by the industrial works that surrounded us, but that morning we noticed a new and pungent smell – as had our mother who had risen long before us. The acrid smell wafting to us on the breeze was unmistakably that of a fire which must have started after my father had left for work, or he would have ventured outside to investigate and report back. Ronnie and I dressed hurriedly and ran outside with my mother. It was still very early, and against the dark of the morning, in the direction of Ynyscedwyn, we could see a fiery glow. We scampered back indoors to quickly swallow some breakfast before rushing again from the house. It was by then almost light, but the glow was still there, accompanied by the crackling of flames, and a towering pillar of smoke that was edging slowly southwards down the Tawe valley. We were filled with a curious mixture of apprehension, curiosity and excitement. Soon word reached us that Maesydderwen School was aflame, and we sped indoors to tell my mother. I then hurriedly gathered my school books together and, after snatching up our coats, Ronnie and I left the house once more and sprinted towards the school. We soon joined other pupils running in the same direction. On the main road we met workmen who had passed the school and who confirmed the rumour, and by the time we reached the Aubrey Arms we could see the flames leaping up behind the bare branches of the trees surrounding the Gough estate. From that point we had to run through a screen of dense, billowing smoke. We all sensed that it must be the school that was aflame, but we had to verify it for ourselves. It did not take long. Tearing past the new Croesffyrdd Estate, we entered the lower drive of the school, and stopped aghast. What a sight it was ! The large rambling mansion was ablaze from top to bottom. We ran forward, but I was so struck that I could not bear to go beyond the Monkey Tree, against

80

which I sank and gazed in wonder at the fire while Ronnie ran ahead to see if he could do anything to help. Firemen had established a cordon to keep at a safe distance all but staff and senior pupils, for part of one of the ground floor classrooms had already collapsed. Chalked in white on the board inside it were clearly visible the previous Friday's French lesson. In the middle of the building, etched by flames, was the solitary figure of Mr Rees frantically gathering up books and hurling them out to the crowd in the courtyard below.

Joining the majority of school members in the field a short distance in front of the burning building, my initial numbness thawed into a strange sense of liberation as I realised that it would take some time before we could again attend school. It never occurred to me that we might never return to Maesydderwen. Later that same day, we were informed by teachers that the school would have to be completely rebuilt, and were instructed to go home and study on our own as best we could until alternative arrangements had been made. The Gurnos School Elementary children were quickly moved to the Drill Hall in Lower Cwmtwrch, but it took six weeks to erect in the girls' playground the new classrooms required before we could all be housed, so we did not recommence classes until the start of the summer term. During the intervening period, I was very much at a loose end. I tried self study, but found it difficult to concentrate without a classroom atmosphere, and retained practically none of the knowledge that I attempted to memorise. Moreover, there was the distraction of moving house, for the pull of helping my mother prepare our council house for occupation proved greater than that of school work. Our house move finally occurred in May, two weeks after we had returned to school. For that brief fortnight, I could reach school in five minutes flat, but when we moved to Glanrhyd, which was a mere five minutes from burnt-out Maesydderwen, it again took me as long to reach school as it had when I used to walk from the Gurnos to Maesydderwen !

Chapter Nine

HOLIDAYS

My father worked three shifts in every twenty-four hours, for fifty-one weeks of the year. Railwaymen were entitled to one week's holiday, although my father also gained a special dispensation to attend the final Railway Ambulance Competition – all such local events having to be organised by the men in their spare time. By special agreement, the Railway Company also allowed the men to travel up to the annual Flower and Vegetable Show, held in rotation in the four towns of Llandrindod Wells, Llanwrtyd Wells, Builth Wells and Shrewsbury. Sometimes the whole family would go – for me the main attraction was the journey, for we caught the train in Victoria Station, Swansea, and travelled the Central Wales line on an ex-L.N.W.R. express. It was a sumptuous experience compared to travelling on our little Swansea Valley trains. We children used to spend most of the journey in the corridors, watching for the landmarks. After leaving Victoria Station, the engine would gather speed, running alongside the familiar features of Swansea Bay as far as Blackpill where it crossed the bridge over the Mumbles railway and road and struck inland, up into Central Wales. We knew precisely where to start looking for the Sugar Loaf mountain, which resembled an upturned pudding basin. As we approached it, the open fields became obscured by cuttings that hemmed us in. Then the whistle shrilled and the windows were rapidly pulled shut as we were plunged into the dimly lit Sugar Loaf tunnel that amplified the 'chugga-di-chug' of the engine. Once, when we were travelling at speed near Church Stretton, on the way to Shrewsbury, the train jerked to a halt. Everyone rushed to the windows, but a considerable time elapsed before news reached us that an old lady had been knocked down and killed while attempting to walk over an unmanned level crossing. We were all shocked. There must have been an enquiry, though I recall hearing nothing further about the incident.

Each year, my father was entitled to a total of four free family rail passes, on which we could travel anywhere on the L.M.S., and in addition we received P.T.s – Privilege Tickets – issued at a reduced fare for dependents of railway employees. The Flower and Vegetable Show would use up one free ticket, as would our summer visits to my father's family at Pembrey, but we did sometimes manage to travel somewhere special. On two occasions we took the

On a Railway Trip to Scotland – The Forth Bridge. Eileen's mother is on the extreme left of the third row, behind the spectacled boy wearing a cap. Eileen is third to the left of her mother, with Ronnie immediately behind her.

Quay Parade, Swansea, c.1920.

overnight train to Scotland – although we only had a very short time to look around before catching the train back. The year we visited Rothsay, we arrived at dinner time to find a meal of fresh salmon laid out for us, but we barely had time to devour the half of it before we had to rush off in order to catch the last ferry boat to connect with the South Wales train. Another year, when we visited Edinburgh, and were passing under the great Forth Bridge, a wag called Jones 'Cray' (his home town was Cray) shouted to all and sundry, "Mind your heads, boys bach !"

Also in the summer months, Auntie Edith, my mother, Ronnie, Harry, and myself regularly took a Saturday afternoon jaunt to Swansea Sands. From the Gurnos, we used to travel down to Pontardawe every other Saturday morning to see my grandmother. If the weather was sunny, we would afterwards meet Auntie Edith and Harry at Pontardawe railway station and catch the next train to Swansea, alighting at St. Thomas' station in the Dock area of the town. From the platform, we clattered down the dark covered steps to the pavement outside and branched right onto an iron girded drawbridge spanning the river Tawe. This was a different river from the one we were familiar with further up the valley. At Ystalyfera, our friends would be swimming in its clear swift running waters, home to trout and minnow, but from the St. Thomas' bridge we gazed on a river, widened and deepened to carry boats between Swansea Docks and the numerous industrial concerns upriver, which was turbid and sluggish, its surface etched with lazy interlacing circles of multi-coloured oils and waste. Over the same bridge ran railway tracks which we followed past large flour warehouses as far as Victoria Station, where the lines disappeared into the Docks. The sight of Victoria Station always filled us children with excitement for it was from there that we used to start on our rare trips on a L.N.W.R. express up to central Wales. It was not far from Victoria Station to the Rutland Street depot of the Mumbles train the engine of which, as we neared the depot, we could hear and see hissing in impatience as it waited to take the next train and its lucky passengers off to the Mumbles. We would linger a while absorbing the enchantment of this scene before continuing our journey. Following the Mumbles railway line we drew level with the forbidding walls of Swansea prison, a small distance beyond which we turned left through the archway that ran under the main L.N.W.R. tracks and immediately emerged onto Swansea sands.

Our favourite spot was midway between the archway entrance and the St. Helens slip. There the sand was not only clean but, piled up against the railway embankment, was warm, making a cosy resting place for my mother and Auntie Edith. There, we children would listen for, and watch the signals dropping for, an oncoming train, before scrambling up the embankment to the railings through which we looked out for the great gleaming L.N.W.R. passenger engines pulling their long loads. These giants, with their spacious and elegant cream and

Cousin Harry, Eileen and Ronnie on Swansea Sands, c.1926.

*My mother and Auntie Edith, reclining in the banked-up sand against the
L.N.W.R. embankment, Swansea Sands.*

brown carriages, would have dwarfed our little valley engines pulling their red and corridor-less L.M.S. carriages. As we stood there, waving at the trains flashing by, friendly drivers and firemen would wave back, as did passengers standing in the corridors to catch a view of Swansea Bay. Not far away, towards the St. Helens slip, were a few brightly coloured boat swings and a couple of stalls. The swings were not the real attraction, for we possessed swings at home – the council had installed some in the Welfare grounds, and we also made tree swings from rope. What lured us was the ice cream stall, for we could not get Swansea Bay cornets at home. We knew that, in their own time, our mothers would despatch us to buy a treat for ourselves and, occasionally, for them. I can visualise now that ice cream cornet – yellow and creamy, yet crisp, delicious to the tongue.

However, the highlight of the trip remained Swansea Bay itself, a glorious stretch of golden sand which ran to the sea and curled with it round to Mumbles Head. From where we pitched, we had in sight the entire sweep, including Mumbles Pier and Lighthouse. The bay was shallow, so that when the tide was out, it was far to the sea's edge. This made not the slightest difference to Ronnie and Harry who, in no time, had changed into their swimming costumes and were running to the sea. Being more timid, I preferred to await the incoming tide before venturing into the water although, regardless of the state of the tide I would change into a swimming costume and don a special pale blue silky hair net, across the front of which ran a pretty band. The net had elastic at the back to keep it in place and came right over my forehead. In or out of the sea, I kept it on, and thought myself the 'cat's whiskers' ! I never learnt to swim, mainly because I was terrified of deep water, but I thoroughly enjoyed splashing about up to my waist, or sitting at the sea's edge feeling the flow of sand and water through my toes and swirling around my feet, legs and bottom. I envied those who could swim, but nothing would persuade me to venture in any deeper. By the time Ronnie and Harry had emerged from the waves, their swim suits hanging incongruously low, leaden with water, I would have fashioned a large sand castle, decorated with shells and flying a home made flag from its highest turret. As the sea flowed steadily closer over the shallow sands we would frantically attempt to protect it by throwing up outer walls and moats – to no avail, for the tide remorselessly swept aside the outer defences and encroached upon the inner fortifications. Like King Canute we tried to defy the inevitable, until no trace of the castle remained. Then we dried and changed, before devouring the picnic our mothers had prepared. And all the time to the back of us we could hear the familiar sounds of main line and Mumbles trains. To us it was a slice of paradise !

We might, on special occasions, catch the Mumbles train. Then, if we were accompanied by Harry and Auntie Edith, she and my mother first paid a brief visit to Swansea market for laver bread and cockles to take home. These purchases having been made, we would rush down Rutland Street, in the process often tripping up over the railway lines leading from the loco sheds to the Mumbles railway proper. There would always be a train hissing and ready to go, with others waiting in a queue. Five minutes before each departure the depot bell would clang out loud above the noise and bustle. We would clamber up the curved iron stairway to the upper deck, despite it being open to the elements, and choose seats as close as possible to the front and to the engine. Specks from the latter would inevitably fly into our eyes and cover our clothes, but that was part of the fun of the trip. Our mothers, who became experts at removing the fleck from our eyes, did not complain about the state of our clothing for they were out to enjoy themselves as much as we were – of that I'm certain.

From the top of the Mumbles train we could see clearly in all directions, and as we ran alongside and above the Mumbles Road, the buildings appeared close. The gas works loomed huge and when we rumbled by Swansea Prison the bars across the small windows were clearly visible. I always felt a twinge of pity for those incarcerated within. Leaving the prison behind, we pulled into St. Helens slip where the train normally halted for some time – occasionally the crossing gates would shut and we would watch an express shoot past. From our train we could clearly see the lovely arched bridge that spanned both the Mumbles road and the main L.N.W.R. tracks, enabling pedestrians to cross in safety from Victoria Park to Swansea Bay sands. Close to where the bridge steps descended into Victoria Park lay a large flower clock, its numbers (in Roman numerals), hands and border in striking scarlet. It always kept time. Once the train had cleared Patti Pavilion, which also stood in Victoria Park, we could see directly into the Vetch rugby and cricket grounds. From then on, I turned to look in the opposite direction, towards the main railway line, the sands, and the long curve of Swansea Bay. At Blackpill we undercut the L.N.W.R. line as it turned right over the Mumbles road and branched inland on its way to central Wales. This marked the climax of the trip for, from Oyster-mouth, the train pulled slowly into the final stretch of the journey, past high, rugged limestone cliffs to the landward side, and the sweep of Swansea Bay on the other. It came to rest almost at the entrance to Mumbles Pier itself, making such a fuss that we children always felt sorry for it. That little engine hissed, creaked and groaned as it ground to a halt, just as though it was telling you how mightily tired it was !

When the train stopped, we clambered off and ran forward to thank the driver and his mate, and to inspect the front of the vehicle. On the few occasions our mothers could spare the money, we would pay to walk out along the pier, but our normal itinerary was to turn right up the broad white steps which led us

The Mumbles Road Train, c.1925.

over the top of an incline and into Bracelet Bay. Here we would settle for the day. It was a small cove, bordered on one side by the lighthouse, clearly visible as it projected from the rocky outreach of Mumbles Head, and on the other side by the coastguard station, but it possessed all that a child could wish for – sand, pebbles, pools and a labyrinth of caves to explore. Then, at the end of the day, we had the joy of the long ride home on the Mumbles train, as far as Swansea, followed by a trip aboard the little valley train up to Ystalyfera. More often than not, my father would be there waiting for us and, holding my parents' hands, I would walk drowsily home.

Another summer highlight was the Sunday School outing. We visited Barry once, but the favourite destination was Porthcawl because of its dunes and wide expanse of beach. In the early days we used to travel down by charabanc – long open-topped vehicles – from Ystalyfera. Our excitement at seeing them would mount as we clambered aboard. What a ride it was down the valley. The climax of the journey was reached some time after we had turned off the main road near Pyle, as the sand dunes came into view. When, at last, the charabancs pulled to a halt, we rushed out, threw off our shoes and ran delightedly onto the sand. We would jump on it, roll in it, and sift it through our fingers and toes. We would hurl ourselves from the dune tops, to sink deep into the soft dry sand or to twist and slither our way to the bottom. As we fell, we brushed against clumps of sedge grass and tripped over straggling dewberry plants – the fruit of which was eagerly plucked and devoured. We emerged from the dunes onto the beach which, with its short run to the sea, was so different from Swansea Bay where the retreating tide emptied miles of sand. The Porthcawl sea, wide-fronted and calm, was ideal for swimmers and paddlers alike. Children remained in full view and within easy reach of their mothers who felt free to relax and enjoy them-selves. For our fathers, most of whom were at work, we bought sticks of Porthcawl rock from the beach stalls. Finally, there was the return trip on the charabanc to look forward to. It was a sad day when they were replaced by buses.

Of course Christmas was special. Then the chapel children sometimes acted short plays and, on one occasion, the adults prepared a highly ambitious operetta. I remember my mother making up costumes for it: Firstly, she begged the butcher for a bag of real rabbit tails, which she proceeded to sew onto brown 'Bunny' outfits that she had already prepared. She also made elf costumes from green material, and pretty crepe paper dresses for the fairies. But I only faintly recall the show itself – it was called 'The People of Pillory', and one of the choruses started with the line, "Oh, Mr Bunny, you're so very funny". At least one Sunday before Christmas a gigantic Christmas tree was erected to the right hand side of the pulpit. A large silver star was fixed to the top, and it was garlanded with decorations. The Sunday School Christmas party was held after Christmas. By then, the chapel tree was heavy with presents for Sunday School scholars. Each gift had a name written on it but, try as we might, we could never discover whose was whose because Mr Feltham ensured that each present was partially hidden by foliage or decoration. The tea party was held in the Sunday School room, but for the games we moved into the main body of the chapel which had been cleared for the purpose – the pews having been stacked beneath the balcony. Mr Feltham and Mr Peyers organised the games, though many unofficial activities also occurred amongst the dimly lit pews at the back of the chapel. Finally came the moment we longed for – the distribution of gifts from the tree. All the presents had been chosen with care, and they were well received. Of the many I gained over the years, the one I most valued was a shoulder strap purse of real soft leather. It was beautiful and for years I wore it hung from my neck, later using it as a simple purse, without the strap.

Every Christmas, Ronnie, Harry and I went carol singing in Pontardawe. We so regularly did the rounds of the houses in the vicinity of our grandparents' house that our singing sessions became an established annual event. People would anticipate our visits, invite us into their homes and ply us with mince pies to consume on the spot and with oranges to take away. Others gave what were to us considerable amounts of cash. However, we gave value for money. Both Ronnie and Harry played the mouth organ with proficiency, and we all sang – we possessed a broad repertoire of carols, all the verses of which we had committed to memory. We would sing one carol after another before each house until the door opened. We finished up with croaking voices, but also with sufficient funds to purchase quality Christmas gifts for our parents. The sole exception was 1926, the year of the General Strike. I cannot remember whether we even bothered to go carol singing that year but I do recall that, by Christmas Eve, Ronnie and I had still not been able to buy anything for our parents. Late that evening, with only a half-penny between us, we ventured out to the shops in Gurnos Cross searching for a card. We found what must have been the last remaining card, so cheap and grubby that I felt ashamed to give it to our parents. However, it was all that we could afford.

Good year or bad, at home we could only ever afford to pin up a few paper chains and some sprigs of holly for decoration. On Christmas Eve, we would hang up our stockings and sing 'Jingle Bells' as, candles in hand, we climbed upstairs. Besides filling the stockings, Father Christmas would also leave us a single present apiece – I would invariably wake early the following morning to find mine at the foot of the bed. One Christmas I discovered there a reddish carton, the size of a box for an adults' shoes. Lifting its lid, I glimpsed inside a set of four tiny aluminium plates, saucers, knives, forks and spoons. I was keenly disappointed for I had anticipated a bigger present. Replacing the lid of the box, I curled back under the bedclothes to await the arrival of my parents who always came in to see what Santa Claus had brought. They were surprised to find me tearful but, upon my explanation, my mother opened the box and lifted the tray that I had seen to reveal underneath a miniature tea set, comprising a tea-pot, a jug and four matching cups and saucers. I had long asked for such a set and cheered up immediately. Also, I then realised that I still had not opened my stocking which always contained, amongst other goodies, nuts, an orange and a sugar mouse. In addition, our parents usually bought us the Bobby Bear annual, and a relation of my father's, called Auntie Mary, would send us a box of 'all sorts' which was sheer magic to open for it contained a jumble of second hand, but not too worn, oddments. My favourite one year was a half finished piece of embroidery. We were most downcast when, one Christmas, the box failed to arrive and we realised that it would never come again.

I cannot recall exactly when I stopped believing in Father Christmas, but I know that for several years Ronnie maintained the pretence of believing for my sake. The first doubts entered my head when, as one Christmas approached, I noticed some parcels under my parents' bed as I climbed the stair. Their attempt to hide them was foiled by the fact that the counterpane did not quite reach the floor. I pondered over this discovery and its implications, but was unwilling to discard my belief. That Christmas morning I awoke to find not only thick snow all around, but also tracks leading up the road away from the house. This was certain proof of Santa, and my belief in his existence was sustained for yet another year!

Chapter Ten

GROWING UP

The Christmas of 1931, our last in the Gurnos, I received a very special present. Beautifully wrapped in a box lay a doll, a negress, in rich brown velvet. Her limbs were accurate in every detail and she was exquisitely proportioned. Tight black curly hair hugged her head, her ears were pierced with 'gold' earrings, and beads hung from her neck and wrists. She wore a dress of emerald green satin below which her tiny velvet feet barely showed. The dress had short puffed sleeves, a tight bodice and a wide skirt trimmed with a pleated satin border, as well as a tiny opening in the back to take a handkerchief. It would have been a sacrilege to have used her as a handkerchief satchel, so I kept her as she was, a wonder to gaze upon. The doll was a gift from Alfred.

I first met Alfred in 1928, when I was nine and he was fifteen or sixteen years old. He was a second cousin to friends who shared our surname and who lived in nearby Gorof Road. They inhabited a bungalow, a novel structure in those days and every time we visited her, Mrs Baker, a short plump woman, never tired of showing us around it, especially the verandah. It was through her that Ronnie and I were introduced to Alfred who had travelled up from Swansea to spend some of his holidays with his valley relations. Mrs Baker's own son was a mere toddler, and she felt that in us Alfred would have company nearer his own age. Alfred Leyshon's father was a railwayman and, when we first met, Alfred invited us down to Swansea. At the time he lived in one of the smallest houses I have ever seen, built right against the rock side of Kilvey Hill, but his family were soon to move into 42 St. Leger Crescent, a council house on an estate lower down the hill, closer to St. Thomas' Station. As he showed us around his tiny home, Alfred told us about his younger sister, a pretty girl who was studying ballet. At night she not only sleep-walked, but talked as she did so. He would talk back to her in the belief that it might help. Despite the sheer stairs, she never fell and she always returned safely to her bed.

Alfred used to stay with the Bakers of Gorof Road for a fortnight every summer and, despite the four year difference in their ages, Ronnie and he quickly formed a close relationship. The two boys had much in common, while I used to enjoy the antics that Alfred, an amateur dramatics player, would employ to entertain us. He possessed a carefree vigorous nature, and would organise Ronnie and me in a variety of outdoor activities. He had an air gun of which I was nervous but with which he and Ronnie had a great time. He also arranged cross-country runs over rough terrain. These proved almost too much for me, for the course ran through thick brambles and bushes which tore my clothes and scratched my skin, but I would doggedly complete the run, albeit well behind the boys, finishing on the common ground behind the bungalow. We would also picnic out and, while munching sandwiches and gulping back 'pop', Alfred would answer our questions about his school life in Swansea. It appeared that he and Ronnie were about the same level academically, but that Alfred was most interested in sport. He was keen on cricket, swimming and most outdoor sports, but his greatest love was rugby football, for which he had been awarded his schoolboy cap. One summer, he brought it with him to show us. I had never before seen a cap with a long tassel attached. We used to have such a good time together that parting became increasingly difficult at the close of each day. Alfred would 'see us' almost to our door before we would return to 'see him' home – a game which continued until it was quite late. In the half light of those mid-summer evenings Alfred would inevitably start play-acting. He was a natural actor and would skilfully switch from one character to another. Most of them were comic and had us in fits of laughter, but other characters would make me squeal in fright, a reaction which would only spur him on to make me scream all the more.

The summer of 1931 was the last that Alfred spent in the Gorof. He had talked to us about starting work as a 'floor walker' in a brand new chain store in Swansea High Street. Somehow, I could not picture the carefree athlete in front of me as a sedate, well-dressed man, roaming one of the large town shops all day and I curtly dismissed the idea from my mind. That summer also happened to be the last we spent at the Gurnos. As a family, we had long been high on the priority list for a council house and we at last received a letter informing us that we were to be allocated one of the fourteen new council houses to be built on a site close to the bottom entrance of Maesydderwen school. Much as we loved our little cottage in the Gurnos, it was becoming too cramped as Ronnie and I grew up. When building commenced on the new houses, my mother used to meet me after school and together we would walk over to the site to inspect the progress being made, particularly on plot number 'thirteen'.

Indeed, as it looked likely that we might move in before my thirteenth birthday, which fell on March 7th 1932, I would run the words "number thirteen – thirteenth birthday and number thirteen Croesffyrdd, Glanrhyd" repeatedly through my head. Perhaps the year would bring us luck ! Anticipation was also sweet for my mother for she would at last possess a home with modern amenities – a proper kitchen, a bathroom, hot and cold water and, above all, three bedrooms. We excitedly planned how we would decorate our new home, though

*My father attending to raspberry canes at the bottom of his garden
in Croesffyrdd, c.1932.*

with such meagre means at our disposal we had to keep our feet planted firmly in the land of reality. My father, in his turn, would gain a manageable garden attached to the house, although as the site had been founded on a bicycle racing track we knew that large slabs of concrete would have to be broken up and lifted from the ground before he could work the soil. In addition, though it was never mentioned to us children, I knew that my parents worried that they would struggle to find the cash needed to pay the extra rent for the new house. But at least my father was still in work – a regular railway job with assured, albeit small, wage packets.

Alfred promised that he would visit us in our new council house though, as he would have to fit such a visit into his holidays from work, he could not tell us precisely when he would come. Following his return to Swansea, he kept a further promise to correspond regularly. However, it was to me that he wrote, and we exchanged letters throughout the ensuing winter and into the new year. How eagerly I anticipated those letters, written in a polished left-handed script and conveying in every word Alfred's fun loving nature. However, I would carry them away to be read in privacy so that I could read and re-read them, notably the endings signed "Yours, with love, Alfred". I would then sit down and write a prompt reply, similarly signing off with "Yours, with love, Eileen". It was that Christmas that Alfred sent me the negress doll.

Five months later, in May 1932, we moved to Glanrhyd. We enjoyed an early spring and the weather remained fine into the summer, the sun shining on our new house and garden. I anticipated most possessing my own bedroom in which, as a last minute surprise, my mother had hung two pictures, prints of the Mediterranean viewed from garlanded verandahs. I appreciated her thoughtfulness – we had so little money that blankets still had to be made up from the best parts of my father's old railway overcoats. I particularly remember one balmy evening just after moving house, when I had said good night and climbed up to my bedroom. I walked over to the window. The full moon lit up Darren mountain almost as if it were day. The night air was warm and scented and I decided

My father enjoying a rest in our back at Croesffyrdd, c.1932.

94

to stay and gaze out at the moon. I sat on the window sill, knees drawn up to my chin, and meditated. After a while, it seemed that I felt the supernatural presence of my creator. I remained there, watching the moon until, sometime in the early hours, it sank behind the mountain. Only then did I undress and fall into a deep contented sleep. It was, in all, an important period for me. I was heading for my thirteenth birthday and felt somehow more mature. Though still a child, womanhood stirred deep within me. It was a strange experience. I felt like a spring flower, sap rising from the soil beneath, poised to blossom. It was as if all I needed was the energy of the sun's rays to transform my being, and I yearned for the new horizons this promised to open for me.

Alfred and I maintained our correspondence, with my letters becoming longer. Now that we had moved, I was looking forward to the time when he would come and visit us. In my new room, I would often sit in bed at night, gazing contemplatively out of the window. Then something startling happened: I woke up one morning and all that I could see was Alfred's face. I knew instantly, and with an awesome certainty, that I loved him and would go to the ends of the world with him at my side. I was quite stunned, for I had never before had any such vision. Wherever I looked I literally saw Alfred's face before me. I felt ecstatic, a delirious joy possessed me and I seemed to walk on air. I told no one of my experience, hugging the knowledge to myself as if it were the most precious gift on earth. With that in my bosom, nothing in the world could mar my happiness.

Shortly afterwards, my summer holidays began and Alfred sent word of when he would visit. I suppose we still harboured a mental picture of him as he had been when last we had seen him, dressed in shorts and a sports shirt, for when he arrived we hardly recognised him. Before us stood a grown man, in a fitted suit complete with waistcoat. I kept staring at him, but he appeared per-fectly at home, even in his suit, and soon we realised that underneath it was the same fun loving Alfred of before. For me, it was a wonderful afternoon, but time fled only too quickly. We barely had time for tea and for Ronnie to take a few photographs out the back before Alfred had to leave. I accompanied him down to the Capitol cinema in Ystalyfera, from where he would catch the Bryn-amman to Swansea bus. Down the Wind Road I half walked, half skipped, by his side, I was so happy. He, in his turn, laughed and teased me until, all too soon, we were approaching the bus stop. Suddenly he looked down at me and said, very simply, "Eileen, one of these days I'm going to kiss you". I stopped, dumb-struck with surprise. I had not expected him to say anything like that. The kind of love I felt for Alfred demanded no more than to be near to him. I remember wondering if I had heard aright, and his words passed again, like music, through my mind. Surely he must love me too ? I was vaguely aware of the roar of the bus as it passed the Aubrey Arms and rounded Gough Corner.

Alfred's one and only visit to Croesffyrdd, 1932.

I was still standing, rooted to the spot, when it pulled in. Alfred climbed aboard, turned around on the step, and laughed at me. I ran forward, reaching for his outstretched hand, and ran alongside the bus until it gathered speed and I had to let go. His last words were, "I'll write soon". I turned for home, my cup of happiness filled to overflowing.

Alfred's letter arrived virtually the following day. He wrote thanking us for a lovely afternoon, and asked if I could go down to Swansea for an afternoon. My parents gave their consent, and Ronnie walked me as far as Ystalyfera Station. I wore a light costume my mother had made, an off-yellow, almost burnt gold, colour which I felt suited me. As my normally taciturn brother closed my compartment door, he remarked, "Gosh, you're beautiful!" "Don't be daft", I retorted, but I could not help but be pleased at the compliment. How well I remember that journey down. First came the curve round from Ystalyfera, across the river to Ynysgeinion Junction, at the foot of the steep-sided valley, where I thought of the tiny passenger train that we children had taken for granted, making its daily climb up the mountain to Colbren and on to Brecon. From the Gurnos the train had not been visible, though we often heard its whistle, but since our move to Glanrhyd, which was much closer to the track, we had the pleasure of seeing it chugging away up to Ystradgynlais Halt. They had announced the termination of the passenger service and soon we would only see freight trains pass that way. It was a sad thought, but quickly dismissed, for I had a much more exciting preoccupation. I kept imagining Alfred waiting to greet me on St. Thomas' Station, and wondered where he might take me, hoping that it would be to one of the big new cinemas in town that we had heard about – that would be perfection. And I thought over his words, "One of these days . . ." – he had promised me a kiss.

Soon the train had left Glais and was ploughing through blackened industrial wasteland. Previously, my happiness had brushed aside all other sentiments, but as the train approached Upper Bank, my heart began to beat wildly and I felt suddenly shy. When the engine slowed into St. Thomas' Station I hung out of the window, but could not see him. I waited until all other passengers had disembarked, but still there was no sign of Alfred. I had been so sure that he would he there. There must have been a good reason for his absence, but what should I do now ? Thinking that he would surely appear soon, I decided to wait. Each minute that passed seemed an eternity and, after half an hour, I resolved to go to his house which was not far from the station. As I walked, my disappoint-ment started to evaporate for I determined that Alfred must have had a sound excuse. However, my nervousness returned as I approached St Ledger Crescent. Perhaps his parents had only issued an invitation out of politeness, following Alfred's visit to us. If this was the case, I would have to remain on my best behaviour and wait until I had returned to the station before I could be alone with Alfred. Not only was the neighbourhood deserted, but the house, at the front window of which I had half expected to see someone looking out for me, appeared unoccupied. Had I mistaken the time, or the day ? No, I was certain that I had not. Should I approach the front or the side door ? I hesitated, as I did not know which entrance I was expected to use. As the front room appeared to be empty, I walked along the side of the house to the kitchen door. Perhaps I would hear voices inside ? But when I reached it, there was no sound. My heart sank. I had visions of returning alone to St Thomas' Station and arriving home unexpectedly early.

I decided to knock on the front door. To my surprise, it opened, and there stood Alfred. Casually dressed, shirtsleeves rolled up to the elbows, he looked as if he had never had any intention of stepping a foot outside the house. However, he appeared his normal self, and invited me inside, giving no indica-tion that anything was amiss. Reappraising the situation, I wondered if perhaps there was no reason for me to have expected Alfred to meet me, and that I had merely taken such an action for granted. He probably reasoned that I had known him long enough for me to walk straight to his house, without preliminaries – it was, after all, only a short distance from the station. Alfred's parents and sister were out, and he made me sit down while he made a cup of tea. By the time that he had re-emerged from the kitchen, my disappointment had quite evaporated, and I was looking forward to whatever Alfred had in store for the rest of the afternoon. As together we drank tea and ate a slice of cake, I was hoping to be asked to go to the pictures or, as it was a glorious day, to walk with him along Swansea sands. Instead, after finishing his tea, Alfred moved to a cupboard, extracted from it an armful of old school exercise books, and presented them to me. Confessing that he knew that I was particularly interested in biology and geography, he wondered if they might be of use to me. I felt quite bewildered. On the one hand, I knew that I should have been grateful, that Alfred had attended one of Swansea's finest grammar schools, that his books were beautifully illustrated and written up in his distinctive handwriting, and that he had gone to considerable trouble sorting through them. But on the other hand, they were the last thing on earth I wanted just then. Surely this was not why I had been invited down to Swansea ?

Alfred sensed my disquiet, for he placed the books in a pile on the table, sat down beside me on the sofa and, drawing me up onto his knee, asked what was troubling me. Unable to answer, I could only shake my head. He then turned my face gently towards his and kissed me. A hint of the intensity of my emotions must have transmitted itself, for he pulled me away for a moment, and stared at me. Then he drew me to him once more and kissed me as I had never been kissed before. No longer able to contain my feelings, I blurted out that I loved him, but to my dismay Alfred immediately withdrew and grew serious. He said that, fond of me as he was, he did not love me. In fact, he was going out with a young lady of his own age. He saw her regularly. Her name was . . . Each statement pierced me like a dagger. Alfred's voice appeared to grow fainter. He was being fatherly now, doling out advice: "Promise me, Eileen, that you won't go round telling boys that you love them . . . Watch out, Eileen, for any man who tries to take advantage of you . . . Don't let anyone touch you . . . do you understand, Eileen ? . . . Are you listening ?" But I was not interested in other boys – it was him I loved. I felt that he meant well, but by now his voice was remote. I could hardly hear him, and I no longer cared – I wanted to put my hands to my ears and block out sound altogether. My brain was numb, my heart broken – I still breathed, but my mind and body felt lifeless. My eyes were open but unseeing, my world was shattered, my dreams broken.

I do not remember leaving Alfred, nor the walk to the station and the journey home. I do not recall what I said or did when I arrived. Some days later, after my father had lit a bonfire in the garden, I crept out, carrying all Alfred's letters, and fed them to the flames. I watched each in turn curl up, blacken and crumble into dust. I wished I could do likewise. All I desired was to sink into oblivion. There is more than one way of dying !

Chapter Eleven

LEAVING SCHOOL

Life without Alfred

From that time on, as I kept the sweet secret of my love for Alfred to myself, I suffered the lonely misery of a broken heart. I was thankful more than ever for the sanctuary of my tiny bedroom in which I spent most of my time. Fortunately, my mother was preoccupied with Ronnie who was about to start in Swansea University. Not yet sixteen, he and his pal were going to study for their Higher Certificate and then their degrees. Up until then my mother had skilfully made him suits out of my father's discarded railway uniforms, but now he was to be fitted for a proper one. I could retreat to my room without attracting their attention, though it was different with my father. I loved greeting him when he got home from work and although he said nothing about my sudden withdrawal, I felt he knew something was wrong. He was soon to know everything.

One Saturday morning, not long after my visit to Alfred, my father took me into Swansea. Arriving at St Thomas Station, we went down the steps on the town side and were about to turn right across the river bridge, when my heart gave a sickening lurch. Who should I see on the opposite side of the bridge walking towards us but Alfred ! I pulled my father back into the covered shelter of the smelly station steps.

"Please, daddy," I begged him, "please stay in front of me for a few minutes !" He did what I asked and could see Alfred passing on the other side, unaware of our presence. He then very gently took my shaking arm by the elbow and guided me along into town. I knew that he understood and was grateful that he didn't pry.

My mother, too, had confirmation, just before Christmas. I was upstairs, as usual, when the postman brought a package for me and recognising Alfred's handwriting, my mother called up, "Come down here, Eileen, I've got something that will cheer you up !" As soon as I saw the beautifully packed parcel, I thrust it back at her.

"No, I don't want it !" I choked and ran back upstairs, flung myself on the bed and sobbed into my pillow. My grief was out for the first time and though I felt exhausted, it made me feel a little better.

In school, the whole of that Autumn term had the same nightmarish quality as the rest of my life at that time. Our beloved Maesydderwen having burnt down, my friend Marjorie and I now had to walk back to our old Elementary School in the Gurnos. What a great friend she was! Always quiet and dignified, she asked no questions and put up with all my misery during those dark days.

At the beginning of term, I didn't want to go back at all. I started getting recurrent styes on my eyes, frequent colds and there were mornings when I had such bad headaches that my mother gave in and let me stay at home. I remained all day in my room, huddled up on my bed, riddled with guilt. Even in my favourite subjects I found it impossible to concentrate. The following year we would be sitting the Central Welsh Board School-Leaving examination but this did nothing to ease my dread of school or shake me out of my inability to work. From having been in the top seven pupils in class in both our fortnightly tests and end-of-term exams, I now plummeted to practically bottom! Miss Jenkins, our kind French mistress, realised that something was wrong and took me to one side one day.

"Whatever is the matter with you, Eileen? Your work is atrocious!", and though she showed genuine concern, I could no more confide in her than anyone else.

Mr Rees, our headmaster and the main Maths teacher, had changed greatly since the school fire but was still capable of being devastatingly tyrannical in the cause of his subject. He was the only teacher who still managed to scare me but even he could not penetrate the shell I had built around me. I had always enjoyed all three Maths subjects, delighting in solving the problems by using logical steps. But now I was abysmal and I remember the feeling of great shame when on the morning of a test, I would beg Marjorie to give me a quick revision lesson. Not that it helped me, for my mind would blank out in sheer panic. She told me to stop worrying and cross every bridge as I came to it, but at the time it was advice that I just couldn't take in.

Things began to slowly pick up in the New Year of 1933, when I started to apply myself to work again. I wasn't helped by the negative attitude of one of our other Maths teachers, a seargent-major in the Territorial Army. Sarcastic at the best of times he would roar across at me, "You're not as good as your brother, are you?" Though I never resented the fact, to be told it in front of the whole class was a different matter. It simply fuelled my resolve to leave school. I was forced to look fairly and squarely at my situation and realised that if I wanted to train as a nurse, I would need that School-Leaving Certificate. Somehow or other I had to pass it, for wild horses wouldn't keep me in school a minute longer than necessary.

As far as languages were concerned, Welsh was out! From the very beginning we children had been discouraged from putting any effort into learning it.

"Welsh is no good to you – don't waste time on it! If you want to get on, concentrate on English. That's the language of the future in this country!"

French I liked and felt I could do enough to scrape through. The Leaving Examination required passes in both English Literature and Grammar but I was quietly confident in those. All three Maths subjects had to be passed, though they only counted as one. I knew I had fallen back dramatically but was determined to make up lost ground. Five passes was the minimum required and I felt that Geography and Botany were possible, giving me no room to spare.

I had loved History before starting secondary school but it had been killed stone dead by the obsession with dry facts and figures, list upon list of dates and a disproportionate amount of homework, especially on the weekend. Detention was given at the drop of a hat by the mistress, who obviously felt that doling out lines in their hundreds would inspire us to greater things.

My plan was to work relentlessly and work I did, driving myself ever harder both in school and at home. Many a time, at ten in the night, my father would plead with me to stop. Even in bed my brain would go on working and I always woke up tired. The other thing on my mind was my parents' financial situation. Although as a railwayman my father had regular work, his wages had been cut and we now had the council house rent to find. I was worried in particular about my mother. At mealtimes she would bring in food for my father, Ronnie and me, before retreating to the kitchen on some pretext or other, telling us to get on with the food while it was still hot. I soon realised that she was living on leftovers, making me more determined than ever to find a job and bring in a little money to help out.

Ronnie was doing his bit by working hard in University, studying at home to the background of classical or operatic gramophone records. This soon led to conflict because it was all done in the living room, which, as the only room with a fire, was the communal room. Ronnie demanded silence when his music was on, which meant we dare hardly breathe, let alone talk. The cold of winter had forced me downstairs and I resented having to comply with my brother's directives. My parents' attempt to keep the peace between us often backfired and I became increasingly rebellious. On weekends I would listen to jazz or the latest dance music and would turn the wireless up if Ronnie was around, out of sheer spite. I knew it would infuriate him, but somehow couldn't help myself. Deep down we loved each other and I blamed myself for causing strife and misery within the family.

Meanwhile, friends helped. Muriel and her family had moved up the valley from their beloved Kilvey in Swansea. They had lived first in Ystalyfera before moving to a new house next to the railway line in Gurnos, not far from where

My dear friend Muriel.

we used to live. Muriel and I were firm childhood friends and I loved visiting them occasionally. They were not ones to stand on ceremony and always made me feel welcome. Her father, Mr Jenkins, like mine, worked on the L.M.S. Railway and had to move to where the work was. I don't think they ever settled in the valley but I was simply glad that they were there. We were also becoming friends with Mr Bisgrove and Mary who had just come to live in nearby William Street.

That year, too, Jackie Jones of childhood days reappeared. After an absence of four years, he turned up to visit the Mathias family. Bert and Jackie had been buddies from the time that he and his mother had come to live there. Mrs Mathias and Jackie's mother had soon become firm friends, coming as they did from thoroughly English backgrounds and Jackie had quickly become integrated into the Railway community, joining in with everything except our privileged railway excursions. After the General Strike of 1926, however, his step-father Dan Jones had fruitlessly scoured the valleys for work, before being taken on in a carpet factory in Kidderminster. Not long after, Mr and Mrs Matthias had got word that he had died from a serious chest complaint caused by working in the pit. We, the Bakers, had heard nothing of Jackie or his mother for a long time.

Mrs Matthias, however, had kept in touch and bumping into her one day in Ystalyfera, she told me that Jackie would be down sometime during the summer holidays. She insisted that I come down and meet him and out of respect for her, I duly turned up. The afternoon tea outside in the hot sunshine was a constrained, polite affair, with no enthusiasm on my part. It had been a year since my friendship with Alfred but I was still in love with him. That would have been the end of contact with Jackie, except that he wrote to me time and time again, signing himself 'Jack', which sounded very grown-up! I wondered why he persisted and when I reluctantly replied, such was my mood that I wrote in a perverse, often frivolous manner. He kept the correspondence going and deep down I was ashamed of myself.

The two boys I would speak to, however, were **Kenny Cornelius** and **John Battenbeaux**. Kenny was a cripple I'd known all my life from the Gurnos railway cottages and like us, his family were on the priority list when the new council houses were built in Croesffyrdd. When we moved in, we soon made friends with John, living in nearby Glanrhyd with his large family. About my age, fourteen, he was already working to support them. He was quiet and unassuming and we soon discovered that he could whistle like a nightingale and had a gift for poetry. One day, very shyly, he let Ronnie and me read some of his beautiful verses. However, it wasn't very long before he and his family moved away.

With Christmas over, I knew that 1934 was going to be a crucial year for me, five months in which to catch up and prepare for my C.W.B. examination. March came and went and with it my fifteenth birthday. The French Oral, always the first exam, loomed on the horizon but I wasn't unduly worried about it until we heard that the examiner would be a real Frenchman, in place of kind Dr Mary Williams from Swansea University. On that day in early June, I was shaking from head to foot. Alphabetical order seemed to seal my fate – as a Baker I was first in ! I was confronted by a genuine Frenchman, very tall, imposing-looking, with a Vandyck beard to boot. Zut alors ! The only thing missing was the smell of garlic, and in my panic I'm afraid that my tongue literally stuck to the top of my mouth and stayed there. I understood every word but was powerless to answer his questions about Spring in our country and the beautiful daffodils. In French, he told me to leave the room, where Miss Jenkins and the next sacrificial lamb were waiting. As she looked enquiringly I shook my head and ran ! The dreadful truth was that no matter how well I did in the coming written paper, it wouldn't count. I had already failed in French !

One by one the examinations were taken and after an agonizing wait for the results, I found to my relief that I had passed in the remaining subjects and scraped through. Miss Jenkins, the French mistress, asked me what I intended doing and for some reason I blurted out, "I wouldn't mind working in Wool-worth's !"

"Oh, Eileen, you're far too good for that !"

Inwardly, I didn't agree but should have explained about the financial situa-tion at home and that I needed a job, any job, until I could start nursing. I'm sure I left her feeling let down, hurt and disappointed in me and this com-pounded the guilt and misery I felt.

Throughout the year, Jack's letters had kept me fully informed about his activities, especially with the Young People's Group in Baxter Church. On top of their Christmas parties and walks in the countryside, he talked of the pictures they had seen – had I seen them ? Had *I* seen them ? It cost nine pence to go to the pictures, something that would take me months to save up for ! When I had the chance I loved going, especially to the spectacular musicals which even-tually reached Ystalyfera.

I found his letters both interesting and irritating, some of it sour grapes, no doubt, for I would have loved to learn to swim in proper swimming baths ! The only sport I was proficient in was table-tennis, learnt by playing with Ronnie on our old, wooden living room table. We became experts at landing the ball either on the crack that ran right across it or on the rounded edges, when the ball would fly off at unexpected angles. We also spent a lot of time playing cards, so my life was quite different to Jack's. Even had I lived amongst Jack and his friends, I would probably have shied away from the crowd. I loved my own company and would spend winter and summer holidays reading good books, drawing with my treasured box of Reeves' pastels or absorbed in embroidery. So when the letters came, full of accounts of interesting activities, I felt there was nothing for me to say and I often didn't reply. I did tell him that Vic Matthias had been taken to hospital after a baker's van had hit his bike on the way to university with Ronnie. Jack had invited the pair of them to stay in Kidderminster on the return leg of their cycling tour up north. Each summer holiday they would go somewhere different, making use of their railway passes to travel as far as possible and then cycle around their chosen area. I took advantage of Ronnie's absence to tune into programmes that I liked, including all the Music Hall items. American jazz and blues appealed to me, as did Henry Hall's dance band and a new programme called 'In Town Tonight'.

Starting work

When I left school, I went down at the first opportunity to see Mr and Mrs Thomas who kept the newsagent-cum-sweet shop in the Capitol Buildings next to the cinema in Ystalyfera. Opposite stood the bus stop, which would for ever be a painful reminder of treasured moments with Alfred. Mrs Thomas's wonderful teaching had enabled Marjorie and me to skip a class in Gurnos Elementary School. She had married late in life and they now ran the shop together, working all the hours under the sun. I was delighted when they took me on immediately, for four evenings a week. I worked from five until ten and halfway through the evening, was invited into their living room for a cup of cocoa and a biscuit. They had a huge grandfather clock which chimed every quarter of an hour and by the time it announced that it was a quarter to ten, I was whacked and ready to go. But it was well worth it, for at the end of the week I could take 2/- home to my mother, more if I worked a Saturday !

My mind was still on the future and what to do for the next two years, until I was old enough to start nursing. Of all the hospitals I had written to, the Matron of the Eye Hospital in Bristol had been the most encouraging, urging me to read about Ophthalmic Nursing and to write again six months before my seventeenth birthday. I had already passed every available St. John's Red Cross exam in the area and read all the medical books my father kept in the house, including 'The Home Doctor', a *Daily Herald* gift book. My parents wrote to Breconshire Education Authority, asking if I could assist the teachers for a year in an elementary school. I was told that I could start in Yniscedwyn Infants, Ystradgynlais, in September, under the supervision of the headmistress, Miss Jones. I would be expected to observe and participate in all three classes, but because I was 'under-age' and therefore a 'Teacher-Learner', I would receive no remuneration. Had I been eighteen, I would have been entitled to the grant given to 'Pupil Teachers'. Mr and Mrs Thomas were pleased for me and suggested adjusting my hours, knowing how important my little wage was.

At this time we were seeing more and more of Mary Bisgrove, who was a little older than Ronnie and living in William Street. Her father was a very tall, straight man, having recently returned to work on the railway after serving in India with the Dorset Regiment. An old friend of my father's, he was a widower who relied on Mary to look after him. Because she was so mature in her ways and often in the company of my mother, with whom she had become firm friends, she seemed a lot older than she was. Her father suffered from recurring bouts of malaria and had an ulcerated leg which flared up from time to time.

Muriel shares a joke with Mr Bisgrove.

105

My mother unstintingly gave of her time to help Mary and like my grandfather in Pontardawe, was very skilled in treating ulcers. Whether he was poorly or not, he was always a joy to be with and would regale us with tales of their time in India, his eyes sparkling out from a face of bushy eyebrows and meticulously-fashioned handle-bar moustache.

Mary, too, was a lovely person, with pure white skin. When we first met, her hair was unusually short and very thin, apparently due to a recent illness but it was now starting to grow back again. She wore very thick glasses, without which she could hardly see. In 1934 she took me to visit her aunts who kept a little shop in Huntspill, Somerset, and it was there that I learnt the secret of how to put fizz into pop bottles. Out the back was a special gas cylinder fixed to the wall and Mary showed me how to use it. Simple ! The following year we visited her relatives in Poole, Dorset, and at the harbour I was treated to a spectacular fireworks display. On these visits I got to know more about Mary's family. Her father had been born in Glastonbury, son of the first station-master on the Somerset and Dorset Railway Line, before the family had moved to Temple-combe. On leaving school, Mr Bisgrove had worked as a student teacher and then in a bakery before being posted to India, where he spent many years. It was the death of his wife that saw him and Mary returning to Britain and they moved to Glanrhyd with an influx of railway workers. We remained friends for many years.

At the end of August, not long after my visit to Huntspill, Ronnie and Vic arrived home. There was a lot of news to exchange, not least a first hand account of everything that had happened to Jack and his mother since the death of Mr Dan Jones. It had initially been hard for them, but they had obviously made some good friends both in Baxter Congregational Church and in Kidderminster Welsh Society. Jack's mother had recently married another Welshman, a Mr Davies from Pontypool, and Jack now had a stepsister, Muriel, slightly younger than him. Jack had won a prized scholarship to the King Charles I Grammar School, where he was now known correctly as 'John Laurie Campbell'. Ronnie was full of praise for his prowess in all kinds of sport and he and Vic had taken it upon themselves to invite him down to Ystalyfera the following August.

Ronnie was pleased to learn that I'd be starting in Yniscedwyn, which would mean a walk of about two and a half miles, the bus service being a bit patchy. Imagine my surprise, when two days later he came home with a beautiful new lady's bike worth £4, a New Hudson 'Black Lady', paid for out of his hard-earned pocket money. What a brother that brother of mine was ! Knowing that I was terribly nervous, Ronnie helped me get used to her and before long I began to love that dependable steed. In the early days at the school I had every reason to be thankful not only for my bike, but to Mr and Mrs Thomas for reducing my hours to a Friday and Saturday. I was ready to drop at the end of the day and often longed to rest my body against the huge guard of the classroom fire.

It didn't take long, however, for me to get really involved and I enjoyed every minute. I found myself resenting the weekends, impatient to get back to those lovely children. Miss Jones, who had a particular responsibility for the reception class, took me under her wing and made sure that I gained experience in all three classes. Miss Davies was in charge of the middle class and remembered me and Ronnie from her time in Gurnos Infants. As time went on, Miss Jones gave me more and more responsibility in her class – the 'Babies' as it was known – and gave me invaluable guidance. She plied me with books to take home, one by a man called Freud, which I'm afraid I couldn't make head or tail of and soon put down !

Now that I had a bike, Ronnie sometimes took me with him on a fine Sunday to Cribarth, high up in the Tawe valley overlooking Madame Patti's old home in Craig-y-nos. Cribarth is a great rugged outcrop of limestone rock on which Ronnie was basing most of his thesis for a B.Sc. degree. These little outings were stimulating and absorbing. Not only did I lose any fear of cycling while he was by my side, but I loved hearing him talk. He explained to me about evolution, showing me fossils to prove his point, and it all made such good sense. Not, however, to Mr Thomas, teacher of the senior girls'

Ronnie on his beloved bike.

class in Sunday School. With the new-found knowledge ringing in my ears, I was foolish enough to challenge his views. I told him that I couldn't believe everything in the Old Testament word for word and despite his reaction, went on to say that I wasn't even sure about the existence of God any longer. That did it ! I can still see him now. To prove his point, he summoned up as much of the wrath of his Maker as he could, before standing up self-righteously and savagely pointing to the door.

"If that's how you feel, my girl, the best place for you is outside of that door !"

My attendances at Sunday School having become more infrequent anyway, Mr Thomas had just given me the perfect escape route. I got up, walked out and never went again !

For my mother's sake, I continued going to a mid-week meeting called 'The Young People's Guild', in which someone would simply prepare a 'paper'. When my turn came, I talked on the life of Elizabeth Fry and though our minister, Rev. Melville Philips, congratulated me on it, I found it an ordeal. Hot with embarrassment, I muttered something unintelligible, before hurrying my mother out and home. Soon after, I stopped going to church altogether and though I knew my mother was upset, felt it would have been hypocritical to continue. I think she understood.

In contrast, I was finding the training and experience in Yniscedwyn Infants far more enjoyable and rewarding than I'd ever imagined. Up in London, the story was of the engagement of the Duke of Kent to the beautiful Princess Marina. National news of the Royal Family, of the world's biggest liner, the *Queen Mary* and of Amy Johnson's flying exploits, didn't hold a candle to the unfolding of those young minds, learning and grasping things so eagerly.

News that did upset us in our valley in that year of 1934, however, was the terrible mine disaster at Wrexford Colliery in North Wales, when an explosion and resulting fire killed more than two hundred and fifty men. I remember feeling so grateful that my father didn't work down the pit. All around us, colliers were still out of work and living in abject poverty. I felt lucky to have been taken on in the school.

That first term was making an indelible impression on me. As we got nearer to Christmas, we could hardly contain the children's excitement and I found myself deeply moved by the simple nativity play and accompanying carols. Then, on the last day of term, came the Christmas party. The partition dividing the two classrooms was pushed back to create one large room in which we fixed up coloured electric lights, the first I'd ever seen! These shone through the looped decorations, holly and mistletoe. Miss Jones placed a tiny Christmas tree on a table in the centre of the room, while around the sides we turned the desks together to form tables and covered them with snow-white crepe paper. The children now had plenty of space to move around easily, their eyes shining as they feasted on the fairy-like scene. They excitedly chatted to one another across the tables, the multicoloured hats they had made in class perched precariously at all sorts of different angles! And then the magic sound of sleigh bells could be heard, before Santa appeared at the door with his heavy sack, waiting for Miss Jones to let him in. Three cheers for him, then, before he gave out the presents. There was an extra child there that afternoon and that child was me!

Christmas at home that year was the first carefree one that I had enjoyed for years, with no homework to do or dreaded school to go back to. Back at Yniscedwyn, Miss Jones had decided that on top of the traditional songs, Welsh versions of Cinderella and The Three Little Pigs would be performed on St.

St. David's Day 1935 at Yniscedwyn Infants School.
In 1956 it became a Welsh-medium school and is now known correctly
as *Ysgol Gymraeg Ynysgedwyn.*

David's Day. I was designated to help with the props and I thoroughly enjoyed myself making the costumes with crepe paper, using rolls of cotton wool for the wigs. Miss Jones was so pleased with the final rehearsals, that she arranged for a photographer to come. It was a great success !

Throughout 1935 Jack continued to write, though my replies were still not very forthcoming. It was obvious that he was looking forward to his August visit and he had asked a friend to accompany him, as it was such a long way to cycle. I hoped that he wouldn't be disappointed. All we could offer was the beauty of the valleys and the hills, especially beyond the coal pits. If it rained, as it often did, didn't Mrs Matthias' immaculate living room radiate warmth and comfort, just as ours did ? There was for ever a glowing welcome in my mother's living room, a big black iron kettle sitting half on the hob, half on the fire, cheerfully reminding the waiting teapot that they would not be idle for long.

It was Silver Jubilee Year for King George V and Queen Mary and though my brother took me to see a huge firework display in Swansea, there was very little to show for it where we lived, apart from a few bonfires. In Singleton Park, Ronnie blew a fuse of his own as he realised the cost of all those rockets and Catherine Wheels. Every day we saw men in our valley struggling to feed their families, someone on the dole only able to claim four pence a week for each child. How could it be justified ?

109

Visit to London

Whitsun half-term came and my father had a couple of days off. I was delighted when he decided to treat me to a flying visit to London, staying two nights. Leaving very early on the Sunday, I remember that we were flat out by the time we arrived at a small guest house near Euston Station, though that didn't stop us from going to the pictures! Monday morning saw us doing a lightning tour of the city on top of a London bus and seeing the big crowds around Buckingham Palace, clearly enjoying the Jubilee celebrations. Some of the decorations remained, reminding us of the elaborate preparations that had gone into staging the festivities. The Royal Family was, indeed, very popular, but a world apart from our South Wales valley. The afternoon trip down the Thames was the highlight of the visit for me, everything looking so different from the river. At Greenwich we saw the Naval College, visited the museum and what was known as 'The Painted Hall', a magnificent room with oil paintings from ceiling to floor. Most were of admirals and captains, but there were many others in dazzling colours, depicting wrecks and battles at sea. Outside in the main square, the time was given every minute in electric light figures. My father, who had served in the navy during the war, could have stayed in Greenwich for days, but the return boat was waiting. Before catching the train the next morning we managed to fit in a quick trip to the shops to buy presents. A very happy father and daughter eventually reached their snug little house in Gurnos at half past ten that night!

Back to school after the Whitsun break and the last lap for me there. It was at this time that I had a frightening experience on the bike. Every morning I had to go round a blind corner, immediately followed by a dip before the road rose again and levelled, to reveal a row of houses with a wide pavement on the left. I had just reached the top of the incline, when a girl of about eight or nine came running full-pelt out of nowhere, straight into my front wheel! The impact brought us both down but no real damage was done because I'd been going slowly. However, her loud screams brought her startled mother running to the scene, protectively examining her little girl before turning to me for an explanation. The truth seemed to satisfy her, the girl soon stopped crying and I helped her into the house, before shakily forcing myself to remount the bike. Although the mother had told me not to worry, for the next few days I dreaded passing that corner, expecting to be confronted with some bad news.

All too soon the end of the summer term was upon us and the end, too, of my year as a Teacher-Learner. I took my leave of both staff and children with great sadness and gratitude. It had been a wonderful, wonderful year! What was I to do next? While working in the shop, I had taken the opportunity to look at various job advertisements in the papers and periodicals and found plenty for companion-helps, nannies and domestic servants of every description. My preference would have been to work with children but the minimum age required was seventeen. Perhaps I would apply for one of the helper jobs.

Jackie Jones visits us again

I was not the only one who was accident-prone during that summer of 1935. Having done well in their exams, Ronnie and Vic set off on one of their tours, this time on Vic's tandem. On a particularly steep scree in the Lake District they skidded on a narrow bend and grazed themselves badly. Seeking medical help at the next village, they were advised to go home immediately in case of infection and the heavily-bandaged bicycle twins arrived by train with their tandem in tow. When Jack and his friend cycled down on August 10th – having been warned by Mrs Matthias to take care on any bends, as she didn't want another pair of 'wounded soldiers' on her hands – Ronnie was too stiff to go part-way to meet them. So Marjorie and I strode out purposefully, spotting them right on time, on the long stretch of road between Ynyscedwyn and Ystradgynlais. It was a happy meeting. The twelve hour journey didn't seem to have over-tired them but we didn't keep them talking, directing them to Croesffyrdd, where we would catch up with them later.

Marjorie wouldn't come back, and I found Jack and Evelyn had already exchanged a lot of news with my mother. She had, of course, supplied them with tea and cake and they were looking very much at home. Mr and Mrs Davies and Muriel had also come down for the week and were staying in Oystermouth. They planned a trip up the valley to visit Mr and Mrs Matthias on one of the days and wanted Jack to join them in Swansea on another. That meant that we had to make the most of those few warm, sunny days of late summer. If we didn't see Jack and Evelyn in the morning, then we'd see them in the afternoon or evening. We walked everywhere, climbing our local 'mountain', the Darren, and visiting my father in his signal box. As a family we took to Jack's friend, who was seven or eight years his senior and had graduated at Oxford with a degree in Modern Languages. None of that seemed to matter – as my mother said, he had 'no side to him' – and he joined wholeheartedly in everything that we did. Quiet and kind, he made us laugh a lot that week with his delightful sense of humour and we were sorry to see them go. My brother was now fit enough to accompany them as far as Brecon.

For Jack, however, it was not 'goodbye' but 'au revoir', because within eleven days he was back ! Ronnie met him just south of Leominster to where Evelyn had accompanied him, and the two of them made their way back through heavy rain to the Swansea Valley. It was lovely to see them relaxing in front of the fire after a hot bath and I hoped that the Unemployment Exchange wouldn't find me a job before Jack went home. I needn't have worried !

For the next five days our valley was cloaked in drizzle, yet we managed visits to the Matthias family and took short walks all round. Jack was introduced to our friends Marjorie, Muriel, Mary, Eurwyn Lewis and Johnnie Battenbeaux, all of us quite used to popping in and out of one another's homes. On the Friday, when the rain wouldn't let up, my mother invited them all to tea. They stayed on into the evening, when we played table tennis and then cards, so that everyone could join in. Outside, the rain beat against the window, while inside, all was warmth and laughter. From time to time I caught Jack looking at me intently, often at the meal table. I found it a little disconcerting, though all I was really worried about was whether he was enjoying himself. I had warned him that we had little to offer in comparison with Kidderminster and the weather was limiting our options !

We managed a short ride to Abercrave and Craig-y-nos on the Saturday afternoon, after a game of improvised cricket in the morning. The sky was still heavy with grey clouds but Ronnie was able to point out Cribarth, shrouded in mist, and tell Jack about the interesting limestone caves nearby. On our return, we found Johnnie, who had brought some of his poetry over for Jack to read. Hemmed in for the next two days, Ronnie and I decided to take Jack to see *Forbidden Territory* at the pictures on Monday evening, by which time a week of his holidays had already gone.

Tuesday dawned and blue sky at last ! Ronnie roped us into a long and interesting fossil hunt, cut short only by the fact that Eurwyn Lewis had invited us for tea. The same age as Ronnie, he was also a student at Swansea University and lived with his parents two doors down. He was a huge lad with a club foot which restricted his walking. He was so strong, however, that he could hop very quickly on his good foot, almost like a kangaroo. He had a sharp wit, a wicked sense of humour and all the girls regarded him as a dreadful tease. I would often return home to find his huge bulk leaning on our front railings, elbows back, ready for his bit of sport. He wouldn't let me into the house until he had teased me unmercifully and tried to get me to go out with him. That, I always refused, for I was a bit afraid of him and didn't wish his invitation to tea to become a habit.

Jack and I were left to our own devices for the next two days, after Ronnie and Vic had decided to use up one of their remaining passes to go to Ireland. We climbed the Farteg on the Wednesday and took the little-used road across to Crynant in the Neath valley. The fact that we were the only living souls up there in that wilderness merely added to its beauty. Once at the top, we left the road and wandered at will across the browning surface of the mountain until we found the highest point. The gentle wind caressed our faces and flirted with our hair as we strolled on happily. Neither of us felt the need to talk much and the calm was broken only by the occasional screech of a bird, or when we surprised one of the ragged mountain sheep. I remember how much at peace I felt and I think Jack was the same. From the conversations we did have, I got the impression that he was drawn to missionary work, but I was content to enjoy the moment, the soothing silence and the warmth of the sun. Down the valley we could see the strangely beautiful colours of the Mond Nickel Works, bright yellow and orange mingling with the hazy blue of the sky. In that second, you could almost forgive the putrid, poisonous gases that were reducing our beautiful trees to grotesque, lifeless shapes. On a clear day we would have been able to make out Swansea docks and the glint of the sea.

Hungry, we sat with our backs against a warm boulder and enjoyed the sandwiches and bottle of water we had brought. We stayed there, soaking in the sun, loathe to leave it. But leave it we had to, for Jack had been invited to tea by Fred and Ben Evans. By the time we got home, washed and brushed up, it was later than we thought, so we decided to cycle down. Mr and Mrs Evans made such a fuss of us and time in their company flew. Pushing our bikes home, we planned a visit to the Cwmdu Falls the next day.

We set off early, catching a Swansea bus as far as Godre'rgraig, from where we would follow the Gwred river. The path alongside the stream was narrow and we walked in single file for a mile or two, the sight of the crystal clear water making up for the initial disappointment of finding a rubbish dump. Before long, the faint rush of the falls became a crescendo, the rain of the past week having replenished it after a relatively dry summer. The sight was spectacular, the waterfall unexpectedly high for such a small river, the narrow rock walls and shale slopes forming a kind of grotto around it. Because the light was poor, Jack was unsure whether his photographs would turn out and on we scrambled to the top, glad to be in the sunshine again.

Soon the valley broadened out between two undulating hills and we realised that we were behind the Alltygrug Mountain. Once again the comforting warmth of the sun, the gentle attentions of the breeze and the muted babble of running water had a soothing effect. For the first time in three years, I was aware of a great easing of the pain caused by my love of Alfred Leyshon. Jack, too, was helping to fill that gap, someone I found quietly companionable and trustworthy. For a short while, up on those hills, we could revel in the timelessness of it all. It was very good to be alive !

We had only been inside the door for five minutes when Ronnie arrived home, assuring us all that his brief trip to the Emerald Isle (no sooner had they set foot on dry land than they'd come straight back !) had been worth it. The following day, it was his turn to show Jack the sights, his favourite limestone caves at Craig-y-nos. Having reached Madame Patti's castle, we turned left towards a farm that Ronnie obviously knew well. He introduced us to the farmer, before getting permission to visit the caves, and we strode across a field to a tiny river. We followed the stream upwards, before it suddenly disappeared into the hill through a small opening in the limestone. Could this be the entrance to the caves ? It was here that my elder brother laid down the law, telling me in no uncertain terms that it was no place for a girl, and that I had to wait outside. Feeling crushed, yet trusting Ronnie's judgment, I sought out a dry spot and stretched out in the sun. Complete with strong boots, waterproof jackets and a large torch, the boys stooped low to enter the mountain.

After what seemed an age and just when I was beginning to worry, they reappeared, shading their eyes from the bright sunlight. Jack was visibly impressed with Ronnie's tour, which had taken in stalagmites and stalactites and at the point where it was unsafe to go any further, a huge cavern with a pool of deep, deep water. Stripped of their damp clothes, they joined me in ravaging the sandwiches and gulping down the pop. As we lay down in the soft ferns and closed our eyes, I felt Jack's hand clasping mine. I let it stay but as yet couldn't respond to his tentative hold, for I was still very unsure of myself. If it proved to be the tiny seed of something that might develop, fine, but for now I was content to have him as a good and trusted friend.

Jack's mother married a third time after the tragic death of Dan Jones. Jack is on the far right next to his mother and new stepfather, Mr Davies. Next to Mr Davies is Muriel, Jack's stepsister.

Next morning he left, and with Ronnie again accompanying him as far as Leominster, the house felt so empty. I sat at the back door with my box of Reeves crayons and sketched the view of the Darren. This was for Jack, to remind him of his holiday with us.

With Ronnie and Vic on yet another short cycle tour, a letter of thanks to us all arrived from Jack. He enclosed a photograph for me signed 'Laurie', as well as a local 'Situations Vacant' column and grateful though I was, I couldn't see myself fitting in with his competent, sport-loving friends ! Down at the Labour Exchange the same day, there was just one job that I could apply for, that of a companion-help to a family in Porthcawl. I wrote off immediately but never received a reply. Restless, bored and at times irritable, I was in no mood for Ronnie's high spirits when he arrived home, especially as he assumed I would sell a big wad of tickets for the Variety Show he and Vic were helping to produce. I nagged him to death about writing to Jack so that I could enclose my picture. It wouldn't have crossed our minds for me to send the picture independently, as our upbringing would never entertain such a waste of postage. Things came to a head on the Saturday – a week after Jack's departure – for I felt that by this time Jack would really be looking forward to a letter from us. All week Ronnie and I had been bickering over the silliest things.

Forbidden fruit

With nothing to do and all my friends either back at school or working, I asked my father if he could get me a Privilege Ticket to go down to Swansea. A few hours away from the house on my own would do me good. With very little money in my purse, I made for the High Street Woolworth's. It was still a great novelty to one and all, and such a big store that you could spend hours just looking ! I resisted the temptation to jump on the escalator and visit the splendid cafeteria upstairs, choosing to wander around the ground floor. Time and again I found myself drawn to the make-up counter where, for next to nothing, you could buy tiny round tins of rouge and face powder. I can still recall the smell, cheap and pungent, but so enticing to a fifteen-year-old girl who had never used make-up. As I made my way home, the tins felt like forbidden fruit in my pocket !

Early afternoon and everything was quiet in the house. I sneaked up to my bedroom, where, driven by a mixture of excitement and guilt, I started to experiment in front of the tiny swing mirror. A little rouge to start with, then more and more as I found I couldn't stop. At first I felt a queer sensation in the pit of my stomach, something I'd never experienced before. Then, as I plastered it on thicker and thicker, I felt truly sick. Before long the place started to resemble a circus dressing room, with me as the clown ready to go on and make everyone laugh! Ashamed, my thoughts turned to how I could get it off. Soap and water was required but our bathroom was downstairs. Slowly, I opened the door and listened; everything seemed quiet. I crept downstairs but as I reached the bottom, who should come out of the living room where he'd been studying, but Ronnie! He let out a yell, rushed up to my room and threw the rouge and powder out of the window on to our tiny patch of grass below. Raging, he hurtled back down and called me everything, not letting me get a word in edgeways. I knew I was worthy of his contempt but he had no right to go into my sacrosanct bedroom or throw away things that belonged to me. I had no trouble matching his anger!

I went to the Harvest Festival at chapel the next day, the first time I'd attended for ages. I just wanted to get out of the house and hide inconspicuously in the packed congregation. Monday's trip to the Labour Exchange was fruitless, so I called in at the shop to scour the columns in *Llais Llafur*, our local paper, and wrote down the details of a job in Birmingham. Back home, I tried to tell my mother about it but was told to be quiet by my brother, who was listening to classical music. If he did! Still simmering from Saturday's incident, I jumped down his throat and before he had the chance to retort, turned his record off. Fuming, he sprang out of his chair and chased me. He had picked up the nearest thing to hand, which unfortunately for me was a long, hard, steel Meccano rod. What remained of the bean stalks at the back provided but a poor hiding place from the vengeful Ronnie and within seconds he was whacking me hard across my bottom. The pain I suffered was nothing compared to the surge of revulsion I suddenly felt for my brother. At that particular moment I hated him, never wanted to see him again. As he made for the house, I stumbled out of the garden and down the Wind Road, determined to put as much distance between myself and home as I could. At the end of the street, with dry sobs heaving up from deep inside of me, I bumped into my father on his way home from work! Obviously shocked, he caught me and held me tight for a few minutes until I was ready to speak. When I blurted out that I was leaving home, he quietly asked me what was wrong. Starting with Saturday's events, I told him everything, after which he took me gently by the elbow as he had done in Swansea three years before and led me home. I never knew exactly what daddy said to Ronnie, but he apologised to me and was very subdued. In the cold light of day I felt unsettled, for I knew I could never hate my brother. On the contrary, I realised how deeply I loved him.

Lovely Bangor

My mother reminded me that it was time to write to the Matron of Bristol Eye Hospital, so I sent details of my exam results and 'Teacher-Learner' experience.

At the same time, I had a reply from the Mrs Smith in Birmingham I had written to, saying that if she required my services she would come down to see me personally that week-end. In the meantime, however, I received a surprise invitation to spend a week with some old railway friends of ours who were now living in North Wales. Mr and Mrs Cray Jones had been our first neighbours in the new council houses, living at Number 14. Their two children, Gwynfor and Gwenno, were soon joined by a new arrival, Gareth, who seemed to spend as much time in our house as his own! How we loved that little family and my parents had kept in touch after they moved.

Before going, we thought it would be wise to find three people willing to provide a reference for me and by the Friday the Rev. Melville Phillips and Miss Jones had agreed. I found the word 'referee' intriguing, with a ring of importance to it and the next day, Miss Rose Williams, ten years my senior and now teaching in Birmingham, was added to the list. Having heard nothing from Mrs Smith, I felt at liberty to set off on Monday morning, accompanied as far as Crewe by Ronnie and Vic, who were using their last railway pass to go to Oban. I spent much of the time in the corridor, for there was still tension between Ronnie and me!

At Bangor Station, the whole family overwhelmed me with their welcome. The children, much bigger of course, were all attending school and after they had gone to bed that night I had a long, long chat with their parents. Mrs Jones understood my need to leave home and seemed to think that their milkman might have work for me. When I was introduced to him the next morning, I found a polite, chatty young man with a decided North Wales accent. Mrs Jones brought up the subject of work and he told us that his wife might well be glad of some help. At half-past one he was back with the empty milk van, ready to take me to meet her. She turned out to be lovely – homely, young and a little harassed – for not only did she have to pull her weight on the farm but had two little girls to look after! I was drawn to them all immediately and by the time the farmer had taken me back to Mrs Jones, everything was settled, providing that I got permission from home.

The next day, Mrs Jones and I saw the children safely to school, before catching the bus into Bangor, where we toured the cathedral and looked at the view of Anglesey over the Menai Straits. I found the city a little drab, not helped by the rain which swept in from the west, forcing us into the shops. Having collected Gwenno and Gareth, we had another lovely evening together. I couldn't hide my delight at having found work so quickly. Not any old work either but looking after children, on a farm, with such likeable people and with the Jones family so near. It seemed too good to be true!

And that's what it turned out to be – too good to be true! Even as I was reading my mother's reply the next day, telling me to accept the job and not to be 'trodden on', there came a knock on the door which was to turn my world upside down. A telegram had arrived for me which said, "Cancel job – come home Saturday – writing."

There was no 'reply-paid' telegram with it and I was not only baffled, but upset. Mrs Jones, who had been standing near me, told me not to worry, but to wait for my mother's letter which would explain everything. Although I felt she was right, I didn't know how I was going to face the milkman and his wife. The very last thing I wanted was to let them down.

The mystery was solved when the post arrived the next morning. Although Mrs Smith had not written, a letter had arrived from an acquaintance of hers, a Mrs Hands, who had said that I sounded 'just the kind of girl she needed, one to help her generally in the house and at the same time be a companion to her thirteen-year-old daughter Peggy.' Both my parents and Ronnie, back from Scotland, felt that on balance the job in Birmingham would be the better one. I wish that they had asked me first, for I felt instinctively happy about the situation in Bangor. However, I felt obliged to abide by my parents' decision. Mrs Cray Jones was a tower of strength when we explained to the young couple. They were most understanding, wishing me happiness in my new job. I hoped that they would soon find someone to help them out.

Early Saturday morning saw me being waved off by the whole Jones family at Bangor station. I was sorry to leave them and had a lot to thank them for. During the three-hour break at Shrewsbury, I visited the Cathedral with a lady I had got to know in the same compartment. The stained glass windows were magnificent. When the train finally drew into Swansea, my mother and Auntie Edith were there to meet me, having taken the opportunity to buy a few items for my Birmingham venture.

I was to start there the following Wednesday and my mother would accompany me, having given Mrs Hands the time of our arrival at New Street Station. At home, I was able to read her letter for the first time. Certainly, it sounded friendly and genuine enough and my family were quick to point out that I would be only an hour's journey from Jack. However, my thoughts went back to the little Welsh family on the farm and I couldn't help wishing once again that my parents had consulted me before arranging anything. Still, I had to make the most of it and I wrote to Jack to let him know that during his school dinner time, I would be pulling into a station only twenty miles away. I was sure that he'd be happy, but my heart was still in Bangor.

Chapter Twelve

BIRMINGHAM

Deceived – work as a 'maid'!

On Wednesday, October 2nd 1935, my mother and I left 13 Croesffyrdd early. The train reached Birmingham dead on time, but there was no-one answering Mrs Hands' description on the platform. Eventually, we decided to make our own way to 174 Hamstead Road, Handsworth, a friendly bus conductor putting us down almost outside the house, in what was a very long road.

A plump young girl, who could only have been Peggy, answered the door. She told us that her mother had gone to meet us and hadn't yet returned. When Mrs Hands came in about half an hour later, she didn't try to hide her displeasure, blaming my mother for not being precise enough in her instructions. My mother, as ever, was straight. My father had told us that there were two main line stations in Birmingham, New Street and Snow Hill and the letter had made everything clear. Mrs Hands had gone to Snow Hill. What a perfect start, I thought!

With little time to spare before catching her return train, my mother asked Mrs Hands to show us around the house. This seemed to calm her down a little and after we had seen the ground and first floor, I was shown my bedroom, a pretty little room done out in pink. It faced the main road and my immediate thoughts were not of the pink bedcover, eiderdown, curtains or even the thick pink carpet, but of the deafening noise of the traffic outside. When my mother specifically asked about my duties, Mrs Hands replied that it would involve general housework and to be a companion to Peggy, helping her if necessary with her homework. I would initially be on a month's trial and if I proved satisfactory, could stay on until I started nursing. She would, however, require a month's notice when I came to leave.

Apparently satisfied that I would be in good 'hands', my mother had to leave hurriedly. As we said goodbye, a terrible pang of loneliness engulfed me. It was as though something had torn away my insides and I wanted to run after my mother as she disappeared across the road. But that would never do – I had resolved to leave home and I had to stick it out through thick and thin! I went to bed that night in a desolate state and with such a bad pain in my stomach that sleep was impossible. When the traffic started to build up in the early morning,

119

I felt wretched. How on earth was I to face my first day ? I didn't have very long to find out, for soon my new employer was knocking on my door and demanding that I get up. I was to realise before long that what she had told my mother was a pack of lies !

The very first thing she wanted me to do was to wear a cap and apron ! This I flatly refused to do. I didn't mind working hard, but had not come all this way to be dressed as her maid. I would wear an apron, certainly, even a sack around my middle, but not a maid's uniform. Having lost that battle, Mrs Hands informed me that the bedroom I had slept in that night was in fact Peggy's and that from now on I was to sleep in the attic. She led me up a narrow winding stairs where a latched door opened up onto a wide area with two tiny attic windows. A pane of glass was missing from one of them, there were no curtains and the floor was completely bare. The only piece of furniture was an old iron bed with a meagre supply of grubby-looking blankets. On an old chair next to it, an ugly, half-used candle smirked at me from its mucky holder, seemingly held together by a wad of candle-grease. At least the room was quiet, situated as it was at the back of the house, but the sight of that dingy bed filled me with dismay. My heart, already heavy, was now like lead !

Downstairs again, my new Mistress proceeded to give me my orders. I was to be the first to rise ! I would start by cleaning out the dining room grate and lay-ing it with paper, sticks and coal, to be lit later in the day. Then I would clean out the 'Triplex' stove in the kitchen and make sure that it was lit in time for breakfast. It apparently heated the water and the two ovens beside it and was what she used to do her cooking. She also had a gas stove but this was used sparingly. The back kitchen was a large room containing a gas boiler, a deep sink, a large iron mangle with a handle and two massive wooden rollers, with a big bath nearby. Everything, in fact, that you would need to do the washing and it came as no surprise to me to hear that this is where I'd be spending my Mondays. The big rack of pulleys in the kitchen above the fire was there to dry and air the clothes and in the evenings I was to do the ironing !

Outside was sufficient garden for a clothes-line and an outhouse, where I would find coal, sticks and stacks of old newspapers to light the fires – oh, and a chopper for the smaller bits of wood. This last bit of information horrified me ! At home and at my grandmother's place, I had helped with the housework from a young age, but the fire had always been done by my mother long before Ronnie and I ever got up ! As for cutting up sticks and carrying coal, that was my father's job, with Ronnie helping when he could. I might have felt happier if the fire was a straightforward one, like ours at home, and not the intimidating Triplex monster that was Mrs Hands' pride and joy. With its tiny grate, levers and a wheel in the black plate below, it didn't look capable of heating either the water or the ovens and without the big welcoming glow I was used to, it hardly seemed like a fire at all.

By this time I was feeling bewildered, but Mrs Hands hadn't quite finished with me. I had to see the saucepans I would use, the vegetable rack and the food in the larder. I would prepare the vegetables in the kitchen sink and learn to cook the sort of meals that the family liked. So much for the letter she had written my parents! The word 'slave' had not been mentioned and as for her beloved Peggy, I was already feeling that she was the last person I could feel companionable towards, very much a replica of her mother. The feeling seemed to be mutual, for ever since I had arrived, Peggy had looked at me as though I was something the cat had dragged in! I thought that first day would never end, and though I was dog-tired by the evening, I was only able to sleep fitfully between those dreadful itchy blankets.

Next morning, I crept downstairs early and managed to clean both grates before tackling the dreaded Triplex stove. Kneeling in front of it, papers on one side, sticks on the other, and a bucket of coal in attendance, I tried and tried to get the thing to light. With hardly any matches left, a feeling of panic engulfed me and tears began to roll down my cheeks. I didn't even try to stop them. My hands were dirty, I didn't know where my hanky was and what was more, I was so miserable that I wished I was dead.

That was how Mr Hands found me, the first of the family to get up. Fortunately, he was a kind man and patiently showed me step by step how to light that dreadful little fire. He made it seem so easy, and the kindness he showed, together with the warmth of the fire, made me feel much better. From that morning on, the Triplex held no terrors for me and I managed to light it first time. Later in the day, I scribbled a letter off to Jack, telling him that my one half-day would probably be a Thursday. I hoped to see him the following week – could I come for tea? And please would he write me a long letter on the week-end?

Mrs Hands was keen for me to meet another 'maid' that day, so that we could be company for one another. She wasn't very pleased to find that I had friends in Kidderminster whom I hoped to see as much as possible. I had no intention of spending my precious half-day in any other way and though I must have been introduced to the other 'maid' (as Mrs Hands called her), I certainly never met her again.

It was no exaggeration to say that my new employer expected me to do everything. After an exhausting day's work, I had the pleasant task of ironing or keeping Peggy company when her parents went out. My slave-status was compounded when Mrs Hands began 'loaning me out' to her sister who lived in the vicinity. I was to scrub through for her, which meant scrubbing the tiles from the front door through to the kitchen. If I so much as demurred, Mrs Hands would threaten me with the police, and though deep down I knew that was absurd, her manner frightened me. During those first few weeks I was on trial and my pride would not allow me to give in and go home.

Kidderminster was my salvation. Jack and his mother always gave me a marvellous welcome, taking the sting out of my misery. Every week I received loving and encouraging letters from home, but I never let on what things were really like. If they did find out later, as I suspect they did, it wasn't from me. During the second week, I caught the train to Kidderminster, which conveniently stopped at the nearby Handsworth and Smethwick station. The eighteen mile journey took just over an hour, stopping at ten small stations. It would give me just a few precious hours in Kidderminster, as Mrs Hands had insisted I be back by early evening !

Boiling point !

A week-end shortly after my first visit to Jack will for ever be etched in my memory. I was alone in the house with Peggy, who wanted me to help her with her homework. I cannot recall whether it was Algebra or Geometry but I do remember that it was very simple. Simple, that is, to anyone but Peggy, who seemed to me to be an extraordinarily dull girl, 'twp' as we would say back home. We sat down at the kitchen table together and went back to the very beginning of the problem, taking it a step at a time. I realised that Maths was not one of her strong points and so tried to be patient. We spent the whole evening on it but it was no good – she either couldn't or wouldn't understand. In the end, completely exhausted, I'm afraid I stood up and shook her ! I knew I was wrong to do it, but something had snapped and a tearful Peggy informed me that her mother would hear all about it. As I went to bed, I resigned myself to the fact that I would be out on my ear in the morning !

The next morning, it was a very irate Mrs Hands that lost control, shaking me by the shoulders and angrily threatening to call the police there and then for daring to put my hands on her daughter ! I was so frightened and felt so intimidated, that I felt I must talk to someone as soon as possible. Jack had given me Evelyn's address in Birmingham where he was teaching in a grammar school and I arranged to see him the following Thursday. I also wrote to Jack, explaining why I wouldn't be over that week and mentioned in passing that his usual letter hadn't arrived that Monday. His reply confirmed that he had, indeed, written on the Sunday and couldn't understand why I hadn't received it.

Over tea and cakes, Evelyn listened intently. He was very concerned that I was working for such a person but dispelled any fears I had that Mrs Hands would go to the police. He told me to cheer up and as a surprise, took me to the new Gaumont Cinema in the heart of Birmingham. What a treat that was, a completely new experience that allowed me to forget my troubles for the rest of the evening. Everything about that huge cinema was exciting. As the swing

122

doors took us through to the foyer, we found ourselves sinking into deep plush carpets and up a wide imposing staircase, for Evelyn had bought the most expensive tickets. It all made me feel important. Inside, the decor depicted underwater life, deep sea colours of blue, green and turquoise, exotic plants and fish, with unseen lights giving them a marvellous rippling effect. Then, joy of joys, a cinema organ rose up from the pit, its famous organist (I'd heard him on the wireless) immaculately dressed and bowing several times at the end of his repertoire to acknowledge our enthusiastic applause ! As he descended out of sight, huge gold-trimmed velvet curtains silently glided back to reveal a screen as wide as Swansea Bay. The lights dimmed to nothing, followed by that thrilling moment before the first film starts. I forget what the main film was that night, but I'll never forget the warmth, comfort and relief that Evelyn's kind-ness and wise advice had brought me. I didn't have occasion to bother him again, though I knew he was there if I needed him.

I returned to 174 Hamstead Road with renewed confidence. I would stick it out somehow and knew that I would never allow myself to touch Peggy again. Having spoken to Evelyn, Jack's next letter was full of concern, telling me that his mother would do her best to find work for me in Kidderminster should I decide to leave. Strangely enough, though she could still be moody and un-predictable, Mrs Hands' attitude towards me began to change for the better, her little servings of praise almost making life worth living. Then something hap-pened that almost made me leave on the spot !

The morning after I'd written to Jack to reassure him that things were not so black, I got up early as usual. Having cleared and set the dining-room grate, I moved on to the Triplex in the kitchen. As I carefully drew out the tray onto a spread-out newspaper, I noticed some charred remains of a torn-up letter. On one tiny scrap, its edges burnt and curled, a few words in Jack's handwriting leapt up and hit me in the face ! In vain, I desperately scrabbled around to see if there were any more legible fragments. So this is what had happened to Jack's letter ! Kneeling in front of that grate with the one little piece between my fingers, I felt dazed at first and then angry. I painstakingly sifted the remains of his letter into an envelope, placing the one discernable piece towards the top, licked it down lightly and hid it.

When Mrs Hands came downstairs, I confronted her, but knew her well enough not to show her the evidence. At first she denied everything, flaring up into one of her tempers and again saying she'd fetch the police to me. This time I was ready for her and though inwardly quaking, I told her in no uncertain terms that it was I who could report her. My words had an immediate effect, eliciting a promise never to interfere with my letters again and she indicated that with the trial month almost complete, she would like me to stay. On my half-day off she was willing for me to catch a later train back from Kidderminster ! She begged me not to tell her husband, for he would be angry. I don't know why, but I began to feel sorry for her, sensing that I was looking at a very unhappy woman. She then asked if there was anything else I'd like ! In retrospect I could have asked for a lot more but at the time it took a great deal of courage for a young girl to challenge such a bully. Sheets and a pillow case would be nice, as well as something to cover the windows before I froze to death. She couldn't understand why I wanted to put the mattress on the floor, until I explained how uncomfortable the old bed was – in fact, I don't think she ever bothered to go up and see the attic for herself. She told me to help myself to the linen and do what I liked in the room but try as I might, it was impossible to make such a barren ice-box very habitable.

That first month had been so fraught that even when things seemed to be improving, I felt unsure of myself. Was it right to stay on in the house of someone who had shaken me deeply by burning something so precious ? It was pride, again, that won. I wouldn't go home. I wouldn't be beaten. The last thing I wanted was to let my parents down and so, rightly or wrongly, I decided to stay.

The following Thursday, Jack met me straight from school on his bike. As we walked back to Worcester Road, he listened while I told him first hand what had happened. I managed to convince him that the incident had cleared the air and that Mrs Hands would never have the same power over me. I even felt sorry for her and I told Jack that we should now get on and celebrate the end of my trial month. Jack being Jack, he made two things clear. I had to let him know immediately should anything untoward happen again and from that point on he would number his letters. It was with a much lighter heart that I went to the pictures with Jack and his mother and an added bonus that I could watch *The Scarlet Pimpernel* all the way through, there being no rush to catch an early train back. Little wonder that that night I left my beloved beret on one of the seats at Kidderminster station !

Ever since leaving home I had found that I missed Ronnie more than I ever thought possible. For his nineteenth birthday in November, I decided to have a professional photograph taken for him. My next half-day coincided with Jack's half-term and he was able to join me for a lovely day out in Birmingham. On our own together for a change, we visited the Art Gallery before having tea and watching *The Florentine Dagger* at the pictures.

During the remainder of the month, there was hardly a ripple on the previously turbulent waters of life at 174 Hamstead Road. In fact, I was invited to spend many an evening in the family's company, either in the dining room or the lounge. Years of practice at playing cards and table-tennis on our cracked kitchen table at home paid dividends and I proved a match for both Peggy and her older brother – much to the family's surprise. Life was becoming more bearable and as they began to take interest in me as a person, I was introduced to many of their relatives and friends. It was only then that I realised they were Jewish. Mr Hands' brother owned a string of shops in Handsworth village, one of which was a tobacconist's. When Mr Hands confirmed that I was good at figures and his brother replied "very good", I should have realised, perhaps, what his enquiry was leading up to.

Not long after, I met up with Rose Williams, one of my referees, who had written inviting me for tea. She was interested to hear about Jack, for she had known him since he had first arrived in Ystalyfera in 1923. During the 1926 General Strike, hers had been one of the families kind enough to buy tea from us, a venture that my mother went into in order to make a little money while my father was out of work. Ronnie and I hated selling door to door, but the Williams' were always kind, inviting me in for a piece of cake each time I called on my round. Rose was now teaching in a grammar school in Birmingham and I was surprised to learn that her younger brother Eddie had joined the Air Force.

During the good old chinwag we had that afternoon, the conversation turned to nursing. She had heard nothing from the Matron at Bristol and wondered when I would be starting. I had taken it for granted that I would be enrolling immediately after my seventeenth birthday the following March, and I was a little alarmed when Rose advised me to write again. She said that most hospitals took batches of new recruits every three or six months and that time was moving on. My parents agreed and I wrote off as soon as I could. The prospect of having to wait a further six months was almost unbearable and staying on with Mrs Hands was out of the question !

On a Friday in mid-December, I had a wonderful surprise when Ronnie appeared at the door. He was on his way to London to do a week's research and had made a circuitous route on a PT (Privileged Ticket) through Mid Wales. He had put up at a cheap boarding house for three nights and the first thing he had done was to seek me out. I was so proud of my brother as I introduced him – tall, handsome and though only nineteen, in his degree year at University. I appreciated the extra time off I was given that weekend and when he left on the Monday, I took myself out of sight and had a good weep.

Immediately following his visit, I was asked, or rather told by Mrs Hands that I was to help out as a 'cashier' in her brother-in-law's shop every Saturday up to Christmas. I was given no extra money for this – by that time I didn't expect any – but it was a relief to get away from the house and the family for a while. It was something I had already done with Mr and Mrs Thomas, though I found the run up to Christmas exhausting, with Mrs Hands fussing and piling up the work. For a second time, she tried to give me second-hand clothes instead of wages and against my better judgment and ignoring the immorality of it, I capitulated. I could see hanging over her arm, an orange-coloured woollen jumper and what looked like a winter skirt. Goodness knows, I could do with

125

My tall, handsome brother (taken a few years later, in 1944).

some warm clothing and I knew that my meagre wages would not stretch to anything of such quality. I never wore them to Kidderminster, neither did I tell Jack what I had bartered.

Having given him a few weeks' peace to get on with his studying, I was glad to see him once his end of term exams were over. He'd skipped a year, so I hoped he'd done well. The train was held up by severe frost and snow on the line and poor Jack, already with a dreadful cold, had to hang around waiting. We hurried home and stayed in that evening exchanging news, before all too soon it was time to brave the elements once more. How I hated that dreadful, slow-stopping journey back to Handsworth and Smethwick. I can still sense the phantom feel of it, the barely-lit, near empty carriages, with only chilly breath to keep you company. The weary porters ghosting out on to dim, foggy plat-

Handsworth and Smethwick Station.
(Photograph courtesy Andy Doherty, 'Rail Around Birmingham and the West Midlands'.
Picture taken in 1957 by John Edgington).

forms, waving their dismal old lamps as they called out the name of their little halt. The grinding of brakes, the banging of doors and the sluggish chugging again on to the next stop. I didn't mind the first few stations, for they were the Kidderminster side of the line. It was when I started hearing the Birmingham-sounding names being called out – 'Rowley Regis and Blackheath', 'Oldbury and Langley Green', 'Smethwick Junction' – that I drew my coat tighter and tighter around me in anticipation of the dreaded 'Handsworth and Smethwick' call. The physical effort of getting up and opening the door became harder and harder and I wondered how much longer I could go on doing it.

Upstairs, in my attic, icicles had begun to form around the windows. I was so thankful for the dressing gown that my mother had insisted I take with me, double thickness and reversible, all wool and unbelievably warm. It had belonged to Dr Walsh, that fine Irish doctor from Ystradgynlais, to whose children my mother had been nurse-maid, before she married my father in 1914. The Walsh's were very fond of her and years after the children had grown up, continued to take an interest in us all. Dr Walsh was our doctor and though we rarely had cause to bother him, was always glad to see us and never charged us a penny. He was kindness itself and it was a sad blow when he died. When my mother went up to comfort his wife, she insisted on giving her his dressing gown !

It was much too big for me, of course, but I didn't mind. Morning and evening I used it as a kind of tent under which to dress or undress and in bed it doubled up as a blanket. I would pull it up tight over my ears, which were in danger of dropping off. Unfortunately, it couldn't stop me from getting chilblains, which started on my feet before spreading up the backs of my legs, until the pain was unbearable. It didn't cross my mind to tell anyone about them and during the day I spent a fair bit of time in the warm kitchen and could forget about them. Towards Christmas, it was so busy that I had no time to think about chilblains or anything else. Mr Hands was a Jew, but only in the sense that he was a hard-headed businessman. They celebrated Christmas like everyone else. My only respite came on a Saturday evening, when Mr Hands would bring a big Marsh and Baxter pie home with him for supper, something I later realised was a family tradition in the Midlands. This was the first time I'd seen a pork pie, and though I never liked them, was grateful that I didn't have to cook on a Saturday.

Happy Christmas !

Mrs Hands was difficult to work with at this time, one minute chatty and almost pleasant, the next irritable and snappy. Perhaps the fact that all the nearby relatives would be descending on Christmas Day made her so moody ! She demanded that the dining-room table, which could be extended to a fair length once the 'leaves' were in, be laid properly. I had to clean all the silver, which for Christmas Day itself, included candlesticks. By the time it was all set out on Christmas Eve, it looked lovely, but my goodness, what a lot of work it entailed, and it was muggins doing most of it ! I kept all my mail together, in order to have something special for myself on Christmas Day. I had given Ronnie presents for the family, having embroidered a table-cloth and two matching cushion covers for my mother and carefully chosen something for my father and Ronnie out of my limited resources. On Christmas Eve, Mrs Hands presented me with a list of chores for the following morning ! I was up early, for both the kitchen and lounge fires had to be lit, the one ready to cook the feast, the other to keep the family gathering glowing. There was a gas fire in the dining-room, an upright oblong gadget, nothing much to look at, but giving out an amazing heat. The guard around it and the lighting of it were Mr Hands' responsibility. The family were going to eat a huge goose, which had to be stuffed and cooked at the right time. Once this heavy creature was safely in the largest of the two ovens, I could relax a little. The vegetables had been prepared the evening before and were ready for the giant saucepans on the gas stove. All I needed to remember now was to put the pudding to steam.

I don't know when exactly the impact of that Christmas Day 1935, my first away from home, hit me. I think it was seeing the Hands family gathered early in the lounge in their dressing gowns, opening their stockings and greeting each other like any normal family. It is a family time and I didn't resent their happi-

Christmas 1935, without my loving family.

ness, it was just that I don't recall them wishing me a Happy Christmas and I certainly didn't receive a present. Once dressed, Mrs Hands fussed in and out of the kitchen wearing one of her many smart outfits, to make sure that the preparations were going smoothly. Whether or not they were aware of it, I felt very much alone and the hiraeth for my family suddenly hit me. The reality of serving in the kitchen of the Hands household on a Christmas morning instead of being with those I loved, was more than I could bear. Had I wings, I would have taken flight !

Work was my salvation and I set to, washing the dirty pots and pans and putting them away, another thing on my list ticked off. By the time the guests began to arrive, everything was on schedule. Clad in a huge apron, it was Mr Hands who took over then. He sharpened the carving knife on the steel, laughing and joking with me as he did so. On the few occasions that our paths crossed, he and I got on fine. Mrs Hands and Peggy helped to carry everything out from the kitchen, while I carried on at the sink. Eventually, late in the afternoon, all was quiet in the dining room and there was not much noise in the lounge either. After all they had eaten and drunk, I supposed that the guests were sleepy. Peggy's brother slipped out for a walk after dinner with his fiancée who I had not seen before – a real beauty, slim and vivacious. The weather was now quite mild after the recent snow and heavy frosts.

In the privacy of the kitchen I had a chance to open my mail. Oh, the love that those letters from home conveyed ! Sad though I was and very near to tears, that love enfolded me and I was grateful. Despite everything, I knew that I belonged to the most caring family in the world. Thoughtfully, most of the gifts were in the form of postal orders, with instructions to get whatever I liked or needed. The first thing that came to mind was a pair of bed socks ! The rest of the day slipped away quietly and I began to look forward to Boxing Day in Kidderminster.

The family having gone out for the day, I managed to get away about one o'clock, leaving the house tidied and clean. The weather was pleasant, the train was on time and Jack was all smiles on the platform. That lovely day with Jack and his family was my Christmas Day. Despite having got rid of his cold, Jack was given two handkerchiefs, one from me and the other from my mother ! I slept soundly in Jack's bedroom that night while he was relegated to a made-up bed downstairs.

The next morning, I was spoilt by Jack bringing me up a cup of tea. Sheer luxury ! Later, we strolled into town, where I could change one of my postal orders and buy some bed socks. At dinner, everyone was concerned because I had no appetite but I assured them that it was a passing phase. How could I tell them how miserable life was at Hamstead Road and that I was already feeling down at the thought of going back ?

After dinner, Jack suggested a walk to nearby Hartlebury Common before coming back for tea, when Evelyn would be joining us. At first, neither of us spoke very much, but when he asked me about my Christmas Day, I could feel the tears welling up inside of me. Sensing my distress, he drew me near to him. I had meant this visit to be such a happy one but I couldn't stop myself sobbing like a baby. I apologised for spoiling his day, but kindly and compassionately, he merely 'shushed' me and told me that talking about it was better than bottling it up. He helped me to look ahead and to realise that it wouldn't be long before I would be nursing. I managed a smile, before we retraced our steps home, his arm still around my shoulders.

For the rest of the evening I put a brave face on it, but as the seconds inexorably ticked away, so that all-consuming depression gripped me again. On the platform, I found it painful to say goodbye to Jack. We wouldn't be seeing each other for two weeks and that seemed aeons away. Huddled in a dingy corner of that ghastly train, I sank once more into the depths of despair.

Back at Hamstead Road all was in darkness, the family still out. Mentally drained and ready to drop, I went straight to bed. Next morning I woke early, remembering almost immediately that there was a lot to do. Mrs Hands was giving what she called a 'buffet supper' that evening and the food had to be prepared and laid out around the dining room. About twenty people turned up and were still there at one o'clock, by which time I was so exhausted that I asked if I might go to bed. I could barely climb the two flights of stairs to the attic and literally fell into that bed on the floor. It was the church bells that woke me the following morning. For the first time in my life I had overslept ! Hurriedly, I dressed, washed and went downstairs. I was not prepared for the mess that met my eyes, both in the kitchen and dining room. Oh, how could they ? Who did they think they were ? Who did they think was going to clear up ? Me, the 'maid', of course, but where was their humanity ? How could they treat a young girl, any young girl, in such a way ? I raged at the injustice of it all, angry towards the Hands and anyone who, just because they had money, thought that they could exploit those who did not.

It took me three hours to get everything tidy. I needn't have worried about getting up late, because the first I saw of the family was late afternoon, when they sauntered down in their dressing gowns. All they wanted was a tray of tea, after which the day was my own, in the sense that they left me alone. I answered some letters, wrote my usual one home and wondered what Jack's letter would bring the next morning. What would he say about my display of self-pity the previous Friday ? I asked my parents whether I should write again to the Matron of Bristol Eye Hospital. If I were to start in March I should be giving my month's notice in very soon, not later than February 2nd, for I had started at Hamstead Road on the 2nd of October. I decided to wait and see what the morning's mail would bring.

Final leg with the Hands'

The postman called regularly at the same time every morning, when I would never be far from the front door. Sure enough, at a quarter to eight, I heard him approach and saw a number of letters fall through the letter-box. Amongst them was Jack's usual plump envelope and one from home, but nothing from Bristol. I read my parents' letter first – their account of Christmas, their queries about me, wrapped in their usual warm love. They felt I should write again to the Matron and added, 'whether you hear from Bristol or not, give in your notice anyway on February 2nd and come home.' Oh, what joy those words gave me ! I felt now that I had served my time. The only sad thing about returning to South Wales would be having to leave Jack.

His lovely, long letter, too, cheered me up no end. The previous week, the talk had been all about the Baxter Church Guild Social, which was the biggest event of the year for the young people. He had decided to forego it, instead asking me over to keep him company. Although delighted, I realised he was making a big sacrifice for me. I worked hard that day, happy thoughts giving my feet and hands wings, and when Mrs Hands strutted into the kitchen mid-morning looking to find fault, she had to beat a hasty retreat. Little did she know that I would soon be leaving her behind for ever !

A few minutes before the last collection that afternoon, I managed to scribble a pencilled note to Jack. As I rushed to the post-box luckily situated only a few yards from the house, I remember how slippery the pavement was. The weather was icy-cold, much more severe than I had ever experienced back home. Back in the kitchen, I drafted another letter to the Matron of the Eye Hospital, trying my best not to sound too impatient. It had been a month since I had last written and I still hadn't had a reply. I took the letter with me to Kidderminster where they helped me word it more carefully. Jack told me about the enjoyable trip the Guild had had to see 'Puss in Boots' the previous Wednesday at the Theatre Royal. He had wanted me to go, but for some reason pantomimes, like circuses, had no appeal for me.

Imagine my surprise the following day, when Mrs Hands swept into the kitchen, pulled on her gloves and announced that she was off into Birmingham to book tickets for Peggy and herself to see the pantomime. Would I like to go and watch 'Puss in Boots' with them ? I should consider myself a lucky girl, as they would be in the four shilling seats ! Although I wanted to tell her where she could stick her precious seats, I politely thanked her, having been reassured that it would probably be on the Monday or Tuesday. The following Thursday would be the last one Jack would have free before returning to school. When she came back – I might have known – Mrs Hands told me that she had booked for Thursday. What was more, when Thursday came, she told me that she considered my little treat the equivalent of my five shillings pay. Oh, she was mean, that woman ! No visit to Jack and no pay that week ! Only the thought of leaving her for good stopped me from saying something unsavoury.

I received an immediate reply from Matron, advising me to continue studying and to get a book on Ophthalmic Nursing, as she didn't think there would be a place for me until the summer. Although disappointed, I was encouraged by her friendliness. I had already read and re-read one book; now I determined to get a more advanced one. I wrote back to thank her, at the same time reminding her that should a vacancy occur in March I would be free to take it. That done and posted, there was nothing more I could do.

I managed to see Jack a week after the pantomime 'treat'. I hurried to finish my work, before taking a bus into Birmingham and buying another book called *Diseases and Treatment of the Eye* with one of my Christmas postal orders. Quickly on to Snow Hill station and Kidderminster, where Jack, wearing his Burberry Mac, had cycled straight from school to meet me. That evening we were able to see *Sanders of the River* at the cinema, before hitting the freezing air again. On the train back, I spared a thought for Jack, who always had to catch up on his homework when I went over. It must have been after he got home or early the following morning that he did it !

The news on the wireless that day had been very solemn, announcing that King George V was very ill. Slogans such as 'The King Is Dead' and 'Long

Live The King !' appeared on all the hoardings following his death. The Prince of Wales would now become King Edward VIII. I was surprised to get news from home that Mr Frank Evans had died, for only two weeks before he had been at my father's birthday tea. Mrs Evans had from time to time come up for an urgent chat with my mother but had kept the fact that she and the boys had been frightened by her husband's increasingly violent fits of temper to herself. I had a vague idea that Mr Evans had been ill, but it was only now that I learned that he had died from a suspected brain tumour.

I relayed the news to Jack and also told him that I would definitely be giving in my notice in February. Each time I saw him after that, there was a sadness about him. Then, unexpectedly, in the middle of February, I received wonderful news from the Matron, telling me that I could start as a Probationary Nurse on March 31st, 1936, providing that my references and doctor's report were all right. I knew that my references would be good and saw no reason why I shouldn't pass my medical examination. I was in for a shock on my following half-day, when I saw the doctor ! There was nothing basically wrong with me, but she was horrified at the state of my legs, the chilblains now worse than ever. She also referred to my 'undernourished state of health' and listened while I described the conditions I had been living in. I assured her that I was really strong and that there was nothing that a couple of weeks at home wouldn't put right. She felt that I would not be able to stick the rigours of nursing, but when I described the regime I had been working under, she smiled and relaxed. I would have gone down on my knees that afternoon to beg her for a satisfactory medical report and I'm sure she sensed my passion to go nursing. Having impressed on me that I needed to build myself up and get rid of the chilblains, she gave me a tonic to be going on with and some ointment for my legs. She would see me again in a week's time – then and only then would she be prepared to consider a satisfactory report. I was so grateful, I could have kissed her ! I took my tonic, the chilblains responded well to the ointment and I took care at night to wrap my legs up in that warm dressing gown. I realised that I should have sought help earlier but the thought of bothering a doctor for such a 'trivial' thing had never occurred to me. A week later, the doctor was pleased with me and with a twinkle in her eye gave me the thumbs up !

The month's notice had put Mrs Hands into a fair old panic. Without my knowledge, she had written to my mother asking if she knew of anyone who could take my place ! My mother had replied to say that she would ask around and when I found out I was angry. Why couldn't Mrs Hands find somebody herself ? I should have left Birmingham on March 2nd, but Mrs Hands begged me to stay on awhile until she found a replacement. Before long, my mother wrote to say that she had found a girl who was prepared to come and that she would see her off safely in Swansea. The poor thing arrived on Saturday, 14th March, and it was I who had to meet her. She didn't say a word all the way to

Handsworth and that evening started to cry, saying that she wanted to go home. I tried my best with her, fully understanding how she felt, but I was going to leave on the Monday, whatever happened. On the Sunday I did my level best to show her how to do everything but as I explained the intricacies of the Triplex grate, her eyes were elsewhere. I began to wonder how long she would last at Mrs Hands' hands.

Meanwhile, I saw as much of Jack and his family as I could. It was getting hard for the both of us and we knew that those Thursday visits were now becoming special. I think it was more difficult for Jack, for I knew he liked me a lot and though I was fond of him, nursing was the most important thing in my life at that time. I was very excited at the thought of starting so soon.

My father had sent me a PT from Birmingham to Swansea for March 16th and said that he would meet my train. Mrs Hands had one last surprise – she was coming to see me off ! At the first barrier, the ticket collector looked at my ticket and asked me which train I was catching. I gave him the time, which I had carefully looked up, and he told me to make enquiries on the platform. He added that the next train for South Wales was indeed in, but that I might not be able to catch it. As there were now a lot of people queuing behind me, I couldn't keep him any longer. Mrs Hands stayed at the barrier, watching me struggle with two cases and a parcel to the top of the platform steps. Looking down at the station I could see one of the new Pullman coaches, proudly bristling with life. My heart sank – only full-fare paying passengers would be allowed on – and I kicked myself for missing it in the timetable. I rushed down to the platform where an official-looking inspector confirmed my worst fears. The next available train was a slow one, which wouldn't get me into Swansea until ten past ten that night ! I explained that my father would be worried if I wasn't on the train but his flat, unconcerned reply remained the same. I was desperate, my desire to get away making even a few hours seem like a lifetime. I rushed along the platform, pleading with every official I could find, but to no avail. Like a condemned prisoner, I ran up to the guard who was looking at his watch with whistle poised, held out my PT and helplessly looked into his eyes. Whatever the reason, he pointed to the guard's van.

"All right, you can get on, but jump in quickly !" he said roughly. I pointed to my cases at the top of the stairs, threw the parcel into the train and hurtled like a mad thing up the steps, where I grabbed the arm of a bystander and begged him to help. He picked up both cases and told me to get on the train. I was barely through the door, than he pushed the cases effortlessly in after me and the train started its journey. I blessed him for the angel he was ! With heart thumping, unable to move, I looked in the direction of the barrier but neither looked for Mrs Hands, nor cared. I was on my way home and in less than four hours was clinging to my father in High Street Station. Oh, it was so good to see him. All was well with my world again !

Chapter Thirteen

BRISTOL EYE HOSPITAL DAYS

Familiar things

Waking up that first morning at home, in my own little bedroom, was wonderful ! The pillow beneath my head felt as smooth as silk, the flannelette sheet – up to my chin – soft as downy, and the familiar *cwthran*, a Welsh, woven counterpane, kept me snugly warm.

Raising myself up on to my elbows, I realised that my mother had let me sleep on. The sun was already touching the Darren, picking out that tiny clump of fir trees, which in its own peculiar way had always spelt out the word 'Arithmetic' to me !

Was this one spelling the 'E' ?

Was it only yesterday I had been in Birmingham ? Would I really be starting as a nurse in the Bristol Eye Hospital at the end of the month ? Was I sure I would be a year older tomorrow ? Yes, all three things were true, but for a short while that morning I was content to wallow luxuriously in my bed.

Later, with my father home from work (Ronnie not yet back from University), the three of us sat down together in our cosy living room. In the quiet, my parents began to ask me about Mrs Hands. Little by little, I was able to reveal what had really happened and could see the hurt in their eyes.

"Why didn't you tell us ! Why didn't you let us know ?" It was then that the tears I had been suppressing for a long time began to flow. We clung together, all three of us, quietly, crying those healing tears until we felt better. We agreed to put Birmingham behind us and look forward to the future.

"And that means", said my mother, "getting ready for your birthday tomorrow !"

With sleeves rolled up, that's exactly what we did. Soon the cake was in the black-leaded oven next to the fire, the pastry rolled out for apple tarts, and the jelly and blancmange well on their way. Dough, in a large earthen-ware bowl covered by a pure white cloth, was rising well in front of the fire, soon to be divided into tins warming on the hob. As soon as the cake came out, in went the tins and by the time Ronnie walked in, the smell of those mouth-watering loaves was irresistible ! My mother laughingly refused him a slice of cake but presented us all, as if by magic, with a delicious casserole supper. I had not noticed it simmering there on top of the fire !

Next morning's post brought me a birthday letter from Jack. Now in his last year at King Charles I Grammar School in Kidderminster, he was doing so well that he was in the top group being primed for University entrance. Ronnie would tease me about him, claiming that he had cycled all the way down from the Midlands the two previous summers not to see the Mathias' with whom he stayed in Ystalyfera, but to see me. Whereas before, I would dismiss this as a lot of nonsense, I was now beginning to feel differently. I had cause to respect Jack for the mature friend he had been to me during the past six months. Whenever I had managed to get across to Kidderminster, I never had to be anything but myself with him. He seemed to sense the depths of misery and unhappiness that often engulfed me. My visits had been erratic, a couple of stolen hours before catching the last train back and though I had not been the best of company, he put up with me and always wrote after each visit. Yes, he had certainly been a good friend.

And now the Baker family were sitting down again, this time for my seventeenth birthday. I had asked for things I would need at the Eye Hospital – a trunk, a pair of comfortable rubber-soled shoes for ward work and three pairs of black stockings. My father had already renovated an old trunk of his which now only needed padlock and key ! Over tea we planned a trip down to Swansea the following Saturday. Ronnie, of course, would be studying, his work becoming increasingly important.

Saturday, bright and crisp, saw us on the train. Our first stop was the High Street Woolworths, a marvellous new store. After shopping downstairs we made our way up to their wonderful, modern cafeteria where we could take our trays and help ourselves to whatever we wanted. We chose a table near the large windows, eating and chatting as we took in the bustling High Street.

Then it was time for my father to go his own way. My mother and I had no problem finding black stockings, but the shoes were a different matter. Rubber soles were only just coming into vogue, but we eventually found a pair that met all the criteria in 'Leonards'. Black leather uppers with a few lace-ups over the instep, slightly built-up heels and, most important of all, quiet rubber soles. Compared with the clob-hoppers I was standing in, these were a pretty pair ! Back, now, to meet daddy at the L.M.S. Station to catch the late afternoon train up the valley. He had bought a new gramophone record, as usual. He and Ronnie shared a love of music, though my brother's preference for Wagner was sometimes a strain on the ear !

I began to realise how restricted life had been at Handsworth Road when I heard my family talking about the rise of Adolf Hitler in Germany. My father, who had served in the Royal Navy in the Great War, had always impressed upon Ronnie and me that there was no glory in war. He was a man of peace who read widely and to find him deeply worried, as we gathered around the wireless to listen to the latest news, came as a complete surprise to me.

The time slipped away very quickly, but not before several friends called, including Muriel. Neighbours, too, were for ever popping in and out. Kenny Cornelius, the crippled boy I'd known from early childhood, loved being teased. He would roll his eyes up behind his ill-fitting metal-rimmed spectacles and chuckle in his high, feminine voice. Nothing missed those eyes of his, for he knew everyone's business ! Now he was quizzing me again.

"Do you have a young man ? Where have you been ? Where are you going next ?"

Unfortunately, I just missed my old school friend Marjorie Reeves, her mother and brother Walter telling me that she had started working with the Civil Service in Cardiff. Down next to see Mr and Mrs Mathias and their sons, Vic and Bert. I carried greetings from Jack and his mother who, although not 'Railway People', had almost been adopted by the Mathias' in those hard years before the 1926 Strike.

All too soon, it was time for me to leave. My trunk had already been despatched and my small suitcase packed, with a pile of my mother's sandwiches at the ready. The evening before I left, my father passed an envelope containing a 10/-

The Mathias' backyard. Eileen enjoying a quiet read with Bert and his parents.

note into my hand, something to 'tide me over' until I got my first pay. They wouldn't listen to my protestations and all I could do was to give them each a great big hug. Ronnie accompanied me from St. Thomas Station to High Street, on the short cut beneath the old viaducts. Handing me my case, he gave me a brotherly hug and kiss, reminded me to write, then stood back as the guard's whistle blew. We waved until the train rounded the corner. Looking up the valley, now in view, my heart welled up with love for everything it meant to me – my family in particular – and I determined to do my best to make them proud of me. Back in the compartment, I removed my beret, unbuttoned my navy Burberry, and settled down to the train journey, a mode of travel I would always love and enjoy.

Bristol !

Temple Meads Station was a huge building that could have overwhelmed me but for the crowds of friendly porters ! It reminded me of a castle, with its long, underground passages leading from the platforms to its impressive front entrance, a dome flanked by two large towers. Outside, the approach was curved and wide, sloping down to the busy street below, in which there seemed to be an endless stream of tramcars, buses and people. One of those trams would take a very excited Welsh valleys' girl to the centre, another to Lower Maudlin Street, all the while taking in the huge buildings and the incessant traffic. Then, quite suddenly, ships of every description came into sight, actually moored to quays right at the very centre of the city ! When I reached the imposing-looking Eye Hospital, I glanced down at my old shoes to make sure they were still shining, brushed my Mac with my hands and straightened myself up before ringing the bell. A porter showed me into an ante-room and before long I was summoned.

"Nurse Baker, please !"

Matron Arnold was a tall, gaunt lady with a large, white linen head-dress which fell stiffly behind her shoulders. Her long, black dress was low-waisted, her hips emphasised by a large bunch of keys. Intimidating, yes, but once I sat down facing her, I found myself at ease. As she welcomed me to the Hospital, she looked at me with such kindness in her eyes that I found myself liking her immediately. She turned her attention to a small wad of papers in front of her. She noted that when I had applied to train at the Eye Hospital, I was coming to the end of my year as a Pupil-Teacher and that had been six months ago.

"What, my dear, have you been doing since ?" What was I to tell her ? Looking at her kind face, I defiantly told her the truth.

"I've been working as a maid !"

Eileen aged 17, soon after starting at Bristol Eye Hospital.

"Oh, my dear," she said, "I wouldn't tell your fellow nurses that if I were you."

I wouldn't forget her advice and never divulged that I had worked as a maid, not because I was ashamed – why should I be ? – but because I very soon realised that I came from a different world to most of the others and that they might not, indeed, understand my background. Sadly, we were not to have Matron Arnold for long. She was already seriously ill and died later that year.

The nurses' quarters next door to the hospital were spacious, airy and very homely, with beautiful furnishings. One of the first things to catch my eye when shown my room, was the pure linen bedspreads, beautifully hand-embroidered with the badge of Bristol Eye Hospital in the centre. The next surprise was to find that the uniform spread out for me on top of the bed was rose-pink ! We had had to send our measurements to the hospital prior to our arrival and I was a little bit apprehensive because of my small, nineteen-inch waist. I needn't have worried, the uniform was perfect.

My first room-mate was Nurse Beynon, who was from Lower Sketty in Swansea. We got on like a house on fire, vitality and warmth flowing from this tall, handsome girl. Although we had to share, the bedrooms were very large, giving us our own space. Each room had a wide sink with hair-washing facilities and a large mirror. Along the corridor were the bathroom and laundry room which were so well-equipped and spacious that I could hardly take it in. Only a matter of weeks ago, I had been sleeping in a cold, bleak attic ! Better not to think about it. Reality soon hit me as I walked to the bathroom with my faithful Mac over my old nightie, for I realised that I was the only one not wearing pyjamas and a proper dressing gown. Our dirty linen was collected once a week and always came back in perfect condition, work that was apparently done by nuns. Imagine how mortified I felt on one occasion soon after my arrival, when I inadvertently left one of my old tattered handkerchiefs in my uniform pocket. Back it came, beautifully starched, ironed and folded and with its very own piece of tissue paper ! At the top of my first shopping list I wrote the word 'handkerchiefs' in capital letters !

We were woken in the morning by a night 'runner' who tapped on each door and told the nurses that it was time to get up. During that heady first week I had difficulty getting used to the idea that I was now 'Nurse Baker', with the status that it brought me in the eyes of the patients. I was to commence duties in Gloucester Ward for women, the biggest ward on the first floor, running the width of the building. Victoria Ward cared for babies and young children while Fry Ward looked after women and older children. Sister and Staff Nurse had overall charge of the three wards, the probationers (of whom I was the most junior in the hospital) working on one ward at a time. The hospital was new and Sister Tucker was determined it should stay that way. As a junior I had to do a lot of cleaning. Not only were the beds to be kept free of dust, but every mortal thing had to be kept as clean as the day it was installed, including every pipe in the sluices, over or under the sinks. Other duties included making beds the correct 'hospital' way, making up special diets, cutting bread and butter in the kitchen, and helping wash and feed patients. Monotonous though it may sound, I thoroughly enjoyed the work. It was child's play in comparison with my maid's duties in Birmingham !

We had a communal sitting room downstairs in which most of the nurses congregated after supper at nine o' clock. Somehow, all tiredness seemed to evaporate once I'd had a quick bath and changed into night gear. The room was so big that the square of carpet in the middle could be rolled back to allow dancing to the wireless or gramophone records. It had come as a great shock to see girls smoking and took some time to get used to the volume of cigarette smoke floating across the room. Some smoked as though they had done so all their lives, lolling lazily on chairs or sofas and inhaling through long, elegant holders, giving me the impression that they came from upper-class families. Others smoked as if their lives depended upon it, pulling away at one cigarette after the other, guiding the smoke back down their nostrils or expertly sending rings towards the ceiling. The chain smokers rarely finished one cigarette before lighting another, leaving dishes piled high with half-smoked cigarette stubs. I thought of the unemployed men at home scanning the gutters and how eagerly they would have pounced on that mountain of dog-ends ! Nevertheless, I lapped up the relaxed atmosphere in which those of us who didn't want to dance could play cards or simply curl up and read. It was 'lights out' promptly at ten-thirty, a rule with which our motherly Night Sister would never allow us to take liberties.

During the day we had two hours off, either morning, afternoon or evening The one evening off-duty a week seemed longer for the simple reason that we finished at six o'clock for the rest of the day. We looked forward to it with anticipation, for it meant freedom to go to the pictures, visit friends, anything, provided that we were in by ten. If we wanted to stay out later, we had to ask for a special pass, something that was frowned upon and difficult to obtain. Besides that, we were always 'clocked-in' by the night porter ! We were also given one half-day off a week, starting at two o'clock, and one whole day a month. One day in April, I had a wonderful surprise when my parents turned up. They were able to look around the hospital and meet Matron, who thoughtfully provided us with complimentary tickets for the Little Theatre's matinee performance. Seeing how happy I was brought them peace of mind.

Another eye-opener was to see the kind of undergarments the other nurses were wearing ! We would hang our 'smalls' to dry in the ironing room, where I was literally hit in the face by tiny panties, fine lingerie and most amazing of all, brassieres ! I was still wearing liberty bodices and began to realise how incongruous they looked amongst all these dainty offerings. I was determined to buy some new clothes as soon as possible. Our salary as probationers was £20, rising to £25 during the second year, which worked out as just over £1 a month. I had gazed longingly at the lovely underwear in the Dorothy Perkins store but knew that the first essential was a pair of pyjamas. They were all the rage and it seemed that every nurse except me had a pair. Clutching my first month's pay packet tightly, I bought my very first ready-made night gear and proudly joined the ranks of the smartly-dressed ! My second month's salary saw me in 'Bright's of Bristol' at the top of Park Street, a lovely store where you could buy almost anything ! My mother had taught me how to sew and I had often watched her make her own patterns while making clothes for Ronnie and me from adult cast-offs. I opted, therefore, to buy material and patterns for a dressing gown. It says something about the size of our bedrooms that I was able to spread that material out on the floor without it being in anyone's way. The pattern was simple – a darted bodice, flared skirt, long sleeves and stand-up collar. Using only my curved nail-scissors, I carefully set to work. The end result saw me regally sweeping down to the sitting room in my paisley silk dressing gown, to gasps of admiration from my fellow-nurses. The fact that I still had no slippers to my name didn't seem to matter !

Having to take my own measurements had made me very conscious of my own body. At nineteen inches, my waist was fine but my bust left me feeling dismayed. Looking at myself in the mirror, I had to admit that I barely had one, thirty-two inches amounting to two tiny bumps ! Some of the other nurses were very generously endowed. It wasn't fair. I was seventeen, had been menstruating for three years and had fallen in love at the age of thirteen. Perhaps exercise would help ! In the end, I fell back on the words of my wise old grandmother at Pembrey who had told me that it was the lean cows that made the best mothers !

One person who tried to make my life a misery was our Staff Nurse, who picked fault with everything I did. After a month, I had been put on the Children's Ward, which I found very rewarding. As time went on, I became confused by being told to do one thing by a senior nurse, another by Staff. In the end I simply consulted the list in the kitchen, where all our tasks were clearly stated. Staff Nurse saw this as obstinacy and sent me to Matron, who, while sympathetic, left me in no doubt that I was still a very junior nurse. It didn't stop her signing me on for the next two years, my initial three month probation period having been completed. The nagging and needling continued until, totally exasperated, I followed Staff Nurse into the kitchen and told her I would report her to Matron if it continued. I went back to the ward feeling sick and shaky, but it had been worth it, because from that point on she left me alone. She reminded me in some ways of Mrs Hands – a bully who would climb down when confronted.

Generally, though, life was good during that initial year. During the summer, I rarely used the common room, the city of Bristol beckoning with its impressive docks and ancient buildings set in odd nooks and crannies. Up steps, down steps, narrow cobbled streets, historical statues, churches on every corner, I was totally enthralled. Not far from the hospital was the wonderful Suspension Bridge, high above the Avon Gorge, with miles of open downs on one side and the beautiful Leigh Woods on the other. Surely it would take a life-time to explore !

Meeting Nurse Payne was a tonic, the two of us having been written up to work together. A West country girl, she was familiar with Bristol and suggested a visit to the zoo on Durdham Downs. It was, indeed, a wonderful place, but left me feeling sad. The most famous exhibit was Alfred the Gorilla. As this magnificent animal restlessly grabbed the bars of his cage, it seemed as if he were looking directly at me and pleading with his large, dark eyes to be set free. It didn't seem right and as we strolled out into our sunny freedom, our thoughts remained with the hapless beast.

Meanwhile, Nurse Beynon had gone home to Swansea to recuperate after a tonsils operation. I was introduced to a new probationer, but she cried from the moment she arrived and in less than a week had run away, leaving her uniform and a note for Matron on the bed. She was followed by an altogether different character, small, pert and very pretty with not a care in the world. She, too, came from Swansea and though our backgrounds were completely different, we got on well from the start. She had come straight from Convent School and was most ladylike in her ways, though her fascination for young men amazed me. She would burst into the bedroom to tell me all about her latest acquisition and before long I began to wonder what the nuns had really taught her ! She was great fun to be with, always making me laugh and we soon found ourselves sharing off-duty times together – during the day, that is – for what Tregonning did in the evenings was her own business !

That summer I nursed an extremely courageous woman who was in great pain with glaucoma. Once better, Mrs Woodcock and her loving husband, a jolly, rotund man, invited me to visit them at home. Only days after her discharge, I received a delightful letter, not only repeating the invitation but giving precise directions to their house. Feeling slightly obligated, I accepted and received a most homely welcome. They wanted me to go again but I had been written up for night duty and couldn't promise. Payne was also on nights, on a different floor, but that didn't stop us enjoying one another's company during time off. I was also able to have a brief chat with Nurse Beynon, who was senior nurse on day duty and from whom I took the report.

I was still on the First Floor and so knew all the patients, but the atmosphere at night was very different, muted in some respects, yet with a great deal of fun and satisfaction. Midnight was a novel experience, for when all was quiet, the clocks of Bristol burst into song. Some were a little early, others a little late, so that the strokes went on and on. The night passed quickly, our busiest time being from early morning onwards. All treatment, washing of patients, bed-making and breakfasts had to be completed before day staff came on at eight o'clock. Having done my shift, I often felt full of energy and during that beautiful autumn would go into the garden to breathe in the balmy air before breakfast.

About a week after starting, I went on night duty as usual. Pushing open the double doors into the corridor, slightly dimmed for the night, I found myself almost stepping on some sort of object on the floor, then another and another. They were laid out in a zig-zag pattern and I carefully dodged them as I followed the strange things around the corner and all the way to the kitchen, from where Beynon was watching me. With tears rolling down her cheeks, she explained that the hospital had been given so many eggs that they didn't know what to do with them ! Gifts in kind like this apparently extended back sixty years, one of the most unusual being a donation of twenty-eight rabbits. No-one knew whether they had been skinned or not but tradition has it that the Matron received a little memo shortly afterwards:

> "Rabbits young, rabbits old,
> Rabbits hot, rabbits cold,
> Rabbits tender, rabbits tough,
> Surely Matron, we've had enough !"

I reckon that Beynon felt the same way about the eggs ! When we got to know each other better, I found that she knew Miss Jones of Mumbles, headmistress in Yniscedwyn Infants. Small world ! I wasn't too surprised to find that she could swim like a fish and learning that I was terrified of water, she suggested we go to Hotwells Baths together. Those mornings proved to be most enjoyable, especially when Payne came along. I never managed more than about six strokes before going under but that, for me, was progress. Tall and well-built, Beynon was never far away in the pool and she gave me confidence. Had we more time together, I'm sure that I would have learnt to swim.

At about this time, a new fire escape was installed in the night nurses quarters, right opposite my room ! One morning, the Hospital Secretary came over to demonstrate how to use it. Secured over a pulley at the top of the building was a long coil of steel rope, covered with fire-proof material, looped at either end. After fastening the top loop around his body, he climbed over the window ledge and lowered himself in an upright position, simply walking down the side of the building. Up came the wire again and three of us took it in turns to descend. Once out of the window, with feet planted firmly against the wall, it was a piece of

At one of the windows!

144

At home in the Gurnos Cottages. Eileen can be seen reaching for her favourite toy, Sunny Jim, while Ronnie and her father busy themselves with the 'Cat's Whisker' listening set.

Eileen's memories of her mother coming home after scavenging for coke on the 'Patches' during the General Strike. The tin works and the Darren are in the background.

*Jackie Jones (later Jackie Campbell and Eileen's husband) aged about three,
sitting on the step of his house in Ystalyfera.*

Towyn Farm where Eileen's grandparents were tenant farmers. Her grandmother is standing at the corner of the longhouse, while her grandfather is working in the field.

A train steaming into Ystalyfera Station where Eileen's father worked as a signalman.

cake ! We all wondered, however, what would happen in a real fire, for it was a very time-consuming exercise.

One night in September, I was assigned to an emergency admission in the Women's Ward and surprised to find Mrs Woodcock, whose eye condition (glaucoma) had flared up badly. She managed a big smile when she saw me, and grasping my hand, told me that I must meet her 'Sailor Boy', standing with the rest of the family at the back of the ward. A tall, tanned, very fit looking man and a younger version of his jovial father, he was in the Merchant Navy and had been away in the Far East. In the dimmed light, there was only time for a very brief introduction, before I had to usher them out. It was that night that I administered my first medicinal leech, with Mrs Woodcock as my 'guinea-pig' ! I had seen the procedure many times, the leeches applied through a tiny hole in a piece of sterile lint to exactly the correct spot at the side of the patient's eye. I was fascinated at how the small creature increased dramatically in size as it clung and sucked away at the blood. It had to be removed before it fell off of its own accord, by applying pressure very gently, until it dropped into a test tube. A dressing was immediately applied to the affected area. These leeches brought great relief of pain and, together with 'Esedrine' drops, were the standard treatment at that time. A new operation involving the removal of a tiny portion of the iris, allowing the build-up of fluid to escape without damaging the retina, was still at an early stage.

While she recovered, Mrs Woodcock's family continued to visit and though evening visiting time finished before we night staff came on duty, 'Sailor Boy' managed to slip back on some pretext or other on a number of occasions. His mother reckoned it was to see me but as he looked like a bit of a lad, I was very wary of him. Before he set sail again, he cheekily told me that he'd see a lot more of me the next time he was home !

In the middle of November, an old school mate from Abercrave, Nan Watkins, started at the Eye Hospital. Matron moved Tregonning out of our bedroom and charged me with looking after her, something I initially resented. However, Nan and I were soon catching up on the last two years and, of course, calling each other by our Christian names. She had missed quite a lot of school with kidney trouble but was now looking fit and healthy. She was very pretty with a ready smile, lovely fair hair and beautiful blue eyes. Within three weeks, however, she and another nurse went down with diphtheria and were whipped off to Ham Green Isolation Hospital. As her room-mate, I, too, was isolated and had a nose and throat swab taken as well as being given the Schick test. At the same time, Chicken Pox broke out on the Children's Ward and another two nurses dispatched to Ham Green. As many patients as possible were evacuated from the First Floor wards, and until the incubation period for both illnesses had well and truly passed, only emergencies were admitted. Once my tests had come back negative, I was transferred to help there, as they were now five nurses short.

Our Christmas Show

Payne and I came back on day duty together about two months before Christmas and were immediately recruited for the Nurses' Christmas Show, in the chorus line for a mini-production of *The Fleet's In Port Again*. It was ironic to think that while we were busy rehearsing, King Edward VIII was slipping quietly out of the port of Plymouth on the morning of December 12th on *HMS Fury*, having abdicated and on his way to meet Mrs Simpson ! In his own words, "Love had triumphed over the exigencies of politics."

I shall never forget that first Christmas. The few remaining patients who were not spending it at home had the benefit of a full nursing staff, for there was no such thing as off-duty leave between Christmas Eve and Boxing Day. The atmosphere was relaxed, joyful and homely, each ward having been beautifully decorated with its own theme. On Christmas Eve, we nurses, dressed in our capes and carrying candles, walked from ward to ward singing carols. It was tradition to start in the Children's Ward and I savoured every moment. The atmosphere was that of a big, loving family. On Christmas Day the consultants took over, playing Father Christmas and his helpers to the delight of the children, before donning tall white chefs' hats while carving the turkeys !

By evening, the most Senior Consultant, under Matron's eagle eye, was carving for us at the staff dinner. The junior doctors in training were sitting down with us and I was opposite a young American. Nearly everyone was smoking, a common habit for both men and women in those days and one live-wire of a nurse had from the start been trying to introduce me to the art.

"Come on, Baker," she would say, "have a drag !" I just laughed and shrugged her off, but she never gave up hope. Now, suddenly, I was being offered a cigarette by the American house-man. Whatever took hold of my mind at that point I'll never know, but instead of refusing, I took it ! I knew that it was a mistake but he was now holding out his lighter. Serve me right ! What happened next would haunt me for the rest of my life. As I put it into my mouth, his loud drawl seemed to announce to the rest of the room, "I suppose you know you're lighting the wrong end of that cigarette !"

Everything went quiet, then laughter broke out, rocking the whole room. It was cork-tipped and I was offering him the cork ! I wanted the ground to open up and swallow me ! I was rescued by the maids bringing round the plates but my new American friend hadn't quite finished with me. With exaggerated solicitude and a wicked grin on his face, he leant forward again, proffering me a tureen of vegetables, complete with serving spoon ! The only comfort I could take was to convince myself that his six months training would soon be over.

Next evening, that of Boxing Day, I was making a fool of myself again in our little musical. The senior nurse, who had done her best to knock us into shape, had a beautiful voice and sang all the solos. The rest of us as the chorus line, dressed in short, frilly navy and white dresses and sailor hats, kicked our legs up energetically, as sailors do ! It was great fun, the applause thunderous, and there, very prominent in the audience, was the appreciative American ! No doubt, he would put in an appearance again at the Hospital Ball, but there were three good reasons why I wouldn't be there. No evening dress, no partner and little faith in my dancing ability !

As it happened, I had been written up for night duty again. I didn't mind, the times spent in the Children's Ward being something special. I never ceased to wonder at those little ones, many of whom were unable to see. Some had been born totally blind, some double-padded after operations. Yet they were so good, brave and adorable, just normal kids ! One of my duties when time permitted, was to iron delicate theatre towels, and as I did so, I would recite lots of the nursery rhymes, stories and songs I had picked up at Yniscedwyn Reception Class, often sending the children to sleep.

The year of 1937 started with a cold spell. Ronnie wrote to me with news that Jack had suffered a bad attack of tonsillitis. A pang of guilt prompted me to write immediately, for I owed him a letter. As I wished him a speedy recovery my mind was on something else that Ronnie had told me. Jack and his friend Chick were contemplating a cycle tour of North Wales at Easter, cycling down to Ystalyfera to spend a couple of nights with Mr and Mrs Matthias. I suddenly realised, with some pleasure, that that was when I would be on annual leave ! He had started work in October as a 'Youth in Training' on a two-year apprenticeship with the Post Office Engineering Department. I felt sad that he couldn't

Jack's workmates in the Post Office Engineering Department.

have gone to University, after having matriculated in seven subjects, nearly all of them with distinction. His parents had had a big say in the decision, influenced by the promise of a safe job with promotion and a pension at the end of it. Like me, he would be starting at the bottom, as one of a gang doing the absolute basics and working his way up. There was no better way to learn, so why worry !

Meanwhile, my eighteenth birthday had come and gone, bringing me lovely letters from home and from Jack, who also sent me a beautifully-bound pocket Testament. This I treasured, taking it on duty with me and dipping into it when all was quiet on the ward. As leave got nearer, the drill was the same. Everything belonging to us had to be packed into our trunks, collected by a hospital porter and despatched home two days before we left. I had to make do with a scrap of waste hospital paper to let Jack know my holiday dates, as my writing paper was safely packed.

Although not full by any means, that old trunk was heavier than it had been a year ago. I was dying to show my mother the beautiful dressing gown, fashionable pyjamas and new, cosy deep-red jersey dress. I had a gift for each of them, too, but those went into my suitcase. I had been introduced to 'Morny' talcs and soaps during that past year, my favourite perfume being 'French Fern', but for my mother I had chosen some perfumed 'Rose Morny'. For both my father and Ronnie I had bought fountain pens.

Spring 1937 – at home with friends

I couldn't wait for that Monday morning to arrive ! Waving good-bye to patients and day-staff, I rushed off duty, had a bite to eat and a quick bath. Wrapped warmly in scarf, friendly old beret and faithful navy mac, buttoned up against the piercing wind, I caught a tram to Temple Meads and the early train to Swansea. I savoured everything about the journey, the familiar sounds of whistles and wheels, each rhythmic revolution taking me nearer and nearer home. By the time I was on the valley bus, excitement knew no bounds. Once past the Mond Nickel Works in Clydach, the valley got narrower and more beautiful every inch of the way. The hills I knew so well grew closer and steeper until my beloved Darren was towering above me on the right. The Capitol Cinema came into sight and it was time to get off. As the bus chugged up towards the Twrch valley, I was on the last lap ! A short walk straight along the Glanrhyd Road and I was at 'Croesffyrdd'.

Watching from the bay window of our council house, my mother had been on pins ! As I turned the corner of the main road, out she came to greet me and we ran to hug one another. We had so much to say, but the first thing she wanted to

Eileen with a fringe, 1937.

ask me about was my hair. I'd forgotten that she'd never seen it cut short with a fringe ! Soon, very soon, I was in our cosy sitting room with a delicious dinner in front of me. My father arrived home from work and when Ronnie walked in later, our family was complete. After giving them their presents, we spent the rest of the evening chatting. Ronnie wanted us to listen to a some piano music by a composer called Littorff, an amazing piece that would for ever remind me of my brother, though it was hardly a soothing lullaby. By that time, however, nothing could keep me awake, and my mother shepherded me to bed. She had already warmed it with hot bricks, wrapped up and straight from the oven. I was home all right !

Next day I opened my trunk, eager to show my folks what I had acquired during my first year. They were both interested in my lecture notes, too, as well as my spanking new textbook on Ophthalmic Nursing. In a year's time I would be sitting my finals and I was determined, if a little anxious, to do well. Muriel called then, looking a picture. She had done her hair differently and wore a very fashionable dress with 'leg of mutton' sleeves, made by her sister Eunice, who though only nineteen, was an accomplished seamstress. Muriel was three years younger, just finishing in Maesydderwen School and had applied to become a Pupil-Teacher.

At home, it was a real treat to listen to the radio, or to records, without the constant racket of the nurses' sitting room. As was the unhurried pleasure of poring over my childhood treasures, safely housed in a straw portmanteau in my bedroom. Most precious of all was still the beautiful, dusky, velvet Negress doll in her emerald green satin dress. She was, in fact, a handkerchief satchel, but was far too good for that ! I couldn't help holding her up against me and thinking of Alfred. He was probably married by now.

The sky was leaden that first week – we even had had a little snow – and we wondered whether Jack and Chick's tour would go ahead. Over the next week the weather improved and a postcard arrived from Bala telling me that they were enjoying the hot sun ! I slipped down to see Mr and Mrs Matthias, Vic and Bert, where I was welcomed with open arms as usual. Even for a quick cup of

Jack on the right and Chick, Kidderminster, c.1938.

tea Mrs Matthias brought out her rose-bud, almost paper-thin china. Vic teased me that they only saw it when I came round ! Bert, a year younger than me, had shot up into a fine, broad-shouldered, good-looking young man. Vic said he intended cycling up to meet Jack and Chick the following Friday for the last few miles of their journey, teasingly adding, "Just to make sure that Jack reaches you safely, Eileen !"

As it turned out, they missed each other, Chick having got a puncture, but the three were reunited in the early evening at Vic's house. This didn't stop them coming up to our house once they had eaten, but Jack and I seemed destined to see one another only during short intervals. That evening the chatter gathered momentum; photography, cycling, telecommunications, metallurgy, geology and music all got a good airing. However, whenever I looked up, I found Jack's eyes on me, quiet, searching eyes, silently telling me something which I thought, I hoped, I wanted to hear. We made plans for the next day, their only complete day with us, though we had already been summoned to Bert's birthday tea !

The weather promising to be good, Jack wanted Chick to see the stunning views from the top of the Darren and they set off first thing on the steeper climb from the riverside at Heol-y-Varteg, a route I had no desire to go on ! Back at our house in time for dinner, Chick said that he was genuinely impressed by our local 'mountain', as the pair of them cleared their plates. The three of us could relax in the afternoon before making for Bert's house. We decided on the pleasant walk along the riverside, hugging the lower reaches of the Darren, rather than use the main road through Ystalyfera. In the evening we briefly visited Mr Mathias in his signal-box lower down the valley from my father's. Normally we wouldn't have walked alongside the railway track, but it was a quiet period between trains and Saturday meant no freight wagons. Both boys were interested in the workings and Mr Mathias allowed us to use the telephone to speak to my father in the next box. Then it was back to our house for cocoa and a bite to eat. The day had gone as planned !

In the quiet time before Bert's party, Jack and I had a chance to catch up with what had happened to us over the past year. Again his eyes rarely left mine and I felt a bond growing between us. We enjoyed the pretty walk and the party, too, though in a sense we were interlopers. Walking home, I knew that Jack was beginning to mean a lot to me and that I would cherish this young man from now on. Before he left for Kidderminster he called in to see me and I was over the moon to hear my parents invite him to stay the next time he was down. Armed with a battalion of sandwiches from my insistent mother, the boys went on their way. The visit may have been short but the memories would last !

Chapter Fourteen

MORE RESPONSIBILITY

If my first year at the Eye Hospital had been the most carefree, happy time of my life since leaving home, the second was to prove the one in which I suddenly grew up. I was now one of a group of Senior Probationers, halfway through our training with a year of theory and practice behind us. We were now expected to take on more responsibility, administering most treatments and occasionally taking charge, especially at night.

I returned to work at the end of April 1937 to find Bristol garlanded for the Coronation. My first free half-day was cancelled, Night Sister explaining that I was to to 'special' two patients, a six-week-old baby on the ground floor and a middle aged private patient addicted to whisky, on the second. The baby was isolated because her eyes had been badly infected at birth, her mother having contracted gonorrhoea. The nurses treating the baby were not allowed to do any

On the roof of the Eye Hospital.

other treatment. My brief was to treat and feed the baby, suitably barrier-clothed, before getting well and truly scrubbed and going on to sit with the whisky addict. She had played havoc in the theatre and her operation had had to be halted. Quite unpredictable and violent, capable of tearing off her dressings, she was given regular doses of whisky to calm her. In her saner moments she was a likeable old woman but we all breathed a sigh of relief when she went home. I returned, then, to being 'relief-runner' and soon found mysef looking after two babies when a thirteen-day-old boy was admitted with the same disease.

We had been told many times not to get too involved with the suffering of patients, in case it affected our ability to help them. While acknowledging this, the plight of these little babies troubled me. It was not their fault, and after they had got better, what sort of home would they be going back to ? And the woman who could only keep sane with doses of whisky. What was she doing to herself ? These questions I started to subconsciously ask to a God I had thrown out four years ago. I had begun looking for answers in the Testament Jack had given me. I eventually got round to replying to his letter inviting me to their new house on the outskirts of Kidderminster. It was another five months before I could get up and see him.

It was at this time that my feet became so painful that I reported the problem. It turned out that I had 'dropped arches' in each foot which soon improved after a spell of treatment, both electrical and physical.

Night duty continued from April to June, but it wasn't all work. Many mornings were spent in the swimming baths and two memorable evenings at the ballet. As nurses, we were given complimentary tickets to Bristol's Little Theatre and The Theatre Royal, but as they had to be used in the afternoon it was impossible for those on night duty to go. At the Prince's Theatre in Park Row, a short walk up Upper Maudlin Street and Perry Street, I was able to see two of my favourites – Gounod's ballet from *Faust* and Tchaikovsky's *Swan Lake*. On my income I could only afford tickets in the 'gods'. These were reached by first going down a dim alleyway at the side of the theatre, lit by a solitary, spluttering gas jet, then up a winding wooden staircase that led dizzily to the top of the theatre. It seemed to go on for ever and was so steep that I felt at any moment I would topple over into the auditorium ! The stage looked like a matchbox in the distance.

I chose to sit on the end of the bench at the very back so that I could slip out to work without disturbing anyone. I stayed until the last possible moment because both ballets were enthralling. The one from *Faust* was performed on a large, curved stairway with the chorus dancers passing ethereally up and down it, dressed in all colours of the rainbow. While on day duty I went to see Wendy Hillier in *Far From The Madding Crowd* in the Theatre Royal, another unforgettable performance.

153

Bristol City Centre, July 1939.
(Author's photograph).

Coming off night duty at the end of June, Payne and I were delighted to find that we were sharing the same bedroom. We were in time for 'Alexandra Rose Day', for which we would sacrifice our off-duty. We had taken part the previous year but at that time neither of us had been nursing long enough to know the ropes. I had started off with a more experienced nurse but we had somehow become separated and I had ended up on a country bus to Bishopston, selling hardly any roses and arriving late for duty. This time, Payne and I were much more confident as we set off with our trays and collecting boxes, dressed in uniform complete with capes. We had discussed our tactics, which worked perfectly. The skill was in choosing a local tram or bus and collecting downstairs, before rushing up to the passengers on the top deck. Then we would get off, returning almost immediately on another vehicle heading towards the Centre. This drill was repeated, bringing us nearer and nearer to the Centre, all the while keeping an eye on the time. The drivers and conductors, obviously well-accustomed to the tradition and its high-spirited nurses, willingly stopped for us and teased us unmercifully. Rarely had I had such fun ! Tired and hungry, but elated with our morning's efforts, we were back in time for our midday meal and afternoon shift.

The summer of 1937 was spent very happily on day-duty, whether in Casualty or Out-Patients. Both the sister, plump and cuddly, and staff nurse, tiny and slim, were helpful and friendly. Staff told me that she had originally trained in a ballet school in her home town of Weston-super-Mare where her closest friend had been Deborah Kerr, the film star ! By now I was expected to treat casualties on my own, this being my second stint. One patient was a worker from the Filton Aeroplane Works, who had a tiny piece of steel lodged in his cornea, causing him great pain. It didn't take long to remove and he was told to return within a week for a check up. Once on the mend there was no need for Bob to come again but come he did, time after time, bringing flowers, chocolates, even silk stockings ! He would move back deliberately to be last in the queue and each time I would gently turn his gifts down and send him on his way. His final bid to take me out came towards the end of one week, as I was clearing up in Casualty. He knew that I was off duty at six and he chatted away, begging me to go to the pictures with him. In some desperation and without Jack's say-so, I told him that I already had a young man who would be meeting me at Kidderminster station on the weekend. As I sat on the train drawing out of Temple Meads that Saturday afternoon, I was amazed when he suddenly appeared at the door of the compartment, having bought a return ticket to Gloucester. We talked and talked, until eventually convinced I had a boyfriend, said that he wouldn't bother me again !

Preparations for our final exam were now taking definite shape. The four consultants giving us lectures were Mr Iles, Mr Garden, Mr Chambers and young Mr Palin, who was already building up a reputation for operating with great success on hitherto hopeless conditions such as detached retinas and glaucoma. His lectures were compelling. He anticipated that corneal grafts would soon become as common as the removal of cataracts and he was experimenting with contact lenses. In Out-Patients I was now allowed to test people for suitable spectacles. The consultant would test them internally while we nurses would examine externally by means of lenses and if our results tallied we would receive due praise, a wonderful feeling !

At home, all was well. Ronnie and Vic Matthias were now taking their finals at Swansea University and had already been interviewed by representatives of the Shell Oil Company. Ronnie would be working for them in Romania before his twenty-first birthday in November while Vic would remain in this country, employed by a British firm.

Sailor Boy

Although Bob had been persistent, at least he had been decent and full of humour. Things were to be a lot different with 'Sailor Boy'. He had been home since Coronation Week, when his troopship had taken part in the celebrations at

155

Spithead. Since then he had been stationed at Portsmouth, coming home on most weekends. Off-duty times had enabled me to see more of the Woodcocks and Sailor Boy had taken me to the big Gaumont Cinema in Baldwin Street several times. I considered him to be a friend and nothing more.

On one Sunday in September, I went out to their village and was given the usual warm welcome. When Sailor Boy suggested a little walk, I hesitated, but his parents urged us to enjoy the sunshine while it lasted. It was one of those warm, lazy sort of days and I could hardly refuse. We walked through some lovely fields behind their house, before hitting a country path which wound its way along the top of a little valley. In a quiet spot overlooking a small stream, he sat down and motioned me to sit next to him. He lay back, his hands clasped behind his head and closed his eyes, for all the world a picture of contentment. The warm sunshine lulled me into a false sense of security and I must have fallen into a light doze.

Suddenly, to my horror, I became aware of his hand on the inside of my bare thigh. Electric waves ran up and down my spine as Alfred's words from five years ago flashed through my brain.

"Promise me Eileen, promise me ! Don't let any boy touch you . . . !"

I hadn't understood at the time but now I did. I started to protest but his lips pressed hard on mine and the more I struggled, the more pressure he exerted.

"Come on, Eileen, it's all right. Trust me !" he kept whispering. But I didn't trust him. His one hand was already under my light summer frock, feeling its way to my waist and the top of my knickers. He didn't know that they were French cami-knickers, part of a one-piece garment from my shoulders down and the only advantage I had over this strong seaman. I wriggled and squirmed until, by some fluke, I was able to roll away, get on my feet and scarper. I ran until I was in sight of the houses. There, I waited for him, panting and trying to compose myself. I had great respect for his parents and for their sakes wanted us to return behaving as natural as possible. Back in the house, Mr and Mrs Woodcock beamed at us and at one another in a way which made me wonder if they were hearing 'wedding bells' for me and their son. As soon as tea was over, I made some excuse to get away.

"See her to the tram, then !" Sailor Boy was told by his father.

We were decidedly uncomfortable with one another at the stop and he surprised me by asking if he could see me again. Instead of flatly refusing, all I could come out with was, "I don't know, I just don't know !"

What I did know for sure was that I felt degraded and terribly guilty. I kept thinking how very easy it would have been for me to have given in to him. What would my parents think of me if they knew ?

'Johnnie' arrives

At the end of that summer a State Registered Nurse arrived to do a specialist twelve month course in Eye Nursing. She caused a stir amongst us because of her prim, strict, dour appearance and the fact that she proclaimed her religious beliefs at every possible opportunity. Working on the same floor, I began to resent her prying questions about my religious background. She had hardly any friends in the hospital but as I got to know her I became more tolerant of her, realising that she had a wry sense of humour.

She belonged to a Pentecostal Church I had never heard of, the Mount of Olives, situated on Blackboy Hill towards the Downs. She invited me along but I found her weird talk of 'Baptism of the Holy Spirit' and 'speaking with tongues' off-putting. However, curiosity got the better of me and I reluctantly gave in to 'Johnnie' (that is what

'Johnnie' on the left with Eileen, picking rose-hips.

she wanted to be known as, her surname being Johnstone), not knowing what to expect that Sunday morning. A more friendly group of people you couldn't wish to meet. She seemed to have one special friend there, Miss Vivien Armstrong, who had come with her family, all women ! She radiated love and friendliness and put me at ease. The pastor, a Scot by the name of Wallace, was just as sincere. Despite the frequent 'Amens', 'Praise The Lord' and 'Halleluias', I felt that the whole service had been direct and meaningful. Before long, however, I felt pressurised by Johnnie and decided to talk things over with Jack. On a late Friday afternoon in early October he was meeting me at Kidderminster Station, not from school this time, but from work. To see the love in his eyes and feel his caring arm around me as he guided me to his new home, was worth all the aggravation from Johnnie.

'Ridgecroft', an attractive semi-detached building, was so called because it had been built, along with several similar houses, on a ridge in the Greenhill district of Kidderminster. At the back was a beautiful garden on which they had worked so hard, with a vegetable patch and delightful trellised lawn. Beyond was a pleasant view of rolling countryside. Mrs Davies and Muriel greeted me warmly and we were soon chatting over a pot of tea in their comfortable dining room, before being joined by Mr Davies, who was now an Insurance Man. Jack showed me his bedroom which would be mine for the night and then sat me down in the front room, where a coal and log fire was crackling away. As he was working the next day and wanted me to hear some music, there was little time for serious discussion. However, he gave me an alternative view to Johnnie's approach to religion, taking a great weight off my shoulders. I was grateful for his knowledge and lucidity and so proud to know him !

Over the evening meal the talk was about the dark green Post Office Telecommunications van that Jack had been allocated, replacing the unwieldy heavy motorbike that he used in the outlying areas. After two lessons over the next couple of days he would be expected to take (and pass) his driving test ! All to get him ready for the Regional Training School at Lancaster Street, Birmingham. Muriel also worked in the city, as a civil servant. Mr Davies startled me by asking if I paid into a Pension Scheme, but after hearing how little I earned, dropped the subject. I didn't want their pity, telling them that with care I could save for what I wanted – the following week I would be going to a concert in the Colston Hall. I dared not tell them that the 7/6d ticket had taken me three months of scrimping !

With Mrs Davies' permission, Jack and I went back into the front room, where we were left alone. He had borrowed some gramophone records of Schubert's *Unfinished Symphony*, and to this day I cannot hear it without remembering that evening; he sitting close to me, gently, tentatively, putting his arm around my shoulders while I clasped his hand and let my head rest tenderly against him. I was sure, then, that there was more than mere friendship between us. The next day, Jack left work early to take me to the station. Our small talk came to an end when the engine pulling my train made its appearance at the end of the platform. Jack gathered me in his arms and kissed me gently.

Muriel, Jack's stepsister, in the back garden at Ridgecroft.

His first letter confirmed how he felt, pages and pages of outpourings of love for me ! We were so busy on the ward that I could only manage a short note in return. We were temporarily without a Sister-in-Charge, so most of the treatment, both in the crowded men's ward and seven private wards, fell on my shoulders. On top of that we had frequent lectures in the evening, though that didn't stop me going to see my concert by the Czech Philharmonic Orchestra. Under Raphael Kubelick they played pieces by Dvorják and Smetana and I so wished Jack could have come. His letters came thick and fast, the very sight of the envelopes giving me a thrill. I wouldn't open them until the evening when I'd have time to read them over and over again. I was delighted when he asked if we could spend a week together the following summer, exploring the Gwred, Giedd and Twrch rivers.

In the meantime, I went to church again with Johnnie and found Jesus' 'Sermon on the Mount' amazing. I wanted to follow Him and His teachings, yet felt unworthy. I envied Payne, an Anglican, who seemed to have no hang-ups about religion and came out of church feeling full of fun. One evening, she persuaded me to drop my studying and catch a train with her to Weston, whereupon she dragged me into the nearest first-class compartment and a luxurious half-hour ride. With straight faces, we handed in our third-class tickets the other end ! Payne's escapades may have been infantile, but they stopped us getting too serious about life. However, wherever I went, I couldn't get Jack out of my mind and wished he could be with me.

At the beginning of December 1937 an Irish sister arrived on our ward from Wolverhampton Eye Hospital. As Christmas approached, she suggested we ask a group of young male patients who worked at Filton Aeroplane Works for ideas about the central display on the ward. Before long, we were working on a model aerodrome, the men supplying technical expertise while we busied ourselves making papier mâche buildings and aircraft.

The Hunt Ball !

One of the private patients at that time was the wife of a Baptist minister in Bridgewater. When her family arrived to take her home, I was dumbfounded to find that daughter Peggy had arranged for me to attend the Bridgewater Hunt Ball with her. Not only was there an official invitation to what was the biggest social event of the Season, but she had even arranged a partner for me ! The fact that I couldn't dance was no excuse – she was going to lend me a very special boyfriend who was an excellent dancer. Out I went to buy a ball-dress that was within my price-range, settling on a pretty pastel blue lace with a large pink ribbon sash, Peter Pan collar and short sleeves. It was simple and I felt comfortable in it. A pair of slip-on pink shoes completed the outfit.

Peggy met me off the train and on our way through town, introduced me to her boyfriend, teasingly asking me not to steal him away from her. I replied that there was no danger of that happening; after all, I had a boyfriend of my own ! A taxi picked the four of us up and at half-past nine I was attending one of the West Country's most glittering spectacles. Everything was decked out in tune with the hunt, right down to the defenceless little fox ! A fanfare announced a colourful prancing parade of hunt members, including the ladies, led by the Master of the Hunt. Complete with whips and horns, they raised the roof with a cacophony of strident baying and cries of tally-ho ! Peggy's young man was kindness itself, shepherding me through the first couple of dances until I suggested he let me sit out the next few. Gratefully, I'm sure, he sought out Peggy and it was a real revelation to see them dancing so gracefully together. Before long, I had been asked to dance by the other young man. I wished Jack could have been there but somehow knew that he would not have been comfortable. Neither was I, in all truth. These people lived in a very different world but I reminded myself that they had been kind enough to invite me. At two in the morning, after many more elegant dances and much cavorting about, it was time for Auld Lang Syne.

Next morning I found myself downstairs, where everything was quiet. A light underneath Peggy's father's study suggested that he was already working and he joined me shortly in the kitchen. Over breakfast we had a long chat. He had lately completed a history of his church – Bridgewater Baptist – and he showed me a book full of autographs of people he had written about, many of them missionaries. A nursing friend of theirs had recently left for the Congo and I momentarily felt a pang of envy. Jack had often talked about missionary work and though I knew I couldn't do it on my own, I felt that I'd like to accompany him. It puzzled me for a while that this learned religious man and the fun-loving Peggy of last night were father and daughter. Then, I realised that I knew very little about them and anyway, why shouldn't enjoyment and religion go together ?

On my return, a Christmas letter from Ronnie was awaiting me, telling me all about life in Romania. He was learning to ski and generally seemed to be having a good time. He'd invited colleagues to a celebratory meal on his twenty-first birthday in November and was now being measured for a dinner suit. Dear Ronnie, he had gone without new clothes for years while he'd been studying but was now in a position to make up for it. I knew that my mother and father were proud of him. They, too, had made sacrifices. This was the first Christmas they'd spent on their own – 'Lonesome' they would write, 'but still enjoying the spirit of Christmas !'

On the two Sundays before Christmas I attended the Mount of Olives with Johnnie. I also visited Mr and Mrs Woodcock, who had invited me several times since that awful afternoon in September. The whole family was there, Sailor

Boy having docked into Plymouth, and I felt very awkward in his company. I had to be back on duty at two o'clock and the family wouldn't take no for an answer when the young sailor gallantly said he'd see me to the hospital. He told me that he would be leaving soon for a two year stint in the Far East and was keen to take me out. There was a Cary Grant film on at the Gaumont and this would be the last opportunity for him to see me. His manner was so friendly and kind, so like that of his parents, that I agreed.

After buying the tickets, he shepherded me upstairs to the best seats in that sumptuous cinema. He was so pleasant that I began to relax and almost forget his previous behaviour. To cap it all, he produced a box of Fry's dark chocolates ! The film was very funny and the evening was a real treat until nearing the hospital, when everything suddenly changed. I held out my hand to thank him and wish him bon voyage but with a vice-like grip on my elbow he started to lead me up a dark narrow alleyway at the side of the hospital. Here, he pushed me roughly up against the wall, asking me if I didn't think he deserved more than a mere 'thank you'. As I tried to explain that I had accepted his invitation as a friend of his parents, he tipped my face up with one hand while clumsily trying to unbutton my coat with the other. I felt sick with shame as I felt his big frame hard against mine. Praying for help, I gathered every bit of strength in my shaking body and gave him one almighty shove, enough to escape his hold and run as fast as my legs would carry me to the safety of the lighted hospital door. In panic, I rang and rang the bell, the bewildered porter calmly enquiring if he could be of any assistance in helping me raise the dead ! Once inside, I leaned against the wall before straightening myself up. I bid the porter goodnight and rushed upstairs to my bedroom, all sorts of things running through my mind. Was this what I'd heard some of the nurses talking about, the kind of repayment some men expected when they took girls out and gave them presents ? Well I'd learnt my lesson ! How could I be so naive ? Never again would I see Mr and Mrs Woodcock or their sailor-boy son. In anger, I stamped my foot on the floor and hissed, "Damn ! Damn ! Damn !"

Many years later, recalling the incident, I remembered that the Woodcocks had written to tell me that their son had sailed at the end of February to China for two and a half years on the troop-ship *Dilwara*. With less jaundiced eyes, I wondered, with pity, what might have happened to him. I regretted not replying to their letter.

My conversion

Not long before Christmas, we bade 'au revoir' to one of our nurses who had recovered well after becoming desperately ill following a mastoid operation. The run-up to Christmas was just as much fun as the year before. For Boxing

Day we were asked to organise a Fancy Dress Parade, to be judged by Matron and dignitaries. With time and ideas short, Payne and I went up to a theatrical hire shop near the Prince's Theatre and after a thorough browse, decided on a couple of Dutch costumes. Payne reckoned she could be the man and I would play the woman. With our Christmas gifts and letters sorted, we turned our attention to the outfits and hit on the idea of imitating wooden puppets. We would need a short musical accompaniment, so sought out one of the senior nurses, who played the piano. While she played *Tulips from Amsterdam*, we attempted a few stiff movements across the room. Our pianist begged for more co-ordination, asking us to use our heads, our brains (if we could find them), as well as every bone in our body. We ended up on the floor laughing those heads off and were promptly warned to behave or there would be no music. We promised, then burst out laughing again ! Knowing her cause was lost, she closed the piano and strolled off with the sheet music under her arm. We were certain she wouldn't let us down.

The tradition of carol singing on Christmas Eve was as wonderful as ever. As a Junior Probationer it had all been new to me but this time it held more significance. As I carried the lighted candle in my beloved Children's Ward, I could hear a verse from the Scriptures: "Suffer the little children to come unto Me and forbid them not, for of such is the Kingdom of Heaven." These words of Jesus stayed with me all over that Christmas, 'forbid them not' whirling around in my head even as I was preparing for our sketch. Ever since my disastrous experiences with Sailor Boy, I had been racked with guilt and shame, unable to tell a soul about it. What Nurse Johnstone had been continually preaching began to make sense to my muddled conscience. Inside, I was crying out for the kind of forgiveness she was talking about. All through the excitement of the Christmas show, I felt strangely detached. In terms of faith, I was a child – could I, too, come to Him ? If only !

Time then for the evening charade. With exaggerated pink faces and bright red spots on our cheek-bones, Payne and I were last on. For a few seconds after the music started, we were leaden – inanimate wooden puppets on strings, going through the motions. Then we got into the swing of it and the reaction told us that we'd done at least as well as anyone else. Now it was Matron's turn, meticulously noting the merits of each act, before calling out the winners. It was us ! To thunderous applause, we received our little wrapped packages of Imperial Leather Soap. Acceptable, if a little unimaginative !

It was now time to disperse. With Dutch cap, flaxen hair and plaits discarded, I rushed upstairs to wash the paint off my face and change. I was bursting to tell Johnnie how I felt spiritually and was glad to find her light still on. Slightly surprised, she listened as I breathlessly explained why I had come. She suggested that we kneel down and pray and in the calm that followed, I gave my life, immature and unworthy as it was, to Jesus Christ. I remember the hour clearly – it was just coming up to midnight on Boxing Day 1937. No words can describe the joy that filled me that night and continued for some time to come. From that time, too, despite our disagreements, I loved Johnnie in an inexplicable, unique Christian way.

I wrote immediately to Jack, at the same time thanking him for his wonderful Christmas gifts; a photograph of himself that I had requested, a hand-sewn pyjama case and a calendar with daily texts. He was genuinely happy about my news, while raising a note of caution. He would come down as soon as he could, though he opted out of partnering me at the Hospital Dance, claiming to be to dancing what Henry VIII was to domestic harmony ! He was up to his neck in exams and about to start an important course in Dollis Hill, London.

Our Christmas dance had been postponed until February and as Payne had gone to the trouble of finding me a partner, I decided to go. This was the last time for me to wear my pretty blue and pink dress and though only a few of the young men were suitably kitted out, it was such a relaxed, friendly affair, that it didn't matter. Neither was the ability to dance a prerequisite and I wished Jack could have been there, two left feet or not !

March was a very much happier month, my nineteenth birthday bringing gifts and letters from home, Ronnie and Jack. Jack had sent me some books, including *God in the Slums* and this time I received *God in the Shadows*. He now had every Monday off and he reminded me in his letter that he was hoping to come down the following weekend. It had been five months since we had seen each other and the thought of seeing him again helped me through my exam three days after my birthday. The following day, Johnnie presented me with a beautifully bound copy of the Bible to celebrate my commitment to Christ and signed it from 'Belle'. Belle ! This was the first time she'd revealed her beautiful Christian name to me.

'Our' clock at Temple Meads

The next day I was meeting Jack at what was to become our special meeting place, under the clock at Temple Meads. With a small rucksack on his back, he looked snugly warm in polo neck jumper, tweed jacket and corduroy trousers. We scanned one another's faces, before walking down to catch a tram to the Centre, arms around one-another's waists. Another tram took us to Clifton and Jack's bed and breakfast address. We rarely spent money on meals but were so ravenous that we succumbed to the temptation of an evening meal ! For the rest of the weekend Jack stocked up his rucksack with food, bars of Cadbury Nut being my contribution. With so little time, every moment was precious, lots of questions to ask and so much to tell one another.

Temple Meads Station.
(Photograph courtesy Bristol Record Office).

We were already looking forward to July and a whole week together at Croesffyrdd. Yet I was beginning to feel sad that in two days' time I would be going on Night Duty for the last time at the Eye Hospital. For those last three months, I would be classed as a Staff Nurse with the increase in pay already earmarked as a down payment for General Training. I'd already had the details from Middlesex Hospital, twelve guineas alone for the down payment, uniform to be paid for and no pay at all for the first six months ! No thank you ! My preference was Bristol General which had a reputation as a Christian hospital with high nursing standards and only required an £8 deposit.

Jack was clearly worried about a war with Germany, something that was becoming increasingly probable. It was a greater problem for him, because I would continue in my profession come what may. I could only advise Jack that he must do what he thought was prayerfully right. We discussed my forthcoming baptism by complete immersion in the Mount of Olives. For me, the symbolism was important, as well as the public confirmation that I had accepted Jesus Christ as my Lord and Saviour. My parents were pleased, my mother having been brought up as a Baptist in Neath, though my father was more sceptical. For him, cruel squires, human scarecrows in the fields and the Anglican Church went hand in hand. Jack was supportive, though didn't feel the need for it himself, having already made clear his commitment at Baxter Church in Kidderminster.

Monday, our full day together, was crisp and sunny. We met early, crossed the Suspension Bridge above the Avon Gorge to the beautiful Leigh Woods.

It was simply lovely. Spring flowers were beginning to emerge and the birds were in full voice. Though we were still so near to the city, we would have got lost in those woods had it not been for the signposts ! And it was back to that city that we had to make our way, in time for Jack's early evening train. Oh, the sadness of parting ! We both felt it more than ever. Jack suggested meeting again on the Easter Weekend but Matron would be entertaining important visitors and had warned us that she expected the senior nurses to relinquish their time off.

The results of my exam compensated for my visit to the dentist which had resulted in one extraction and six fillings. I had won a prize for coming first ! What pleased me more, however, were the generous remarks from Mr Palin. On March 18th, I was awakened from my daytime slumbers to receive my certificate and prize from Matron and the Hospital Committee. I had chosen the latest edition of *Black's Medical Dictionary*, though I could have opted for a silver buckle for my belt. I let Jack and my family know, of course, the greatest pleasure being the happiness and pride my parents felt.

Time went quickly, for we were busy on the wards. Matron's plans for the holiday weekend suddenly changed, enabling Jack and I to meet up. He would arrive at five o'clock Saturday afternoon and was eager to go to the Mount of Olives with me – I think he was curious more than anything else. Being on night duty on the Friday, I went to bed early and arranged to be called at three, in plenty of time for a quick bath and hair-wash. Out to meet Jack then, again under our clock but I could see at once that he wasn't very well. He had been all right that morning, but as the day wore on he had started to suffer with a thick head and was blowing hot and cold. It sounded like flu to me and that put us in a bit of a dilemma – we weren't allowed to take visitors back and anyway, night-quarters wasn't equipped for visitors, let alone sick ones. He wouldn't hear of going straight back home and suggested going to his Clifton boarding house. The lady was as kind as ever and mixed him a hot lemon drink which I took up to him. I had to use all my charm to persuade him to take a tablet, one that had worked when I had a migraine.

Before long he was feeling better and we were able to make the early evening meeting, where we met a delighted Johnnie and Vivien. Jack was again feeling unwell by the end of the service but we accepted Vivien's invitation to evening meal. Jack couldn't touch it and I felt so sorry for him, after he'd travelled all that way ! Everyone was wonderful to him, Vivien giving us a lift back to Clifton, where we sat for a while until he felt a bit better. He even wanted to see me back to the hospital so I threatened to put him to bed if he didn't behave himself ! Leaving the hospital phone number with his landlady, I took my leave. He was more like himself the following day and was keen to go to the Easter Sunday service. Imagine how we both felt when his nose started bleeding !

We had opted to sit at the back, so were able to slip out to the vestry without too much fuss. While he sat in a chair I gently pressed the bridge of his nose. Poor Jack was so embarrassed ! Vivien had again asked us to lunch, after which we took a quiet walk to the Downs, then on to the village of Westbury, where I knew of a cosy little cottage that did afternoon teas. We had the place all to ourselves. I clasped Jack's hand, now cool and normal, and we happily enjoyed one another's company. The following morning we went our separate ways. I prayed that Jack would be fit enough to take what would be his most important exam so far.

Back on duty again, I found that all the private beds had been filled, as well as the Men's General Ward, by men from Filton Aeroplane Works. It seemed that work was being speeded up to such an extent that it was causing a lot more eye injuries, some very serious. That couldn't put a dampener on the men, however. One night, after the two o'clock treatment round, they all decided to take a 'walk' to the toilet, and having no slippers, proceeded in their working boots. Despite the clatter, they had me in stitches ! Once normal order had been resumed, I rang down to Payne on the kitchen buzzer to see if they'd heard anything. She certainly had and was all ears to know what it was all about !

Private patients are a pain !

We had a succession of demanding private patients at that time, who paid no heed to the fact that there was only one nurse on duty at night. One of them, the son of a Jewish oil magnate, would have tested the patience of the Angel Gabriel himself ! He behaved like a spoilt schoolboy, ringing his bell every whip-stitch, despite the fact that his needs were always seen to first. Once he had you in his 'sanctum', he would think of a hundred and one things that needed doing. During his time with us, there wasn't a night when I wasn't at least half-an-hour late starting the treatment in the ordinary ward. Even then, his bell would ring constantly, so that the 'runner' – the nurse assigned to help out anywhere in the hospital – found herself virtually confined to his room. While double-padded, he used to work through the alphabet, giving us different names every day. He told me one night that I was 'Florrie', the day staff having been christened 'Folly', 'Flossie' and 'Floppy'. His childish antics eventually irritated our normally tolerant Irish Day Sister, though even Matron's intervention was like water off a duck's back. He also had a voracious appetite. One of our tasks was serving breakfast to the private patients and I vividly remember him eating four separate poached eggs on haddock one morning. Mind you, he was probably doing the hospital a big favour, for that Spring there had been an almighty glut of eggs !

I was called to attend interview on May 10th at Bristol General Hospital and was told by the Matron that she would be happy to take me, provided that all my medical certificates were satisfactory. It had only been a few weeks since I had received electrical treatment for painful 'dropped arches' in my feet but I was confident that the problem had disappeared. As I walked back across the centre of Bristol, thinking what the Preliminary Training School might hold for me in September, it was strange to see buses rather than trams. Earlier that week, we night nurses had rushed to the front windows of the top floor to witness the very last tram on the Whiteladies Road to Eastville route. People were packed in like sardines, waving, shouting and singing as it trundled down Lower Maudlin Street on its way to the city. It was decorated all over with garlands of flowers and accompanied by a small band.

One of the most important events of my life took place on the evening of May 25th, when I was baptised by complete immersion in the Mount of Olives. My parents spoke to me to wish me luck, on one of the 'new-fangled' phones they hated so much, and I was taken by surprise to find my father sounding so Welsh ! The following Sunday, I couldn't get to church quickly enough, where Mr Wallace called me forward and asked me to tell the congregation how I had 'given my heart to the Lord'. I found myself part of two families, the large church one and the closer, more intimate one of Vivien Armstrong. Beautiful in looks as well as by nature, she lived in a lovely house behind Whiteladies Road with her sister Doreen (Doe), their previous nurse and an aunt. The house ran on greased wheels, every member of the household with her particular part to play. After my conversion, I came to know them well and Vivien would often drive me back to the hospital, always insisting that I had a hot drink before I left. She said that she used the car in the service of God, never turning down an invitation to preach.

If Vivien was outgoing, Johnnie was the very opposite – dour, strict, uncompromising and very hurtful at times. She had even written a list of worldly pleasures, including concerts, that should be given up, quoting chapter and verse. Since my Christmas-time conversion, friends and colleagues had begun to notice the difference in me, leading to much teasing and scorn being thrown in my direction. Our delightful Night Sister, a member of the Church of England and a great lover of music, was another to caution me. She did not realise that Payne and I had often sat outside her bedroom door, knees drawn up, listening to her classical records ! She took me aside for a long talk, telling me that for her, music was a gift from God and she was glad when I told her that I would shortly be going to see the Berlin Philharmonic Orchestra. Payne and I thoroughly enjoyed the evening, when the main course was Beethoven's *Fifth Symphony*. The conductor, Furtwangler, had a completely different style to Kubelick, hardly moving his body at all, his wrist appearing to be the only guide to the talented musicians in front of him. The Czech, on the other hand, threw everything into it, his longish hair all over the place ! I was dismayed that Johnnie could disapprove of something so moving, but her heart was in the right place and she remained very special to me. As 1938 went by, it became obvious that the Colston Hall would not host the Berlin Philharmonic again for the foreseeable future, as Britain and Germany slowly edged towards war. My father had written to say that he'd volunteered in his local ARP group as St. John's Ambulance Instructor. He was concerned for me in Bristol, but apart from a few sandbags appearing outside buildings in the vicinity of Queen's Square, nothing much seemed to be happening.

Alexandra Rose Day at the end of June was different from the two previous years, mainly because buses had replaced the friendly trams, but also because Johnnie accompanied me, making it a much more sedate affair. Johnnie's year of training would be ending at the beginning of September and neither of us knew for certain where we would be after that. Because of her off-duty she wouldn't be able to see me off at the station, so we arranged to go to church together the next day. June 30th saw myself, Payne and our heavy cases on the way to Temple Meads with Vivien and Doe. It was such a sad farewell, yet we hoped that September would see me, at least, back in dear Bristol again. I would never, ever, forget the Eye Hospital and couldn't have wished for a better start in my nursing career.

Chapter Fifteen

SUMMER 1938

Delightful Payne !

The idea of Payne coming home with me had surfaced spontaneously on our final night-duty together. As her home was practically on the doorstep of the hospital, she would be at a loose end for that first week and she'd never been to South Wales. Once on the train, we found an empty compartment near the front, where we could spread out and relax. Because I was carrying gramophone records as presents for my parents, I felt more secure with the extra room. To the chugg-a-chugg-chugg of that wonderful old steam train, I could almost hear one of the movements of Beethoven's *Fifth Symphony*, carefully wrapped as it was in a feather-light woollen shoulder cape.

The Severn Tunnel was a novel experience for Payne, as we negotiated some mini-tunnels before the real thing hit us ! With the windows closed and the compartment dimly lit, we contemplated four minutes of travelling with tons and tons of water above our heads. Out again into the summer sunshine, we were now in Wales ! We opened the windows and looked forward to our week's holiday together.

Pulling into High Street Station, I was delighted to see my father waiting for us. Swansea, too, showed signs of preparation for war – ARP notices, sandbags outside some buildings, but nothing too alarming. Even so, one of the first questions my father asked was whether we had taken part in any emergency drills. We had attended lectures on what to do in the event of a gas attack, but lost sight of the seriousness of it all when some fire officers arrived to teach us the drill. We all had to be lowered in a 'chair' from the top (third) floor of the nurses' home to the small enclosed garden below and found it hilarious. Seeing people edge nervously out of the window was great entertainment !

Soon we were on the valley bus. The nearer we got to home, the more beautiful the scenery, less ugly the scars of industry and less ominous the spectre of war. We were on holiday and Payne and I were enjoying ourselves. It had been well over a year since I had seen my parents and it was lovely to sink into my haven called home.

Mammy and daddy took to Payne straight away – who couldn't like her happy, bubbly nature ? It seemed, too, as if she'd lived there all her life. We only had four full days ahead of us and with the beautiful weather promising to continue, we made the most of it. A climb up the Darren the first day was followed by a trip to the Gower. Payne wanted to see Langland Bay, so we took the train down to Swansea packed with day-trippers like ourselves. A short walk through dockland took us to Rutland Street to catch our beloved Mumbles Train, now electrified. With small rucksacks on our backs, we climbed the wide steps from Mumbles Pier as far as the unique 'Apple' stall to buy a drink. Down, then, to Bracelet Bay, a pebble beach rich in rock pools and a child's paradise if ever there was one. Staring into those pools

Eileen in the back garden at Croesffyrdd, wearing a blouse Ronnie had sent from Romania.

was like entering a private little world of strange sea creatures, plants and shells, all in beautiful, subtle colours; pink, green, umber, white and pale greyish-blue. We could have stayed there all day ! On the lighthouse side of the bay were caves, but the incoming tide spelt danger. So after Payne had filled her rucksack with shells, pebbles, dead star fish and other smelly things, we made our way past queues waiting for tea-trays and on to Limeslade Bay. From here we set off to the left, ice-cream in hand, over the cliffs to Langland. The view across to North Devon was spectacular, though the coastline was blurred by the summer haze. We walked in single file along the narrow path, passing a small inlet before coming to Rotherslade Bay, a favourite with the locals. The long row of bathing huts had all been hired out and the beach was crowded. Langland didn't disappoint Payne. We found a spot for ourselves amongst the contented groups of families, dispensed with our sandals and socks and raced down for a paddle. It being high summer, we weren't prepared for the shock of ice-cold water, though that didn't stop us splashing each other ! We then sat down to my mother's delicious sandwiches and observed our fellow human beings, young and old, having a good time. Which is what we were doing, of course !

We arrived home, happy and tired, to a meal fit for a king. Payne characteristically kept us in fits of laughter that evening, as she recalled all that had happened in the last year. I would tell my parents about what was happening in my personal life after she had left. The next evening, the two of us went up to the tiny bilingual Evangelical Church, only a stone's throw away. I had never taken any interest in it before – it was a Pentecostal Church – and that's where I ended up going for the rest of my time at home. We spent Payne's last day quietly, sunbathing out the back in glorious sunshine.

Mammy and I saw her off at the station and though we missed her happy-go-lucky presence, we now had Jack's visit to look forward to. I needed to prepare for the kind of scrambling and climbing that we intended to do. In Swansea that day we found a couple of women's sports shirts to go with my new corduroy shorts and a couple of pairs of knee-length socks. I had tried on my trusty old clob-hopper shoes and as they were in good shape, I felt all set up.

Love blossoms

Nine days later I was back at High Street, waiting for Jack's afternoon train to come in. It had been exactly three months since I had waited for him under the clock at Temple Meads. This July visit would be our first full week together and what was more, he would be staying at Croesffyrdd ! The moment I caught

sight of him leaning out of the window, this time looking fully fit, I started running. Catching his hand, I walked with him until the train came to a stop. He momentarily set his heavy rucksack down on the platform to give me a big hug, his lips brushing my hair. A pressing stream of alighting passengers didn't allow us any more time, but we were together and that was enough ! Even though we had seen relatively little of each other, our love had been growing steadily since my visit to Kidderminster the previous October. As ever, there was the initial shyness and searching of one-another's eyes.

It was a new experience for us to meet up on a hot summer's day and Jack was looking truly fit and handsome in shorts and shirt. I was chuffed when he complimented me on my summer dress and sandals, for I was wearing one of the cotton gingham dresses I had made two

Jack aged about 17.

171

Around the table at Croesffyrdd.

years previously. It was simple, short-sleeved, drawn in at the waist. And it was around my waist that Jack now held me firmly as we walked happily to the bus. I sent a little prayer of thanks up to my Maker !

Awaiting Jack was my mother's wonderful, Welsh welcome. While I washed up, my mother had a chance to chat to Jack and show him Ronnie's bedroom, in which he would be sleeping. Then we slipped down to Ystalyfera Signal Box to see my father, where Jack took three photographs with his new camera, one of my father waving to us as we made the short journey to the Matthias' Varteg council house. Vic was the only one missing, now employed like Ronnie, while Bert, a Senior Scout, was about to leave for a two-week rally in the north of England. While the men chatted, I found Mrs Mathias anxious that Bert might become ill on his forthcoming venture, through sleeping on damp ground or wearing damp clothes. I tried to reassure her, saying that I had left home at seventeen and come to no harm. Her reply was that boys were different to girls.

"Girls seem to know how to look after themselves. I wish I had a daughter I could talk to as I'm talking to you now !" On the way home Jack told me that Mrs Mathias had always worried about her boys, had even taken him under her wing as a little boy. He added that Bert had hinted that he'd like to join the RAF and we wondered how his poor mother would cope if that ever happened !

We let Jack sleep on the next morning, but he was still up quite early, eagerly poring over a map of the area. The Mathias's had told him about some falls in the tiny Gwred valley, about four miles from Ystalyfera. Jack thought that we could follow a path (or was it a sheep track ?) rising steeply above the falls. At about 1,000 feet we would be behind the summit of Alltygrug, from where we could follow another path around the mountain and down into the village of Ystalyfera. What did I think ? I didn't mind – I'd go anywhere as long as it was with Jack !

The following day, Monday, dawned cloudy and dull with a feel of drizzle in the air. Undaunted, we set off donning berets, Jack's a real Scottish one, me in my old faithful. I wore an old, comfortable skirt and lightweight jacket, it being too cold to break in my new shorts ! We found an old, wooden fence at the side of the road which Jack thought might be our starting point but instead of water on the other side, there was nothing but a large rubbish dump. After doing a 'recce' of the area, Jack took my hand and guided me through the dump until we could see the stream itself, quite beautiful in its natural setting. Spurred on by the faint sound of falling water, we climbed slowly upwards and suddenly the falls came into view, wild and untouched. From a high narrow channel in the rocks, the water fell a sheer forty to fifty feet, hugged by trees jutting out at all sorts of angles. With no sign of a way up the narrow valley, Jack again went to explore. He had always reminded me of a mountain goat when climbing and his experience of shinning up telegraph poles in all weathers during the last couple of years meant that this latest challenge would be no obstacle.

Meanwhile, I was beginning to regret that I hadn't worn my shorts, for how was I going to be able to climb in that skirt, even with Jack's help ? Taking it off would have left me vulnerable to injury, so I decided to turn it back to front to see if the pleat would give me some freedom. Not enough ! The only thing for it was to unpick the stitching and Jack could only stop and stare as I borrowed his penknife and proceeded to apparently mutilate my skirt. He understood better when, with the waist button undone, I could turn the waist band over several times and shorten the skirt. I was now able to bend my knees right up. The crazy plan had worked !

Gripping my hand very firmly, he guided me step by step until we reached the top. Here, he pulled me away from the swirling water and noise of the falls, to safety. Close to tears and feeling shaky, I flung my arms around his neck and asked him to hold me, hold me tight. Secure in his tender arms, my trembling eventually ceased. He looked me up and down and with wicked, twinkling eyes, told me how funny I looked. I had forgotten about my skirt and it was enough to break the tension. Because of the difficult terrain, we ate our sandwiches standing up.

After checking our position, we carefully picked our way across uneven territory, pitted with deep holes and animal tracks, until we came to the path that would lead down into Ystalyfera. Able, at last, to stand up firmly, we stopped to hug one another and laugh at the day's exploits ! Striding purposefully, we made our way back home. Home, back home together. How lovely that sounded ! No trains, buses or trams to catch and no need to say goodbye – at least not for a little while. By the time we reached Croesffyrdd the skies were starting to clear, promising a lovely day for our visit to the river Giedd.

I was already familiar with Cwmgiedd, for as children living in the Gurnos Cottages, we had spent many a happy hour walking along the canal bank as far as the village. Higher up the river, however, was unknown territory. As we studied the map after supper, it seemed that the river disappeared as the valley got narrower, only to show up again about a mile further north. What caught our eye was a series of waterfalls which ran into one another. I decided I would wear my shorts from now on !

The Giedd valley was breathtaking, as hand in hand we tried to find the river's source on what was to be a scorcher of a day. In contrast to the previous day's physical challenge, this was a stroll, the valley wide and the surrounding slopes gentle. At one point we saw on the horizon a shepherd on horseback, working the hills, accompanied by his trusty dog. Beautiful pools now led to a series of small enchanting waterfalls, arousing every sense in the body. As we continued to climb, the chattering of birds gave way to an unearthly silence and I was glad that I had Jack by my side. Our stream did, indeed, disappear, but using compass and map, Jack found the little thing bubbling further up the mountain. We had found the source of the Giedd and it gave us as much pleasure as if we had climbed Everest ! We stood in a noiseless world, just the two of us, surrounded by indescribable beauty, the Brecon Beacons on one side, the Black Mountains on the other. We both knew that we'd come back the next day.

Our 'Shangri-La', Jack on the right soaking up the sun.

One particular pool had captivated us, and it was to this that we returned the following morning. It was perfect for a swim, deep, long and flanked by a flat platform of rock which made an ideal diving board. I watched in amazement Jack's graceful movements in the water and enjoyed watching him rub himself down afterwards. Although slight of build, he was all muscle, with broad shoulders and narrow hips. I could well understand how he had won all those silver school sports cups in his bedroom ! As we sunbathed, everything seemed just right.

I must have dozed off, for I was unaware of Jack until I felt his fingers caressing my hair. I opened my eyes and smiled up at him, his face serious, his eyes intense. He had to clear his throat to speak.

"Eileen," he said, "I can't stay silent any longer. I love you so much, with every fibre of my being. Please tell me you feel the same."

Looking at him, I nodded gently.

"Yes, Jack, I do. I love you very much and I've been longing to tell you !"

Then, drawing him to me, our lips met and I kissed him as if I would never let him go. That was our first real kiss – one of commitment – a pledge if ever there was one ! In that moment I experienced pure love, one that needed no physical fulfilment. We looked at each other, wanting to know if this was really happening, was this really true ? And the answer came, 'Yes, oh yes, yes !' Our lips met again as we rolled over and over in seventh heaven. This was my mate, the man I wanted to be the father of my children

If those Giedd valley hills could talk, they would tell of what happened next. Jack stood up straight and lifting his face to the skies, shouted "I love you Eileen, I love you, I love you !" at the top of his voice. In a few seconds back came the echo as clear as a bell:

"I LOVE YOU EILEEN, I LOVE YOU, I LOVE YOU !"

Pulling me to my feet, he clutched my hand and raced around like a young stallion until, drunk with happiness, we fell in a heap !

The rest of the day we spent talking about our future. Once again the question of a war with Germany came up. I had sensed in Jack's letters that he would be a Conscientious Objector. I now had to face up to the fact that if he stuck to his Christian principles, it would affect both our lives. and told him that I would support him all the way. Then we turned to more pleasant things. When should we tell our parents and friends how we felt about each other ? Jack thought that my parents had already guessed, so we agreed to wait a few days when he would write to them from Kidderminster. If they brought the subject up in the meantime, we would tell them.

Our planned visit to the river Twrch the next day was shelved when my father told us that it was now closed to the public because of open-cast mining. Instead we climbed the Darren, before walking part of the way towards Neath on the Crynant Road. No more talk of war – that had been sorted !

Another two whole days together, but the week was slipping away fast. With the weather still holding we made for the Gower and Caswell Bay. Jack had his customary swim but he much preferred swimming baths and rivers to the sea and didn't stay in long. We chose to laze on the sand, wondrously happy, the sea salt and air adding to the sunshine showered upon us during the last four days. By the time we started for home, we looked as if we had been on the Riviera !

Sitting on the Mumbles train brought back memories for both of us, though it was ten years since Jack had ridden on it, when it had still been steam-powered. We talked about our childhood, centred as it was around Ystalyfera Congregational Church. Jack teasingly reminded me that from the age of three, when he'd first clapped eyes on me, he had made up his mind to marry me !

"And do you still want to marry me ?" I asked shyly.

"You know I do," he replied, "and we'll get married in the English Cong !" We calculated that he would be twenty-four and I'd be getting on for twenty-five by the time that could happen. Did he still want to become a missionary one day ? Yes, if it was God's will. What about me ? I knew that I couldn't face such a calling on my own, but with him by my side I would go anywhere !

Our special week ended with us listening to the whole of Beethoven's *Fifth Symphony*, which involved a fair bit of exercise in winding up the gramophone ! Next morning I woke to find Jack already downstairs, his rucksack packed, and grateful that my mother had washed and ironed his clothes. He gave me a letter for my parents to read after he had gone. All too soon we had to catch a bus into Swansea, before the short walk from Orchard Street to High Street. Those last moments were almost unbearable. We clung to one another until the guard's whistle signalled the train to take Jack away from me. Back home, my mother remarked on Jack's lovely letter.

Muriel called at tea-time to see if I wanted to go to evening service at a tiny mission hall in Cwmtwrch. She didn't realise Jack had been down (he'd just be arriving home). Mammy and daddy gave me a key, as they were going to visit Mr Bisgrove, who was poorly. That service, in a corrugated iron shed miles from anywhere, was powerful. The pastor spoke about submitting to the Will of God, taking up the cross and following Him. Muriel and another friend walked home with me to Croesffyrdd but wouldn't come in because they had planned to go for a stroll. I couldn't face the thought of treading familiar ground without Jack and so bid them goodnight. I would see Muriel on Tuesday. Letting myself in, the house seemed so empty. I went up to my bedroom, fell on my knees and tried to pray, but before long was sobbing like a baby, able only to think of how much I was missing Jack. I wept until I was exhausted, the tears alleviating my anguish sufficiently to allow me to slip quietly into Ronnie's room, fold up Jack's bedclothes and make the bed.

It was good to have Muriel with us for two days even though it rained so heavily that we couldn't put a foot outside the door. I admired her because she had left Maesydderwen School with excellent examination results, despite all the odds. She could easily have gone to university but had chosen a career in teaching and was currently training at Brownhills near Birmingham. Domestic Science was her preferred subject. I told her of my plans to train in Bristol and sensing that Jack and I loved one another deeply, she sympathised with our long wait to get married. A package from Jack arrived the next day, containing all the holiday snaps and a letter, thirty-three pages long. It was a love letter all right!

August Bank Holiday saw me in the Bible College on a day's convention, having been invited by two ladies from the tiny nearby church, Eglwys Dduw. The rest of the week, daddy's annual holiday, I spent in the Mumbles at a boarding house with my parents. Despite my continual inner ache for Jack, we had a lovely time, doing something different each day, including a visit to Caswell, walking back through the beautiful little bay of Pwlldu. The paddle steamer was another adventure, hugging the coastline as far as Tenby before crossing the channel to Ilfracombe. Each evening we spent in the gardens in the village, adorned by fairy lights, listening to the local band. I distinctly remember tapping my feet to *The Lambeth Walk*.

When we got home, we found several letters awaiting us. Ronnie would be home at the end of the summer and Johnnie, who was about to leave the Eye Hospital, talked about meeting up in Bristol sometime in August. The 15th of that month was a celebration on two counts, my mother's forty-fifth birthday – though she could have been taken for much younger – and my parent's twenty-fifth wedding anniversary. It was a shame Ronnie couldn't have been there but we only had to wait another nine days to see him.

Jack, meanwhile, had written to say that he might be able to get a lift down with Ippy (Cliff) in his Morris Minor on the last weekend in August. Realising that there would be a 'full house', Jack said that they would bring plenty of food, and that they would have their sleeping bags with them. What a weekend! It was sheer joy to have the family together again, and to see Ronnie looking a picture of health after his year abroad. For now I could forget that he'd soon be off again, this time for Borneo.

Late on the Saturday afternoon Ronnie suddenly cried out that they had arrived. Sure enough, there was Ippy parking his black Morris Minor at the side of the house, Jack guiding him safely in. Oh my! Words cannot describe the joy I felt at being with Jack again. As they brought in a small hamper packed with food, their eyes lit up with delight on seeing how cosy my mother and I had made that little sitting room for them. The house was soon full of youthful, happy chatter, mammy and daddy supplying one and all with freshly-brewed tea and pieces of home-made cake.

Cliff (on the right) was the only person we knew that had a car!

It didn't take long before Ronnie and Ippy were deep in conversation about Christianity and the same debates surfaced that my brother and Jack had written about in their letters over the past year. Ronnie was concerned that I was being drawn into extreme religious fundamentalism, much of which was anathema to him. Later, I was to be grateful to those three young men for helping me through the maze of conflicting religious teachings and easing the turmoil which at times drove me to distraction. Before taking leave of one-another Jack and I planned as far ahead as possible, tentatively arranging to meet up on June 13th (1939), his twentieth birthday. In the meantime we would write at least once a week, even if it were only one line !

A bit of a crisis

Ronnie's stay was overshadowed by a family crisis. Not long before his arrival, our grandmother in Pontardawe had been taken seriously ill and my mother had gone to stay with her. Even after she rallied, my mother called nearly every day, taking it turns with Auntie Edith to look after her. Then, one day, there was a knock at the door. I could sense the urgency in our neighbour's voice as my mother answered it and knew something was wrong when she called out to me in a queer, shrill voice. I rushed downstairs. Poor mammy, she was white as a ghost and almost in a state of collapse. I took her into the living room, sat her down by the fire, covered her with a rug and made her a cup of tea. At first, all she could utter was "Auntie Edith !", then taking hold of herself, said that she must go to her at once. Mrs Lewis was the only person in the row who had a telephone in the house, due to the fact that her husband was an Ambulance Man. At midday, he had been called out to Auntie Edith's house in Rhydyfro to find that she had attempted suicide and had phoned his wife with the message that there wasn't much hope for her ! I helped my mother into her outdoor clothes, gave her handbag and off she went to catch the next train to Swansea, telling me not to worry if she wasn't home that evening. She would give my father the news at his signal box.

We were a sombre trio as we waited for Mr Lewis to come home after his shift. It seemed that Uncle Jim had had a row with one of the neighbours, who he felt had insulted him. It must have been serious, violent even, for it upset my auntie so much that she had gone into the house and drunk almost a bottle of Jeyes Fluid ! This had burnt the lining of her throat and mouth with the result that her air passages had become swollen and she hadn't been able to breathe. Unable to sleep that night, I left the light on to read. At about midnight, I heard my mother's footsteps coming up the lane and went to meet her. Before long, daddy and Ronnie had joined us and my mother told us in a relieved voice that Auntie Edith had regained consciousness at about half-past seven.

She made slow but steady progress after that. Two days before I left for Bristol, Ronnie and I went to see her, her lips still black and swollen. She broke down when she saw us and said how ashamed she felt. I reassured her of our support and told her to put it all behind her. We stayed for a while before going on to the University to see Ronnie's professor. Then we headed for town, Ronnie having asked me to help choose new clothes for his Borneo adventure. I remember that we ended up in quite a prestigious gentlemen's outfitters and the final bill must have been considerable. Even so, when Ronnie produced a £20 note, the assistant held it as though it might bite, scampering off like someone out of a Dickens novel, bowing and scraping as he returned with the change ! Outside on the pavement, we started to laugh uncontrollably, releasing all our pent-up emotion.

During my last week at home my father bought me a beautiful new trunk to replace the wreck that was now falling apart. When I left for Bristol, it was difficult to part not only with my beloved parents, but Ronnie too, going as he was to the other side of the world !

Chapter Sixteen

OLD FRIENDS AND NEW

Back in Bristol, this time in Charlotte Street, at the top left of Park Street, I looked forward to seeing all my friends again. In the Training School, five of us, all budding General Nurses, met up and were soon using each other's surnames – Camp, Emette, Fletcher, Comely and Baker. Comely had not long arrived from Kenya, where her parents had been missionaries with the Church Missionary Society. Her two sisters, one a doctor, the other a midwife, were working in this country and having lived with the Kikuyu tribe as children, spoke their language fluently. When I first met her, she was dressed from head to toe in old-fashioned, black clothes and I wondered, perhaps, if she had come from an orphanage ! As she hesitatingly inched towards me, she looked up to speak and revealed a Madonna-like face ! Her skin was smooth and olive, her round cheeks flushed with glorious natural colour and her large, soulful

Ruth.

eyes were of the most beautiful velvet brown. She and I became great friends and were soon on first name terms, Ruth and Eileen.

I was also glad to get back to the Mount of Olives, despite being drawn between conflicting points of view. On one glorious Autumn day, I found myself one of a number packed into Vivien's large car, heading for the countryside south of the city. Her family owned Carters and Son who had produced the drink 'Ribena' and we were now 'volunteers', recruited by the firm to pick rose-hips. These were believed to be as rich in Vitamin C as blackberries. We worked hard, but enjoyed every moment and were rewarded when Vivien produced a wonderful hamper from the boot.

180

On the Downs. From left to right at the back – Emette, Camp and Fletcher.
Front – Comely, Baker and another friend.

We soon became used to walking in uniform, crocodile- fashion, down Park Street, round the centre and along the wharfs to the General Hospital. Sister Tutor was a wonderful teacher, making even the dullest of subjects come alive and one morning I found myself the focus of one of her illustrations. We were studying the heart and while explaining a certain 'impulse' of the 'Sympathetic System', she wickedly looked up at me and said, "That's the impulse that gives Nurse Baker palpitations in the morning when the letter she's been expecting arrives !"

The three months in the Preliminary Training School went quickly and before long we were sitting two written exams and a practical as a preliminary to our training proper. The first ones went well but the Cookery test was a nightmare, because it was based on the principle of 'telling'. Having to manage three things at the same time, I found to my horror that the apricot fool had started to stick to the bottom of the saucepan. I was convinced that I had failed, though in the event we all passed.

During this time, my relationship with Jack became strained for several reasons. Without realising it, the influence of my Pentecostal faith was making my letters to him sound arrogant and self-righteous. I must have implied time and time again that my views were the 'right' ones and much of our correspondence became a vehicle for opposing religious viewpoints. On top of this, Jack was having problems at home, something I picked up on when I visited him in October. That weekend we almost broke each other's hearts by off-handedly agreeing to write only when we felt like, rather than every week. The situation was aggravated, of course, by the fact that we hardly saw one another. At the beginning of November, I became a member at the Mount of Olives, which merely strengthened my fundamentalist views. As well as cutting myself off from anything that I considered 'worldly', including the BBC Symphony concerts being held in the city, I had been growing my hair for over a year, taking to heart the words of St. Paul: "But if a woman have long hair it is a glory to her, for her hair is given as a covering."

At the end of the month, Jack had planned to join me at Croesffyrdd, but at the very last minute he was called to an interview with his Inspector. As I travelled back to Bristol, he was on his way to start a course in London. With Christmas only three weeks away, I wrote several letters to him but heard nothing back and was unaware that he'd gone home for Christmas. Until he wrote, I knew that I would be unable to enter into the festive spirit and though I put on a bright and breezy face, I was inwardly miserable. Christmas morning arrived and my heart skipped a beat when a parcel came in Jack's handwriting. In layers of soft tissue paper was a beautiful brush and comb set, but not the letter I desired more than anything. I kept an eye on the next delivery and saw an envelope with a Kidderminster postmark. Joy of joys ! To know that he loved me was all I wanted to hear and I was happy again. Emotionally, my life was in turmoil, one day up, the next down. Sometimes I wondered whether being in love was worth it all and turned increasingly to my work and faith.

Across Europe, Nazism was spreading like the plague. Towards the end of my time in PTS, trenches were being dug in College Green and soldiers manning anti-aircraft guns on a factory roof near the hospital. Volunteers and workmen were beginning to stack sandbags around buildings and Anderson Shelters popped up everywhere. Millions of people all over the country had been issued with gas masks with instructions to take them wherever they went. As time went by without incident, the initial fear receded and people started to relax again.

In December 1938, I started my General Training on a large men's surgical ward. Small in stature, our dear Matron ruled that hospital with a hand of iron, and exhorted us to maintain her maxim: "The patient must always come first, whether prince or beggar, to be treated with utmost care and attention, at all times." As I came into contact with more and more patients, I came to totally respect her standpoint and felt proud and privileged to work for her.

And what a variety of patients we had ! I remember looking after a very sweet Salvation Army Captain, in for a routine operation. As he was coming round, I prepared to take out his airway and called him gently to help him really 'surface'. I was astonished when he started shouting out the bluest swear words I'd ever heard in my life, before he fully came out of the anaesthetic and was his old self again ! Then there was the sad case of the black seaman. A fellow crew-member, who could manage just a few words of English, indicated that his friend was in a great deal of pain and that his belly had swollen. It was clear that this emaciated figure had once been a big, strapping man. He was immediately prepared for theatre where the surgeons were going to do a laparatory, an exploratory opening up of the abdomen. All they could do was stitch him back up again, having found that he had extensive carcinoma of the liver. From there on, the growth became very rapid and with the poor man in a state of anguished restlessness, the wound burst open. He let out a terrible scream and we quickly drew the screens around him, discovering to our dismay that his intestines were forcing themselves out of the now open wound. I helped to contain them as far as possible, using sterile, saline gauze, but he died in the middle of it – in an alien land, surrounded by alien people who couldn't understand a word he was trying to say.

In no time at all, Christmas was upon us. Most of the patients had been sent home, some for good, others to be at home over the festive period. Only a few remained. I happened to be on duty on Christmas Eve, which was a truly silent and peaceful night until the buzzer went. The first batch of drunks was on its way up ! In they came, most requiring stitching up after a fight or a violent collision with a lamppost or bollard. Most were concussed, all were sick and some needed stomach wash-outs. It had been bad enough for the day staff, but as the evening wore on we became inundated and by the morning all the beds were groaning. I felt cross but was told matter-of-factly that it happened every year !

We nurses were given a wonderful time Christmas Day and once I had received Jack's letter, enjoyed every minute. Sheer size and numbers in the General meant that it was a mammoth affair, quite unlike the intimacy of my beloved Eye Hospital. Nevertheless, it was well-organised, happy and at times riotous, though we didn't have much breathing space before we were hard at work again.

One day in early January 1939, we received a message from Casualty to say that they were sending up an elderly patient with an almost complete urinary blockage, caused by an enlarged prostate gland. One of the surgeons had catheterised him to relieve the pain and he was to be prepared immediately for

Bristol General Hospital. The Dental Department is to the right.

theatre. The message finished with a cautionary warning, "You will need your gas-masks !"

Soon we heard the clatter of the lift gates opening and shutting, before a porter wheeled in the weirdest looking old man in Bristol. There was no need to tell us that he was a tramp, one of the many that inhabited the dock area. He smelt to high heaven and beneath the rags and grime, his colour was grey. He was obviously very ill. Sister decided that it would be quickest and kindest to get him straight into a bath, rather than blanket bath him in bed. Two of us were assigned to the job and from the very beginning were greeted with howls of protestations from this loveable old rogue. He hated being touched by us 'young girls', hated being undressed and above all, hated the sight of a bath full of water ! In he went, however, and we quickly scrubbed him from head to toe, aware that theatre staff would soon be ready. Then the porter took the opportunity to shave not only his private parts, but his hair and beard as well. Though there was still a terrible smell emanating from his nether regions, he was as clean as a new-born baby going up that corridor !

For the first three days, he had a self-retaining catheter, which allowed the urine to flow out into a large glass container at the side of his bed. It was my job to empty that evil-smelling stuff. Once the catheter was removed, he was at liberty to use a bottle whenever he needed, but rebelling against the hospital environment and being told what to do, he didn't want to stay in bed. He constantly tipped the bottle, with the result that we had to change his draw sheet on innumerable occasions. To cap it all, his wound became septic and he was very poorly again. Eventually, after a tremendous amount of effort by the whole medical staff, from the surgeon down to myself, he began to get better. Once his stitches were removed and he was allowed to sit out of bed, he started to cheer up.

I didn't have a chance to say goodbye to him. I was in sick bay myself, isolated with a sore throat and a temperature of 101.4°. After taking a swab of my throat, one of the resident doctors put me on 'fluids only' and four hours later my temperature was taken again. I saw the nurse staring at the thermo-meter, before she shook it down and asked me to keep it under my tongue, leaving it there for a few minutes. After reading it a second time, she rushed out of the room, though I was feeling too woozy to be alarmed. I thought I was hallucinating when I suddenly saw a group of people standing over me, includ-ing the Deputy Matron and the Resident Officer. Their voices seemed to be coming and going, inquiring whether I had a sore throat, or if had I noticed any spots. While they examined me further, I heard somebody say that they had better let my parents know. As the nurse prepared a tepid sponge, I could hear a Gospel group going around the wards singing hymns. I'm not sure if I thought I was dying, but at the words 'While on others thou art calling, Lord remember me', tears began to trickle down my cheek. To complete the drama, the bulb in the light above my bed burst into tiny fragments as the sponge was being administered, landing all over my tummy ! The poor nurse had an impossible job finding all the bits.

My darling mother came up straight away and with treatment and rest I began to improve. Jack sent me a telegram, after my father had told him I was ill. I was given leave on the condition that I saw the local doctor. It transpired that the bacteria affecting my throat were identical to those which had infected our dear old tramp's bladder, though it had been feared at first that I had con-tracted Scarlet Fever !

In no time at all, the next set of nurses were installed from PTS and I found myself working in Dod Ward for male cancer patients. It was my first encounter with cancer and was a most traumatic experience. Not long after, we were un-settled by a rumour of a merger with the Bristol Royal Infirmary. The majority of us had applied to the General because of its unique Christian qualities and felt let down. In an emergency meeting which I was unable to attend, Matron confirmed in a short statement that there were plans for a merger of all of Bristol's hospitals. She, apparently, was against the idea but we simply had to get on with it.

You always hurt the one you love . . .

Things didn't improve between Jack and me. He wrote to say that he was enjoy-ing London, having met Eurwyn Lewis, who was teaching there, and had gone

185

to several concerts with Vic Mathias. Instead of being pleased for them, I had to put my foot in it by questioning him about these 'worldly' pleasures. When my birthday came, he sent me a £1 Postal Order, which upset me. It hurt my pride and I remember telling him that I preferred to receive money only from my family. Over Easter, a big Convention took place at the Mount of Olives and my fundamentalist view of Christianity was still filling my letters to Jack. I was peeved that he hadn't come to see me over the holiday but couldn't twig what was putting him off. Though still in love, we were at that time being hurtful to one another and I began to wonder if our relationship would continue.

Then, in mid-summer, came a personal upset. Influenced by the Mount of Olives, my blinkered beliefs must have continued to irk Jack. He was tender and patient, wishing that I could join the lively Young People's Group, where views like mine were openly discussed. Then his letters suddenly started to alarm me. He told me that he felt an attraction to one of the girls in the group and with his brutal 'Oxford Group' honesty, kept on about her, despite declaring his love for me. Tired mentally and physically, worried not only about the merger but about the possibility of another World War, I was desperately un-happy. It was too personal a matter to talk to anyone about, and with Jack see-ing a lot of this girl, I could stand it no longer. I sent him an ultimatum – he could choose between her or me. Then, as if by a miracle, the Post Office allowed compassionate leave for the August Bank Holiday and I received a tele-gram, 'Bristol. Friday eve. Saturday. Sunday. Jack.'

He had arrived too late on the Friday for us to meet, but early on Saturday morning he was waiting for me outside the Nurses' Home. One look was enough – as we rushed into one another's arms we knew everything was all right. We hurried away, over the Suspension Bridge to Abbotsleigh. There, in the peace and solitude, Jack poured out how he had become infatuated with the other girl. It was all over, such a thing would never happen again – please, please could I forgive him ? Of course I would but could he forgive my self-centred, sometimes arrogant letters ? He said that he understood my dilemma and that though the Bible had been speaking to my heart and emotions, perhaps it was time to let reason fashion my faith as well. Deep down I knew he was right.

For his part, he had written to the London Missionary Society, who had advised him that he first needed to become an ordained Congregational minister. There was a degree course in Theology over four or five years, involving three different colleges in Bristol. Only unmarried students could be admitted ! It seemed that he was serious about it, for he had already started evening classes in Greek. However, all his plans might have to be shelved as war with Germany looked increasingly on the cards. The National Service Act had been passed earlier in the year and Jack knew that he would probably have to register as a

Conscientious Objector. We decided to leave everything in God's hands. It was enough for us to know that we loved each other, agreeing never to let anything come between us again and to meet as regularly as possible. Back, as strong as ever, was that slender, silver thread.

War looms

I felt so much better and stronger for having seen Jack as I embarked on my second year's training. Which was just as well, for everything paled into insignificance as we grouped around the communal loudspeaker in the lounge to listen to the news. German military forces were advancing across Europe and when Poland was invaded and Warsaw brutally bombed, we knew what lay in store. I longed to rush home to see my parents or up to Kidderminster and Jack's reassuring arms, but neither was possible. The following day I slipped out to see Johnnie, who was about to start work as a Health Visitor in Portishead and had a room in Clifton. On the way back I had my first taste of Bristol's black-out in action, something I shall never forget. The night was pitch-black and my tiny torch completely ineffectual as the rain swept down in sheets. Turning up the collar of my mac, I stumbled over curbs to the nearest bus stop. After what seemed an age, two pin-pricks of light peered dimly through the gloom, to reveal a double decker bus with its number and destination blocked out. It didn't stop. On I ran, with an uncomfortable stream trickling down my back, to the next stop which I knew to be 'fare-stage'. Here, a bus to the centre was bound to stop, but I was the last in a long queue of people. When one eventually turned up, there was an unbelievable rush to get on, as if it was the last bus anyone would ever see ! Such was the panic that passengers trying to disembark found themselves being pushed back in. It was frightening.

Across the centre at Prince Street, I was told that no buses were running on my route, so there was nothing for it but to take the short cut through the docks. With my mind on reaching the Nurses' Home before locking up time, I took my life into my hands. What with the blinding rain and complete absence of any lighting, there was no way of dodging the hazards that dockland posed any visiting stranger. I bumped into bollards, tripped over chains and only the sound of lapping water prevented me from falling into the dock. Upon reaching home, I breathed a deep sigh of relief and promised myself a decent torch. All the light bulbs had been removed, so in the darkness I felt first for the door of my room, before fumbling for the bed and falling in.

It came as no surprise the next day (September 3rd) when the Prime Minister, Neville Chamberlain, announced that we were at war with Germany. The waiting was over, we knew where we were. For the first few weeks, schools, cinemas, theatres, public meeting places, even most businesses, were closed. Air Raid Wardens, taking their duties seriously, went around looking for any chinks of light showing and we frequently heard shouts of "Put that light out !" Before long we had replacement bulbs for the corridors and bedrooms but even they had to be shaded on the window side.

As soon as war was declared, all but a few of our patients were evacuated. Extra beds were erected, as the fear of imminent air raids and resulting casualties grew. This state of affairs lasted until the end of October, after which ordinary patients were admitted again, bombing raids having failed to materialise. One of my friends, Lonsdale, was given a holiday at this time and came back engaged ! Her fiancé had registered as a Conscientious Objector in the first call-up for men and had given up his job at the Filton Aerodrome Works. Now awaiting his Tribunal, he had applied to go into the Friends' Ambulance Unit and hoped to be sent to Norway. It would be Jack's turn next, for he was now twenty years old.

By December, schools had re-opened, cinemas were showing films as before and businesses back to normal. Muted street lighting had been introduced, while the edges of curbs, bases of bollards and the bottom edges of the remaining trams were painted white. We began to feel more hopeful, but were never allowed to become complacent. Posters such as 'Careless Talk Costs Lives' and 'Be Like Dad – Keep Mum' kept us on our toes. Later on, that funny looking little man with a single wisp of hair would appear, looking over a wall, asking all sorts of questions such as "Wot – no jam ?"

At about this time, my parents wrote to say that they had been given the option of either becoming foster parents or taking in evacuees for the duration of the war and had plumped for the former. I also learnt that my Pembrey grandparents were being moved out of their longhouse on the burrows into a tiny cottage near Burry Port, having been given notice to quit by the Government. Auntie Fanny, her husband and cousin Betty, who had married an Air Force recruit, had already gone. The bulldozers weren't long moving in and the site cleared for a long runway. Memories came flooding back of those glorious summer holidays spent there, but apparently the land had been sold to the Air Ministry in 1937 and my grandparents were only tenant farmers. Nearby Towyn Farm was taken over as RAF Officers' Quarters.

That idle October proved very frustrating for the nurses on the wards and I was thankful to be in the Dental Department, where it was work as usual. I loved working for Mr Martin who was extremely kind. When he found out that I was interested in missionary work, he started showing me the techniques necessary to extract teeth. When he thought I was ready, he let me take some easy ones out. Then more difficult cases. One day an old sea-salt came in with toothache and I was assigned the job. Having been given gas, he was temporarily

Holidays at Towyn Farm, Pembrey. Eileen in the centre, Ronnie seated. Their Grandma Baker is on the far right, cousin Pam on the far left. Standing next to Pam is Auntie Emma.

unaware of the ensuing pantomime. First I tried, then a student, but neither one of us could budge the offending tooth. Yet another student was summoned, this time kneeling up on a chair to give extra leverage, but to no avail. It took Mr Martin all his ingenuity to remove it, the largest, ugliest misshapen specimen I have ever seen ! By the time the old sailor came round, I was back in the recovery room cleaning him up and gently slapping him awake. As I looked at him, I realised that his face was one-sided and quietly slipped out to call Mr Martin. He deftly, but gently, manoeuvred the jaw back into position. It had been dislocated during the chaotic operation !

There were two, very odd students in the department at the time, one of whom ordered the other about, neither of them serious about their training. They rubbed everyone up the wrong way, the loud-mouthed bossy one unconcerned about what he said, whether in front of fellow students or patients. One morning he started goading me, calling me a 'goody goody' and becoming ruffled when his taunts went unanswered. At the end of each day, I had to clean up and check that all instruments and apparatus were ready for the next morning. My last job was to make sure that all Bunsen burners in the students' lab were safely turned off. I was glad to finish that particular evening, wanting to attend a service at the Mount of Olives, where meetings were becoming shorter and earlier. Later that night, as I was getting ready for bed in the dim light, something caught my eye on the dressing table. By torchlight, I was able to read a message written on a tiny scrap of paper . Matron wanted to see me urgently, so I rolled up the bottom of my pyjamas, put on my sandals and mac and legged it down the corridor, thinking a telegram had arrived. Outside her office, a senior nurse told me that she would make enquiries and returned looking grim. Matron wanted to see me dressed in full uniform ! I went back to my room, all fingers and thumbs as I dressed, trying to fathom out what I had done wrong. I tentatively knocked the door and it was Matron herself who answered, propelling me by the elbow to the centre of her office. She looked at me dead straight and told me that she was holding me responsible for almost having caused a fire which could have spread throughout the hospital ! In finishing her rounds, she had found two Bunsen burners full on in the Dental Department, one white-hot and in so dangerous a condition that disaster could have ensued. While regretting the incident, I insisted that I had carried out my duties to the letter. Next morning, I told Mr Martin what had happened, knowing that Matron would be on the warpath, and he soon found the culprit. It was, indeed, the objectionable student, whose excuse was that he'd been in the lab experimenting ! He and his pal left me alone after that.

Matron, too, went out of her way to be nice. She seemed to be preoccupied and we nurses found it odd that she was starting to administer leave in a totally ad hoc way. One day, she told me that I could take a week due to me immediately and five hours later I was on the doorstep at Croesffyrdd, much to the surprise of my parents ! My friend Muriel called the next day, unaware that I was home, in order to say goodbye to my parents. She was to start in a school near Birmingham as an uncertificated teacher, in charge of fifty-two children under the age of five ! My other great friend, Marjorie, had been moved to the Customs House in London and Ronnie had written from Borneo to say that the oil fields were under threat from the Japanese. Some good news as well – after her suicide attempt, Auntie Edith had made a good recovery, under the watchful eye of my parents.

Back in Bristol, I hoped that my next leave would coincide with my twenty-first birthday in March, but nothing could be certain from now on. I was glad to be busy, for at home it had been all too easy to think of Jack, especially now that he had received his call-up papers. As a result of registering as a Conscientious Objector, he had received a notice to appear before an Armed Forces Tribunal in the New Year.

At this time I found myself being sent as a relief nurse to 'Radcliffe', our hospital's Isolation Block. Here, almost immediately, I witnessed the most tragic death I had yet seen – a case of septicaemia, too late to treat before admission to hospital. The poor young thing, a girl of seventeen, having found that she was pregnant, panicked and used a knitting needle to get rid of the baby herself. This had infected her and she died with no family or friends to comfort her. We had done our best, but were badly shaken.

Before Christmas I was moved again, this time to night duty in Artisan Medical Ward. The surprisingly mild weather suddenly changed in January, with a freezing east wind that refused to go away. Jack wrote to say that all the ponds in Kidderminster had frozen over and that skating was all the rage. Bristol, meanwhile, was enveloped by a permanent pea-soup fog or 'smog'. People with chronic chest and heart ailments suddenly became ill and died. Artisan Ward, in which I was the only night nurse at the time, filled up with men so ill that few survived. I came on duty one night to find that an oxygen tent had been donated, so in effect the staff had to decide which one patient could be saved. Every night, I cleared the desk to use as a display area for the patients' charts and on each one I would put an individual 'kidney dish', already prepared for the patient's next injection. My food came up each night in a metal container but for weeks it went untouched, there being no time to grab a bite. We spent day and night in one hectic fight to save lives.

A man in his early thirties was admitted with acute pneumonia and the doctors agreed to try out on him one of the Sulphonamides, a new drug being manufactured by 'M and B'. There was nothing to lose and as if by a miracle, it worked. Not so lucky were the many others admitted on the point of death. All we could do was to ensure that they were comfortable and try to make their passing less distressful. One night, two days before I was due on holiday, I arrived on duty to find one side of the ward – ten beds in all – completely empty. Their occupants had died that day. I had hoped that less people would die as a result of the weather improving slightly, but not so ! No sooner had I taken the report from day staff, than the internal phone rang. In no time at all, ten desperately ill men were brought up, all gasping for breath, accompanied by Night Sister herself. While the house-man was examining the patient who had been given the new drug, Sister took me to one side and quietly said that I could do with some help. Before long, Nurse Jones stepped diffidently into the ward, a buxom young woman of about thirty-five. I could have hugged her ! Although a junior nurse, she brought with her an aura of quiet confidence and maturity and the two of us fought with all we had to save those men. Every one of them died, however, and when the day staff came on they were greeted by another ten empty beds.

The next morning, I was sent for by Matron and assumed that my leave would be cancelled. She had given me time off for my birthday, something she was normally reluctant to do. I needn't have worried. Firstly, she congratulated me on my standard of nursing during the last difficult few months and then asked me to postpone my leave by just one day, in order to give Nurse Jones time to learn everything. Like most of the nurses, I would have done anything for our Matron !

My twenty-first birthday

Back in my room, a letter from Jack told me that he would arrive at Croesffyrdd on the evening of March 6th, one night before me. I sent a telegram home and went to bed, dog-tired but happy. The following night in Artisan was almost a picnic, with plenty of time to teach Nurse Jones about the ward. She was a lovely person, quickly acquiring the affectionate nickname 'Big J'. Holiday concessions meant that I could finish night duty at six o'clock instead of eight, which meant that on that Thursday morning of March 7th, 1940, my twenty-first birthday, I was off. Literally ! With my case already packed, all I had to do was change, before scampering through my short cut to Temple Meads. I caught the six-thirty express by the skin of my teeth and with everything running on greased wheels, was home within four hours. What a joy it was to see Jack, but this time he looked pale and tired. The severe weather had caused an unprecedented number of breakdowns in the telephone system and he'd had little respite. What I didn't know was that he'd spent the early hours of the previous night in my father's tool-shed ! Having missed the last bus up from Swansea, he had decided to take a taxi, reaching Croesffyrdd just after mid-night. Thinking that I was at home, he had thrown gravel against my bedroom window and then gently knocked the front door. Returning to the back of the house he had found the shed unlocked and decided to climb into his sleeping bag amongst the logs of wood. Jack had emerged at five-thirty to give my poor father a real shock as he returned from his shift ! In no time at all, my mother was up, magically producing a roaring fire and a steaming pot of tea, before despatching the pair of them to bed. When I arrived home, they had just started breakfast and looking at Jack's pale features, I determined to take care of him over the next few days.

In the excitement, I had forgotten about my birthday, but was soon to be reminded. Jack couldn't give me the beautiful wrist-watch he had bought, for my parents had also got me one but I asked him for a Scofield Bible instead. After a birthday tea with Auntie Edith, cousin Harry and an unsteady Mr Bisgrove, Jack and I wrapped up some goodies from the feast to take down to daddy. I loved everything about that signal box – its levers, bells, its very smell. Soon we were drinking one of his special brews, the milk going in last ! On the railway phone we chatted with Mr Mathias, before our customary visit.

Back home, we sat around the glowing fire in a different world ! My mother, bright as a button, made cocoa for everyone. She would retire only after preparing sandwiches – for my father at work the next morning and to help Jack and me on our little trip to the Giedd valley. For the first time since the outbreak of war, my mother was glad of our Emergency Ration Books. Bacon, sugar, butter, cheese and meat were all being rationed, while many other commodities were beginning to run short.

Jack looked more like himself the next morning, insisting on putting everything into his rucksack. I wore my long hair in a bun at the nape of my neck and Jack was soon teasing me that it looked old-fashioned. I told him that it had won me respect in the men's wards, making me look older than I really was, but as soon as we were off the main road, I tucked in behind him and undid the pins. It was not long before he became aware of it flowing down my back and gazed in obvious delight. Holding hands, we swung away up the valley and made for our 'Shangri-La', which by this time was painted in the colours of early Spring. We lingered awhile, before Jack threw off his rucksack and grasping me firmly, asked if I would marry him ! I was slightly taken aback, for we had so often discussed the years of training before this could happen. Yes, yes, but would I marry him at the end of this time ? For a brief moment, the ghost of that first love I had felt for Alfred Leyshon flickered across my mind – and was gone ! What I felt for Jack was different, solid and permanent. Yes, of course I would marry him, God willing, I would, I would ! He held me then as though he would never let go and there were tears in his eyes. We agreed not to get officially engaged, as I thought it would put an extra strain on us, but that didn't stop us celebrating. As we sat happily together, he produced a large box of Black Magic chocolates. My eyes must have been like saucers, for apart from costing the earth, such goodies were practically unobtainable !

Walking on again, I asked him about the result of the Tribunal. He had been given exemption from National Service provided that he remained with Post Office Communications. That was the 'rub', because we knew that one day his expertise would involve him in war-work. Should that happen, he would obey his conscience and take the consequences. We then moved on to the recent freeze, in which he and his mates had worked in temperatures so low that some

The council house in Heol-y-Varteg where Dan Jones' relatives lived.

of the telegraph poles had snapped like matchsticks under two or three inches of ice ! The balaclava and fingerless gloves I had sent him had been a god-send. Even so, there had been times when his fingers had been so stiff that he'd been unable to use them. As we talked, we found ourselves on the foothills of the Black Mountains and could see many areas where the snow had not yet given up its hold. We ate our lunch, sheltered from the wind, in a rough sheep-pen, but as the mist turned to rain we decided to return home.

That evening, my father and Jack discussed the war. It became clear to me how dependent we were on our shipping for a considerable amount of our food supplies. At sea there was not the 'phoney war' which we on land had been experiencing. I realised, too, how much the war was beginning to affect every-one in some way or another and that included us. My grandparents had had to move, my parents were thinking of taking evacuees and my father was teaching colleagues First Aid and Ambulance lessons. Active, too, in Air Raid and anti-gas precautions, he didn't think much of the latest tiny stirrup pumps they'd been issued to fight fires. Against modern incendiary bombs, he felt that they would be useless. Then there was Ronnie on the other side of the world, writing to say that they were on a war-footing with the Japanese. Jack had been called in front of an Armed Forces Tribunal and as for me, well, I just carried on nurs-ing. Having recently seen how devastating the combination of nature and pol-lution could be – with hundreds of Bristol civilians dead in one short month – I think I was becoming resigned to any further horrors that might hit us.

A minor alarm occurred the next day, though it was something that gave my parents and Jack a good laugh. A letter arrived from the hospital enquiring about the false teeth of a dead patient, something we nurses had been taught was neither funny nor insignificant. They had to be accounted for as a matter of law and I wrote back saying that I would return to hospital immediately if required. Later on, Jack was able to cash his wages at a local post office and I accompanied him to visit some relatives of Dan Jones, his stepfather of Ystaly-fera days. As we were now so close to the foot of the Darren, he suggested we climb it by the short steep route, via what we called 'the cave'. This was a narrow cleft through that outcrop of rock unique to the mountain and so distinctive for miles around. Only a hair-brained goat of a young man would contemplate it and his name was Jack. Never letting go for one second, he led me step by step to the safety of the cleft, where he sat me down before taking some

The 'cave' of the Darren.

195

Jack standing on the edge.

photographs of the village below. Watching him standing on the edge of that precipice filled me with terror and when we reached the top, well away from the edge, I flung myself flat on my face until my heart stopped thumping ! For a while, then, we sat close, taking in the soothing cool wind of that cloudless Spring day. We descended by the more conventional path to be greeted by my mother waving a telegram from the hospital. It read 'All well – matter cleared up satisfactorily' which led to more laughter and relief on my part as I settled down to enjoy the rest of the day. My mother and father were more like pals to us than parents, making their 'goodnights' early to let Jack and I be alone. However, the mountain air had done its work and the pair of us were soon asleep.

Jack rather reluctantly accompanied me to the service in the nearby evangelical church the next morning, but warmed to the little band of folk who were so kind and friendly. Then on to visit Mr Bisgrove, still with his military handle-bar moustache, who was approaching retirement as a railway worker. He intended joining his daughter Mary who was in Huntspill, Somerset, with some aunties, preparing a café business. At home, my mother had prepared the usual Sunday lunch of roast beef and potatoes, apologising for the smaller, rationed beef joints. Mr and Mrs Matthias had invited us to tea, after which we accompanied them to evening service. For me it was a bit of an ordeal, returning after seven years to the scene of the showdown with my Sunday School teacher ! I needn't have worried, for apart from renewing old friendships, I discovered that at the ripe old age of fifty-one, the Rev. Melville Philips was a fine preacher. As we strolled back down the Varteg Road, the Matthias' recalled the happy days at the church when we had been children and over supper they continued to spoil us. They adored one another, she revelling in his constant teasing, gently pushing him away and telling him not to be so silly ! Watching them, I prayed that our love, too, would flourish.

Jack had been given special leave for my twenty-first birthday and I promised to do the same for his, on June 13th. This was our last evening together and we spent it alone, deep in love and drunk with happiness. Neither of us wanted the magic to end and it was in the early hours that we eventually said goodnight. That morning, reluctant to part, we decided to take one last walk along the Crynant Road. There, Jack attached a self-timer to his camera, placed it carefully on top of a wall, ran back to me and let the camera take a picture. We only just caught the train at Ystalyfera, waving madly to my father on top of his signal-box steps until he was out of sight. In no time at all Jack and I were waving to each other at High Street Station. Alone, I made the journey home.

I felt empty, Swansea seemed empty, even home wasn't the same ! By early evening the next day, I was feeling no better and decided to ring Jack at work from Glanrhyd phone box. Just to hear his voice sent a thrill through me but I could sense that a call out of the blue had caused him some alarm. I told him that with only a little change, all I wanted to do was to tell him I loved him. My little mission accomplished, I put the phone down and raced home, my heart pounding with happiness. My parents told me to calm down and tell them what Jack had to say.

"Nothing", I replied, "I only had enough time to tell him I loved him !"

When they found out that Jack had asked me to marry him, their delight knew no bounds and they were eager to know more. We were interrupted by a loud rat-a-tat-tat on the door and standing there was a telegraph boy, who waited to see if there was a reply to the telegram he'd just handed me. There wasn't. A quick glance had told me all I wanted to see – 'Just fine to hear your voice. Now drunk again.'

Realising that he'd replied immediately from work, my parents were agog to know when the big day would be and somewhat crestfallen to hear that it might not be for another four years ! They hadn't realised that my all-round training, including Midwifery, would take so long and were genuinely sorry. It was good to discuss the future with them and feeling much more settled, I was able to do some much-needed studying for the Preliminary State Examination in a month's time. I still had another two weeks at home, for this was my annual holiday. Just as I was about to return to Bristol, a letter arrived from Ronnie telling us that he'd been made a Fellow of the Geological Society. How proud we all felt !

Chapter Seventeen

THE BOMBING OF BRISTOL

Casualty

Only a day back into work, a large oblong cardboard box was delivered to me, full of Spring flowers that included daffodils and narcissi. Their fragrance and beauty put me in dreamland but I was brought to earth when I learnt that I would be doing a three month spell in Casualty. So many nurses were off sick at this time that several wards had had to be closed. Most had German Measles but much more serious was the outbreak of diphtheria, the third case having recently been sent to Ham Green Isolation Hospital. Many of the nurses on the wards became depressed under the heavy work burden.

Meanwhile, I loved my time in Casualty, apart from the dreaded 'Tonsils and Adenoids Removal Day'. This would start with me putting out everything for the ENT (Ear, Nose and Throat) specialist and his assistants, before covering the entire floor of the adjoining room with heavy, brick-red mackintosh sheets, one for each child that had an appointment. After having their tonsils removed, they were put on the sheets to 'come round'. I rebelled at what I considered a barbarous way of treating them, the place reminding me of a slaughterhouse. Another thing that upset me was the fact that they came in and went out the same day. The memory of seeing worried parents coming back in the late afternoon to collect those limp little bundles, no matter what the weather or conditions at home, haunted me for a long time. I vowed that if Jack and I ever had children, they would never be allowed to go through such an experience. I was glad when the system changed not long after, allowing the operations to take place in theatre and the children to stay overnight if necessary.

Working in Casualty meant that I had practically every evening off and a weekend twice a month ! How I wished Jack and I lived nearer to one another, as my friend Lonsdale and her fiancé did. I could, however, see a lot more of my Mount of Olives friends, who gave me a surprise birthday party on my first evening back. They had bought me a communal present, a beautiful, black 'Swan' fountain pen with a gold nib and a space to engrave my name. They were delighted that Jack and I were to be married and Johnnie suggested that ours might be the next wedding in the Mount of Olives ! Vivien, by this time, had taken up a lot of war-time duties but her home still remained open house to many, including myself.

198

On the 23rd April we sat the written exam in Southmead Hospital, the oral and practical taking place a week later in our own General. There seemed to be hundreds of nurses there from all over the west of England. Then came the internal exam and I was thankful to be on day duty, so many of my previous exams having been taken while I was on nights. It was at this time that the merger between our hospital and the Bristol Royal Infirmary took place, now officially becoming 'The Bristol Royal Hospital'. Almost immediately, there was an influx of carcinoma (cancer), skin and ENT cases, for we (the General) had become the specialist centre for the west of England. What appalled me most about it all was to see our beloved Matron dressed in grey instead of her black uniform ! Changes were introduced with increasing regularity, Matron announcing that from now on, her nurses would work in both hospitals in order to secure a good all-round training. Casualty Sister found herself being over-whelmed by the large number of new ENT medical students and was further annoyed when I was moved 'just as she had trained me to be a good casualty nurse !'

Two important announcements appeared on the notice board at the beginning of June. During that month, the first exchange of nurses between the two hospitals would take place and secondly, apart from a few wards, our hospital was to be emptied. This was because Hitler's troops had advanced to the very shores of France and we had to be ready for any casualties from Dunkirk. Matron gathered us together for a serious talk, asking us to be vigilant and to be prepared for anything, even invasion ! Any outstanding leave had to be taken in batches, starting immediately, so that the hospital could remain fully staffed. Part of the cellars had already been equipped as an emergency operating theatre and beds were in the process of being carried down. As she took us on a tour of inspection, she showed us the huge fresh water tank that had been installed there. I was particularly fascinated by the size and intricacy of the vast, arched cellars. She then volunteered that the Dental Department would close, in view of a new Dental Hospital having recently opened. We in the General were fortunate, indeed, in having a Resident Warden Post and an Auxiliary Fire Station. The last remark caused one or two titters, for we all knew about the high jinks that had been going on in those quarters during the long, boring days of the 'phoney war'.

One afternoon at about this time, a very drunk sailor stumbled into Casualty, evidently looking for some company, for there was nothing wrong with him. We were being run off our feet and I recall being vaguely amused at first, as he started to tell jokes but was unable to remember the punch-line. Then he decided to entertain us with some bawdy songs, but on being told to be quiet, started to become abusive. A young doctor who had been working tirelessly all day, felt he knew what he would do with a drunken sailor. He grabbed the hapless sea-

The unfortunate drunk had staggered straight out of Casualty (to the left of the building) into the river.

dog by the collar and bundled him out of the door. We half-expected him to stumble back in at any minute but it seemed his little show was over. It wasn't until the next day that the police informed us that it had truly been his final performance. The poor dab had apparently staggered the ten yards straight from Casualty into the Cut and had drowned.

I was among the first batch to be given leave, fortunate to have two weeks in June. I wrote to Jack immediately and back came an invitation from his mother to be their guest during the first week. As I was still on Casualty, I was free to travel up on the evening of Saturday, June 1st, catching a fast train to Worcester. Revelling in the thought that the next stop would be Kidderminster, who should walk into the compartment but Jack !

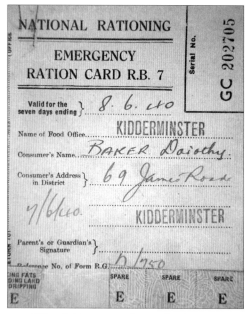

Eileen's Emergency Ration Card covering her week in Kidderminster.

Although unable to be together on his birthday, we made the most of what we had. On the Monday I was in for a great surprise, when he took me to Bewdley and led me by the hand down some stone steps to the river Severn. The boatman was obviously expecting him and led us to a slim and beautiful boat.

Messing about on the river! Eileen at the front of the boat.

"It's all yours, sir!" and indeed it was, not just that day but for the rest of the week, paid for in advance. For five idyllic days he took me sculling, taking me up the rapids to either Arley or Highley. When the sun was at its highest during that heat wave, Jack drew into the shallows and we stepped out into the shade of the overhanging willows. We lay contentedly in each other's arms, happy beyond words and longing for the day when we would be man and wife. On one day, I was allowed to sit at the front going down the rapids, providing I wore his cycling cape. I got wet, of course, but the sun was so hot that it didn't matter. However, it gave Jack an excuse to stop at a little riverside café, where he treated me to buttered scones and jam.

On our last day – a Sunday – we attended morning service at Jack's Baxter Church before taking a walk to the Wyre Forest. In its sheltered tranquillity, Jack again asked me to marry him and for the second time I said yes. I still wouldn't agree to an engagement ring, feeling it would only make it harder for us. Inevitably, we had to go our separate ways, Jack to his work as a Post Office Engineer-in-training, I to my beloved parents for a week. I had given him his birthday present the moment we had met in the railway compartment and each evening we had listened to it – Schubert's beautiful *Unfinished Symphony* !

At home I learnt that Marjorie, who had recently been transferred by the Civil Service from London to Cardiff, was ill in bed. When I visited her, I found that her mother, herself crippled with sciatic, was nursing her downstairs in their dark front room. Though running a high temperature, Marjorie put on a bright smile, but could hardly speak for the cough that kept racking her and I had an uneasy feeling that it was something far worse than rheumatism. Out of earshot, Mrs Reeves confided in me that the doctor suspected TB. Though not surprised, the news shook me. Marjorie was the cleverest girl I knew and was only twenty-one. When I called a few days later, she was weaker but still managed an ethereal smile. Keeping my feelings under control, I kissed her gently on her damp forehead and could barely whisper, "I'll come and see you again next time I'm home. God bless you." Back in the house, choked with grief, I broke down and cried. That evening, I prayed silently for her at the mid-week meeting in the 'Cong', where I was greeted warmly. Afterwards, my mother and I met up with Mrs Mathias and Jack's mother, who was staying with her. All of this prompted mammy to ask me whether we had considered getting married in Ystalyfera. Hadn't Jack mentioned this before, up in the Giedd ?

The next morning brought a tiny package, the handwriting causing my heart to miss a beat. It was a taste of wedding cake from Alfred Leyshon and I genuinely hoped that he and his bride would be happy. My heart was light as a feather when I wished Jack a happy birthday over the phone the next day. I told him that his mother and Mrs Mathias were joining us for a special tea in his honour and that we'd all be going to see *The Proud Valley* at the pictures. Lastly and most importantly, I told him that I loved him with every fibre of my body and that I would never forget our week together on the river. Alfred's ghost had well and truly been laid to rest ! When we arrived home that night, my father was sitting by the wireless, listening intently to the Queen broadcasting to the French 'in their time of sorrow and defeat'.

The next day I returned to Bristol, Jack's mother accompanying me as far as Cardiff, where one of her sisters lived. In Ruth's room that evening, I learnt that I'd been written up to work for a fortnight on Thomas Ward as acting Senior Nurse. It was now a female cancer ward and even though the results of the Preliminary State Exam were not yet out, we were to take on duties of third-year nurses ! For those two weeks I slept in what was called the 'skylight' on the hospital roof, which was the maids' quarters. Also on the roof, a little distance away, were the unique night nurses' quarters, known familiarly as the 'huts', wooden huts indeed, but very quiet and comfortable. As I looked tired, Ruth gave me a pillow and told me to sleep at the bottom of her bed. Unheard of behaviour, but we were living in exceptional times ! We fell, laughing, into bed and were soon fast asleep.

The first day on Thomas Ward went well and in the evening Ruth helped me move my belongings. I wasn't prepared for my early awakening the next morning, the brilliant sunshine streaming through the skylight window. Neither was I prepared for another large cardboard flower-box which arrived while I was on duty. Later, I could open it and appreciate the beautiful roses that Jack had picked from his garden, their fragrance all-pervading. One deep red bud was so perfect, so velvety, that I pressed it against my face and as I started to stroke it, I noticed Matron's presence at the open bedroom door. Wishing to apologise for my new sleeping quarters, she advanced into the room and asked where the roses had come from.

"From him !" I said simply, reaching out for Jack's photograph. She went on to tell me that I would be amongst the first batch of General Hospital nurses to work in the Bristol Royal Infirmary, starting in two weeks time ! She was relying on us to 'keep up the standards of nursing we had learnt in the General'. Because of the increasing threat of air raids over the city, great changes were in the offing and we had to be ready.

Even before the end of that week, the hospitals in the south and south-west of England were put on National Emergency Alert. We were told to expect two hundred casualties from Dunkirk and once again, all but the seriously ill patients were moved to safer venues. We waited three days but no casualties arrived, having been admitted, so we were informed, to more easily accessible hospitals. In the turmoil and uncertainty we all became exhausted. When Sunday arrived, for the first time in two and a half years I felt too tired to walk from the hospital in dockland to the Mount of Olives at the top of Blackboy Hill. Instead, I went round the corner to the Anglican Church of St. Mary Redcliffe. Bristol, the city of churches and clocks, was strangely quiet. The church bells were not to ring again, unless to warn us that the Germans were invading our shores.

At one o'clock that night we were woken by Air Raid sirens for the first time. We spent two hours in the cellars until the all-clear was given. We heard the peculiar heavy throbbing of German planes above and though no bombs were dropped, the reality of war began to sink in. One Air Raid Warden stood up straight and gave us Mr Churchill's speech, which he had obviously rehearsed at home: "We shall defend our island, whatever the cost may be. We shall fight on the beaches; we shall fight on the landing grounds. We shall fight in the fields, and in the streets, we shall fight in the hills. We shall never surrender !"

Stirring stuff, sounding a bit eerie down there, underneath the huge arches. Surely, I thought, it would never come to that. Or would it ? Imagine how I felt when, at the end of the week, we heard that all fighting on the continent had ceased and that the Germans had occupied the Channel Islands ! Next day, all over Bristol, measures were being stepped up to confuse a potential enemy, with signposts being taken away and place-names painted out.

The Royal Infirmary

On July 1st, we made our way self-consciously in uniform across the city, as the first exchange nurses, to the Royal Infirmary. As we passed in front of the Eye Hospital, my thoughts turned to how happy I had been there and how apprehensive I now felt as we approached our new home. We needn't have worried, for the staff were kind and the hospital bright and airy. Equipment was first-class, as was the food, while the Nurses' Home was more like a hotel ! I was assigned to Capern Ward, a large male surgical ward, which to my amazement was full of Dunkirk casualties. The young ward sister was extremely helpful, telling me that as a third-year nurse I was entitled to a long weekend every fortnight, though we were not allowed to sleep out. On my first weekend I cycled out with Ruth to Batheston, where it was said that Emperor Halle Silassie was living in exile. We didn't see anyone that fitted his description !

Bristol Royal Infirmary.

Suddenly Hitler started to vent his anger on London, though he was also to leave his calling card at the other cities, Bristol included. Jack's concern for me was paramount in his next letter. He wondered whether our spirits would remain together, should one of us die. I was reading *Travels With A Donkey* at the time and the following words which I sent to Jack still come to mind:

> ". . . but to love is the great amulet which makes the world a garden, and hope which comes to all, outwears the incidents of life and reaches out with tremulous hand beyond the grave and death. Easy to say; yea, but also by God's mercy, both easy and grateful to believe !"

Marauding German planes now began to fly over Bristol day and night, one swooping so low that I could see the pilot in his cockpit as I peeked out of the third floor window. We were compelled to sleep on mattresses on the ground floor of the Nurses' Home, eighteen of us sharing a rota for getting up if required. Capern became a 'mobile' surgical ward, so that it could be emptied rapidly in the event of air raid casualties. Extra narrow beds were placed down the middle and at each side of the ward.

It was London, however, that continued being bombed, causing Mr Churchill to say, "The vast, vast mass of London itself, fought street by street, could easily devour an entire army – and we would rather see London in ruins and ashes, than it should be tamely and abjectly enslaved." I tried to think how this kind of speech might affect Jack.

I had to reassure my parents that I was all right. While they were worrying, it all seemed so unreal to me ! We were now getting used to the Air Raid warnings and the familiar drone of enemy planes, so much so that we even managed some sleep. Whenever mammy and daddy heard that there had been raids over the West Country, they immediately thought of Bristol. I would have loved to get home to comfort them, but it was too far. Kidderminster, however, was a possibility, and when I arrived on the doorstep at Ridgecroft the next day, Jack and his family thought they were seeing a ghost ! We stole away for a few precious hours, when I was able to give Jack the number of the Nurses' Home, but told him to be specific when phoning as there was more than one Nurse Baker ! Parting was not quite so painful this time, for we realised that we could see each other more frequently.

A fortnight later I was meeting him at Temple Meads, Post Office duty having been lifted again that August Bank Holiday, to enable employees to travel outside their immediate work area. We caught the first bus from the station, now on full Air Raid alert, out to Westbury Village and our familiar little cottage café. Resting our elbows on the old, rickety table, we sipped hot tea and enjoyed the magic of the moment. No matter what was happening

The Nurses' Home at the Royal Infirmary.

around us, we knew that no-one could take away the special love we felt for one another. Presently, the kind old lady brought out a tray bearing a considerable lunch, reminiscent of pre-rationing days. We fell on it like hungry wolves ! We then made for the Westbury side of the Downs, where we found a secluded hollow and rested quietly. The pair of us were tired, Jack having been on duty the night before with the volunteer firefighters. With our heads touching and eyes closed, we relaxed in each other's arms.

After lunch with Vivien the next day, we followed our old route across the Suspension Bridge to Leigh Woods. I remember that when I took my handkerchief out that afternoon, my month's pay-slip came out with it and blew towards Jack. He picked it up to return to me, but pocketed it when I told him it wasn't important. He told me that life at work was becoming increasingly difficult, the quiet times spent in prayer each morning giving him strength to face the day. While some of his colleagues understood his stance as a Con-scientious Objector, others were openly hostile, one in particular having gone to the Union in an attempt to get him sacked. Jack's training would soon take him to London for two important exams, embarking as he was on the fifth out of seven years training. He was concerned about work directly involving the war effort and had to think about the consequences of refusing to do it. All I could do was reassure him of my support. In a thoughtful frame of mind, we walked back to the bottom of the steep flight of steps at the side of the Royal Infirmary, where we said our goodbyes.

Bomb damage in Bridge Street.
(Photograph courtesy Bristol Record Office).

That night no sleep was possible, as we suffered a heavy raid (Bristol's forty-fourth) that continued for hours. We could only feel for those who were in the firing line.

Jack's next letter came from London, where he was again staying with friends in Cricklewood. The last time he had been on a course in Dollis Hill was in 1939, when he had met up with Vic Matthias. They had had a wonderful time, taking night photographs, going to the Proms and exploring London at will. This time it was different, war had seen to that. I was gripped with fear for him, it being no comfort that many thousands were in the same boat. I loved Jack and I hated this war.

Meanwhile, a spanking new wing for day-time nursing staff had been opened, safer and almost de-luxe. Its completion co-incided with the arrival of the next batch of exchange nurses, Ruth included, and I was delighted to be told that I would be staying at the Infirmary for the time being. An important exam was looming but the air raids had made things difficult for us. Several of us had already missed nine lectures, now taking place in the evening. One night, I had been crossing the city on the way to one, when the sirens went. Almost immediately, bombs began to whistle down and I suddenly found myself being pulled down into a cellar. My rescuer, to whom I'll always be grateful, was a former secretary in the Dental Department and it was outside her father's chinaware business that she'd seized me ! The raid was severe, lasting several hours, and I spent the time cheerfully helping an elderly lady wind several hanks of wool into balls, while she told me where to get the best bargains. The impossibility of attending lectures prompted the hospital hierarchy to give us the option of taking the exam the next time round.

Although I wanted to celebrate my mother's birthday with her (their wedding anniversary, too, was on the same day, August 15th), we were not allowed to sleep away. My parents suggested I go up to London to see Jack and with this 'blessing' I wrote to him, though I planned to go up whatever his reply ! He wanted to pay my fare after having seen my pay-slip and being appalled at our wages. As a third-year, I was earning more than I'd ever done and we'd recently had a rise. If he only knew what I was being paid a year ago !

Before the trip, I told Matron Bell where I was going, in case anything should happen. It was still quite early on that morning of Saturday, August 31st, when Jack met me at Paddington. He whisked me into a taxi and before long I was meeting kind Mr and Mrs Francis in Cricklewood. We spent most of that warm, pleasant day in Hyde Park, surrounded by large barrage balloons which made us feel quite cocooned. As we prepared to return to the station, they suddenly started to go up and the sirens began. People were disappearing down shelters as if by magic and with one look, Jack could sense that I wanted to get back to the hospital. Without uttering a word, he pulled me to my feet, held me tight to kiss me and gripping my hand, started running. We ran and ran until, with lungs bursting, we reached Paddington and made for the South-West plat-form. At half past six, the train started to creep out like a snail and we held hands for as long as we could. All I could think of was that I was leaving him there, unprotected, until he could find a shelter. For an hour the train continued to crawl, until we heard a faint 'all clear' and I sank back into my seat, praying that Jack was safe. As though released from a terrible plague, the train picked up speed and tore through the countryside, amazingly reaching Temple Meads at nine-thirty ! As I made my way home, the sirens screamed out, Bristol's balloons went up and searchlights started to criss-cross the night sky. The raid lasted all night, and as day dawned I felt the need to write to Jack. Our letters crossed in the post with the same simple message – 'I love you darling !' written over and over again.

Getting back to work was the best thing I could have done, civilian patients once again filling Capern Ward. Sister allowed me to accompany patients to theatre, where I was able to learn a great deal. The few remaining Dunkirk casualties were well on the way to recovery and a joy to be around, keeping us laughing from morning to night. If they were fit enough, they were given a con-siderable amount of freedom to go shopping, attend shows in the evening and even date the nurses ! One of them, Trevor, whose home was in Pontardawe, had received terrible burns and when he first came in, swathed in bandages, all we could see were his eyes, mouth and nostrils. Now well on the mend, he had gone on an errand one morning to collect one of the nurses' shoes from the local cobbler's, only to find that they weren't ready. Having the afternoon off, I volunteered to pop in again and Trevor promptly stepped forward as escort. We spent a happy few hours shopping for one and all, practically everything, including the shoes and two packets of Lux Flakes, finding a home in the commodious pockets of his Army great coat. On my next evening off, he asked me to go to a Variety Show at the Hippodrome but I declined, sensing he was becoming too fond of me and giving an imminent exam as an excuse. He looked so dejected that I almost changed my mind. Very soon, he was discharged and went home to his parents. Often, when passing through the village on the way home, I thought fondly of him, hoping that he had remained safe in this dreadful war.

Indeed, the whole concept of war came to occupy my mind and I became convinced that Jack's pacifist stance was correct. There seemed to be so much manipulation in the way millions of ordinary people from different countries were being slaughtered. I found it hard to express my views to people, Vivien afraid that I was breaking away from the Pentecostal faith. In love for me, she felt she had to warn me that I was blindly following Jack's 'modernistic' beliefs and we had a frank exchange of opinions. Johnnie, however, was very dogmatic and overbearing, which led to a falling-out one evening over supper, after I had the audacity to quote some words of Jesus: "But I say unto you, love your enemies, bless them that curse you. Do good to them that hate you and pray for them." I implied that these commands had never been carried out by nations, only by a few individuals and that ours was supposed to be a Christian country. In horror, they warned me that I could end up in prison for such views, which was, of course, true ! This was the water-shed as far as my religious beliefs were concerned, though we remained friends.

September 1940 and the ban on sleeping out was suddenly lifted ! Jack was in Yorkshire at a Post Office training camp, miles away but safe, thank God. He had briefly been sent home, from where he had sent a box of juicy plums and pears. On the day that it arrived there had been mayhem in the hospital, compounded by day-time air raid warnings. We were so busy that no-one, not even the patients, had had anything to eat. We fell on the fruit hungrily. Manna from Kidderminster ! I would have loved to have gone up to Yorkshire but it was too far, so my next weekend off saw me heading home. I knew Swansea had been badly bombed, but I wasn't prepared for the scene of devastation when I got off the train. The main exit had been boarded up after taking a direct hit and as I emerged from the temporary side exit, I had to pick my way through the rubble in search of any sign of the valley buses. A feeling of grief quickly overwhelmed me, deeper than anything I had felt in Bristol, for this was 'my' Swansea, these were 'my' people. Eventually, I found a bus and learnt from fellow-passengers about the heavy raids that had completely destroyed the town centre. At Pontardawe the driver pulled into the side of the road, having been told that an air raid warning had just sounded. It was an hour before he got the 'all-clear' and everyone took it for granted that Swansea had suffered yet again.

Back home in Croesffyrdd, things seemed as normal as ever, except for the pleasing effect of strips of plaster on the windows. Two more warnings – in the form of colliery hooters – went off that afternoon and evening but we heard no planes. Gathered round the radio after supper, we heard that London was being bombed continuously and that other cities had been hit. The news was followed by the voice of 'Lord Haw Haw'. Was I sup-

Back home at Croesffyrdd.

posed to love him ? At that moment it wasn't in me to do so. Certainly Mr Bisgrove, whom I visited the next day, was in unforgiving mood. His solution to that dreadful traitor and the Germans generally was to 'burn the lot and leave them to everlasting torment' and I wondered if he'd ever stop talking about them ! In calmer mood, he told me that his two maiden sisters in Highbridge would be delighted if my parents, Jack and myself would stay with them for a few nights. I also took the opportunity that weekend to visit Marjorie, who had been bed-ridden now for fourteen weeks and according to her mother, was very, very weak. Despite that, she seemed to have an inner strength and was holding her own.

The next morning I was up very early, in order to catch the six-forty train to Bristol, a little anxious that my shift was starting less than three hours later. In the event, I was ten minutes late but needn't have worried, for Sister was fine about it. I had always got on well with her and contrary to my initial expectations, almost wished that I could have stayed on at the Royal Infirmary. I soon became aware from Sister Tutor that I was not the only one who had decided to postpone sitting my next exam and that a new system of internal exams had been devised to deal with the situation. After each lecture we would be given a test paper without access to our notes, which under the circumstances we thought was pretty fair.

The next night, Tuesday, September 24th, we heard the now familiar Air Raid sirens. However, this time the heavy drone of German planes became terrifyingly ominous, as they passed directly above us. Imagine how we felt, when almost immediately we heard the lighter throbbing of our own Spitfires, those young British pilots making me question my pacifist stance. We listened to the dreadful whining of the bombs and knew that they were dropping somewhere near. Casualties started coming in to Capern Ward the next morning, six people having been killed in the vicinity of the hospital. The next day there was an alert just before midday, followed immediately by the roar of enemy bombers flying very low and in numbers we had not previously experienced. The dinner trolleys had just been brought up and we were extremely relieved to be given the 'all-clear' minutes later. Sister then decided to go to the first sitting of staff lunches, leaving me in charge. We had barely started serving the patients when the sirens went again, and a second wave of low German bombers screamed by, followed by another 'all-clear'. As we continued with the lunches, wondering if there would be a third alert, we became aware of a cacophony of noise coming from the street below. We rushed to the windows to find that vehicles of every description, headed by a fleet of ambulances, were trying to draw up as near to Casualty (immediately below us) as possible. What a sight ! Some of the bomb victims were lying on top of battered cars, others hanging out of milk vans or lying on top of dirt and debris in the back of lorries. The numbers were so great that people must have just been pushed into anything on wheels. It was all hands on deck ! In next to no time the dinner trolleys were back in the kitchen, those able to walk moved to a patients' lounge and all beds stripped and made up with clean linen.

Soon the phone was ringing and a casualty doctor telling us to be prepared for the seriously injured. How many beds did we have ? Not enough ! The adjoining ward was being evacuated as the first batch was brought up from Casualty, helped by medical students, porters, even painters working in the hospital. One young soldier lying on a stretcher died before we could do anything for him, his lungs having completely collapsed after the blast had sucked in air from everywhere. Another victim, an A.R.P. Warden, refused any help. He stood up proudly and indicated that he wanted to sit on the edge of the bed. I was on one side of him, gently supporting him with another nurse, when he collapsed and died. Five surgeons worked day and night to save the others but there were very many fatalities. We were soon to learn that one hundred and sixty bombs had landed on Filton Aircraft Factory, six of them on the air raid shelters. Hundreds had been killed or maimed, including a complete battalion of army recruits. Two days later, the anti-aircraft gunners were ready for the bombers, allowing only nine bombs to be released, and casualties were light. The noise was deafening, however, and terrifyingly close.

I was resigned to having my next leave cancelled, but grateful when it wasn't. I was able to meet up with my parents a week later at Temple Meads as planned, to catch the train for Highbridge. Jack couldn't come (he was still in Yorkshire where he and a couple of other students were helping teach the latest advances in Post Office technology) but my father could make use of his annual leave. I was concerned that mammy and daddy had colds and looked pale after recent attacks of flu. It took us a while to find the correct platform, because Temple Meads had sustained damage to its tracks during the recent raids. As the train drew in, the sirens went and it would be an hour and a half before it could leave. It crawled all the way, getting us there by half-past ten that night, three hours late ! It was very dark as we started to walk in the general direction of Huntspill but I was certain that I would recognise their house, called 'The Rosaries'. After twenty minutes we managed to flag down a passing bus, whose conductor told us to take a penny ride into the village and make enquiries there. We could have done without his advice, for the house was a mile back along the same road, a stone's throw away from where we had boarded his bus ! A kind local showed us the way and it was near midnight before we arrived. Although her aunties were sound asleep, Mary heard us knocking. We said goodbye to our Good Samaritan who now wanted to get home, and before long were sat at a table covered with a brilliant white damask cloth, proffering cold beef, bread and butter. How good it tasted !

Over breakfast, in the welcoming atmosphere of that warm, cosy house, Mary's aunts told me how much they had hoped to meet Jack and issued us with an open invitation. My parents were keen to visit the Cheddar Cave, but we were soon so tired that we headed back to Mary's café in Highbridge. While my parents rested, I helped Mary, who was being run off her feet. It was a novel experience, carrying trays back and forth and taking orders. My brain got into a complete twist when one lady asked for three eggs, costing 3/3d a dozen. Mary was in fits as I tried to work it out, before coming to my rescue. I had always prided myself on my Maths and didn't like being beaten ! Then there were the village boys, a long queue of them waiting to be served with their half-pence worth of 'liquorice comforts'.

"Liquorice what ?" I asked Mary.

"You know – the torpedoes !" she replied. They were twenty-four a penny and each little boy asked for the same thing, testing both my counting abilities and my patience !

My parents left very early the next day, not wanting to be caught out by any delays on the home journey. The rest of that Sunday at Huntspill was going quietly until fourteen of Mary's relatives suddenly arrived from Poole, in Dorset. Some I had already met and what a jolly crowd they were, relating some hair-raising encounters during air attacks on the south coast. When we were called to eat, my eyes popped out like saucers, as one of the aunts brought in a large dish and lowered it on to the table to reveal a large Michaelmas goose ! If Charles Dickens had knocked on the front door at that very moment, I wouldn't have been surprised.

On the early evening train back to Bristol, I felt warm and relaxed at first. Then, as we proceeded at a snail's pace with neither heating nor light and with night closing in, memories came flooding back of that awful journey between Kidderminster and Handsworth. My instinct now, as then, was to draw my coat tightly around me. At Temple Meads, eerily still in the grip of a black-out, I hailed a taxi, grateful that the skies above us were quiet. I was back in time to give Vivien a quick ring, having forgotten to tell her that I would be away that weekend. It wasn't long before I heard from mammy and daddy, who were feeling so much better for their little break. My mother finished the letter by adding 'the Darren is looking beautiful in its Autumn colours – almost asking for Jack and Eileen to come home and climb it !'

The next Sunday saw me at the Mount of Olives and then back with Johnnie to 'Bethany', Vivien's house, for lunch. Both were concerned about me and it was a relief to share the shocking experience of the Filton air raid with them. I accepted Vivien's invitation to spend my next weekend off with her but before that fortnight was up, something happened to upset me. On the Wednesday of the second week, I had come back from the afternoon lecture in the Infirmary to go on duty in Capern Ward, where I was in charge for the evening. As I read through the report with the night nurses at the end of my shift, I laid the pen down on the desk, not missing it until the next morning. I didn't expect any trouble finding it, but nobody had seen it and I spent a couple of sleepless nights wondering how to explain it to my dear friends. By the time I arrived at Bethany, I was a complete wreck, the side of my face throbbing with pain ! It soon disappeared, as their kindness soothed away my anxiety.

The following week I was commandeered by Matron Robins back to the General, where there was a shortage of senior nurses. Having said my goodbyes to every patient and member of staff on Capern Ward, I was quietly slipping out when one of the young men set up 'Three cheers for Nurse Baker !' I had spent a happy time there and was too choked to say anything. Back in dockland and the General Hospital, I had a room assigned to me in the Nurses' Home, for use when not on duty. However, during the day we night nurses had to sleep in a communal area that had formerly been the Dental Department – either that, or a poky, airless room that had originally been intended to store our trunks. So to cheer myself up, I nipped into town to the tiny wool shop in Bridge Street that the old lady in the shelter had told me about. I bought a pattern for a man's pullover and some of the new double-knitting wool, with the intention of making one in grey for my father and one in Bristol red for Jack. When I would ever find the time to do it didn't matter. It was a pleasant diversion to look forward to !

Back in the General – heavy bombing raids

Several changes had taken place in the four months I had been away, due mainly to the threat of air raids. Because the General was the centre for the treatment of carcinoma in the West of England, the latest apparatus for Deep X-Ray Therapy had been installed on the ground floor, well away from Casualty. In view of the threat of air raids, it had been deemed a matter of urgency to move it, complete with its specially trained staff, to Kewstoke Hospital. The General still took patients of lesser severity, including those being treated with Radium needles, which required great care in their application and removal. A strong slender thread was attached to each needle, so that whenever one was inserted, we could monitor its position. At the beginning and end of each treatment the needles had to be counted and checked and should any session be interrupted by an Air Raid warning, had to be removed and rapidly returned to a special bore-hole storing box, fifty foot deep. The Medical Authorities were keen that patients should, if at all possible, be able to walk unaided down to the Air Raid shelters in the cellars. A very welcome change was that night nurses were now given one and a half hours off every night, which I gladly used to get a bit of shut eye. Sleep in the cramped Dental quarters was difficult, impossible once the sirens started wailing ! Raids on Bristol began to intensify and with them came more casualties. For the first time ever, operations took place on Sundays, as did lectures !

On my first morning back, I found another box of fruit from Kidderminster waiting for me, something Jack had arranged with a friend whose family were in the fruit and vegetable business. His thoughtfulness and love bowled me over and I longed for the day when we could marry. Time was passing quickly and within a year my 'set' would be taking final examinations, qualifying us as State Registered Nurses. The dear Ward Sister in the Infirmary had written on my behalf to a friend, asking for details of the Midwifery course she was doing in Birmingham. It had a good reputation and would be near to Kidderminster, though I had yet to finish my General training, let alone the additional obligatory year at the hospital !

Brave firefighters in Broadmead.
(Photograph courtesy Bristol Record Office).

In the middle of November, the nation was stunned by the news that Coventry had been devastated in one night by five hundred German bombers and that four hundred people had been killed. On Sunday, November 24th, I was at the early evening service in the Mount of Olives with Vivien and Johnnie. It had barely started when the sirens sounded and the deafening roar of enemy planes overhead indicated that this was no ordinary raid. The church had no shelter and Mr Wallace in the pulpit calmly told us that we must go home or to a place of safety as quickly as possible, adding, "May God protect you !"

It was like daylight outside, the sky lit up by myriads of flares floating down from the German bombers. Suddenly, incendiaries began to rain down, pounding buildings either side of Blackboy Hill and Whiteladies Road with deadly efficiency. As the firemen bravely erected ladders, they reminded me of miniature toys as they tried to fight the gigantic flames. As we scrambled towards Vivien's house in Elmdale Road, parallel with Whiteladies, more incendiaries came whistling down. Through streets filled with fire engines and ambulances, and with masonry crashing around us, we at last reached a shelter. During a lull we pushed on, sometimes making a dash for it, then having to crawl against what was left of the side of the road, or stumble over the multitude of fire hoses criss-crossing the area. We had no need of light; the whole of Bristol, it seemed, was lit up by an awful, yet beautiful, orange and yellow inferno.

Once inside the house, we huddled under the stairs as the bombing started again. Suddenly there was an almighty crash right above us and we expected to be engulfed in flames or buried by rubble, but nothing happened. A quick examination showed us that the only damage appeared to be some fallen plaster. Outside, broken pipes were sticking up through a crater made by a bomb that had been meant for us. While Johnnie took charge of the house, Vivien and I tried to find our way back to the hospital. With bombers still coming over in waves, we somehow found a relatively untroubled route through Cotham. Only when I was safely in sight of the General did Vivien leave me. Such kindness was beyond words !

Arriving at the hospital I found that there was some damage – nothing like I'd just witnessed – and that we were taking casualties. We didn't stop that night, for apart from the many fatalities, two hundred had been seriously injured and seven hundred less so. As dawn broke, we heard that two bombs had fallen on the Royal Infirmary's Out Patients Department but thankfully no-one had been killed. A couple of others, neither of which had exploded, had fallen near the Nurses' Home. The nurses, working in whatever they had been wearing when first alerted, were evacuated shortly afterwards. Later that morning I went back to Bethany and was able to see the extent of the destruction in the heart of the city. Vivien told me that an incendiary had actually fallen on the roof of the house that night, but that wardens and soldiers had managed to put it out !

From then on, we night nurses never slept in night clothes, but were always ready to go on duty with our shoes waiting at the side of the bed. Early in the evening of December 4th, we became aware of the ominous drone of German planes, and 'spotters' on the roof informed Matron that wave after wave of heavy bombers were going over, dropping flares the length of the river Avon. Everyone immediately made for the cellars but nothing further happened, at least to us, that night. My particular responsibility at the time was to 'special' a man so desperately ill with throat cancer that there had been no time to admit him to Kewstoke. Indeed, he and a few other seriously ill cancer patients remained in the cellars, some of the ladies sleeping in large laundry trucks ! After his operation, it was important that the tube leading into his trachea was kept clear at all times and I soon became friends with this brave, wonderful man. The following night saw a repeat of the night before and though we suffered no damage, the authorities decided to rapidly evacuate all but the most seriously ill patients. On December 6th we got what sleep we could, before again being awoken by the familiar drone. The sirens started up at about six-thirty and though the noise of our anti-aircraft guns was deafening, no message came from Matron. We therefore assumed that for the third night running somebody else was bearing the brunt of it.

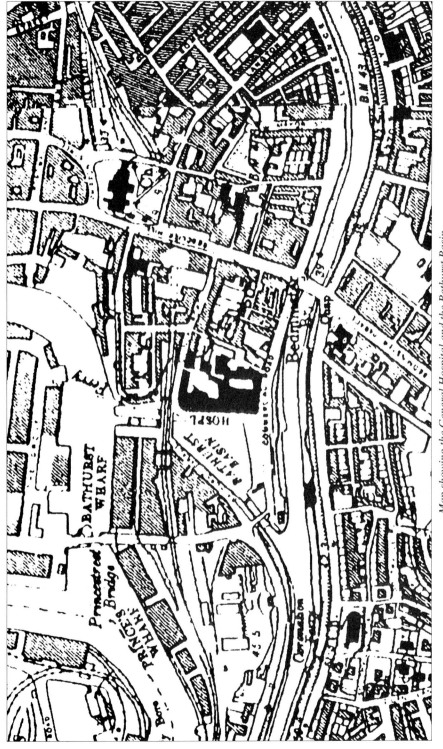

Map showing the General Hospital and the Bathurst Basin.

Then at eight o'clock, a day nurse called us to go on duty and the two of us who had beds against the window stretched out to pull the black-out curtains across. Only then would the day nurse switch the light on. As we reached for our shoes, a wave of enemy planes screamed overhead, flying extremely low. One wag had barely quipped 'I still don't think they're coming for us !', when we all heard the sickening death-whistle of a bomb falling. All except two of us, who by that time were on the way to the bathroom with towel and sponge-bag in hand, dived under the beds. The whole place shook as the bomb exploded. My companion carried on and I told her I'd follow, while our comedian poked her head out from under the bed and said 'I told you so !' Her punch line was rewarded with yet another terrifying whine, this time even nearer, and in an instant we were again under the beds. There was an almighty crash and everything began to shake violently. Suddenly, in blew the window with an awesome force, on to my bed and the bed of the nurse next to me. Splinters of glass fell in a huge shower over us, cutting the leg of my colleague, and we were enveloped by an icy rush of wind. Miraculously, my friend in the bathroom was untouched and off she went to get help. Soon, strong hands were pulling our injured work-mate from under her bed and carrying her to safety. Wardens made a way for the rest of us through the rubble and broken glass, and urged us to hurry down to the cellars, as more bombers were on their way. We heard some screaming coming from inside the wards, which remained a complete puzzle to us, having been told that everyone had been evacuated.

We soon learnt that land-mines dropped in the 'cut', an artificial waterway leading from the river Avon, had been responsible for the explosions. We had copped one that had landed opposite the hospital, about ten yards from us in the Dental Department, which opened directly on to the road. With the tide out, the bomb had hit the soft bed of the basin and part of the explosion had been cushioned. Even so, the blast had come our way, bringing tons of mud and untold damage. Incredibly, there were only three casualties – a woman patient died of a heart attack, our night nurse suffered shock and a nurse on the first floor was knocked unconscious, after being blown the length of the corridor. Her cap was found days later the other side of the building, plastered in mud !

We had no sooner reached the shelters than the electricity failed. Oil lamps we had lit had to be extinguished immediately, after a warden came rushing down to say that the main gas and water pipes had fractured. Fortunately, emergency teams were soon sealing them off but it was imperative that we get out as quickly as possible. The phones were still working and as we contemplated our plight, an urgent call came through from Temple Meads, where a stationary train had been hit. Could we take about a hundred casualties ? All the houseman could do was give them the name of the Medical Co-ordinator, for we were in no fit state to do anything.

Devastation in Wine Street after a German raid.
(Photograph courtesy Bristol Record Office).

All of us who were still 'in training' were called to Matron for a brief announcement. We were to take two days off once the evacuation of patients had been completed, during which time we had a decision to make. We could stay with the General, moving from one institution to another, apply to hospitals in safer areas or alternatively stay at home until the end of the war.

The seriously ill patients were the last to be moved and my tracheotomy man was given a quiet area, away from all the bustle. With the candles I was provided next to his bed and his pillow propped up against a stone wall, he remained cheerful and uncomplaining. We were fortunate in having the huge tank as a water supply but had to go easy on its use. The pressure was low in the sterilizing units but these weren't in such great demand. During the night, the house-keeping sister surprised us all with a wonderful meal of tough meat and cabbage in a bowl of boiling hot water. Matron had been plying us with barley-sugar sweets, but this was a savoury treat ! By early morning, my friend Helen Hesketh was accompanying some of the patients to the Royal Infirmary. After evacuation

219

was complete, I suddenly remembered the knitting that I had left on the window sill above my bed and somehow managed to find it amongst all the debris ! Then I changed and left for home.

Normally, the journey to Temple Meads was quick and easy. Not so this time. As I carefully picked my way through the rubble, moving from one smouldering mound to the next, I thought the soles of my shoes would burn through. It seemed as if there were no buildings left. Evidence of the previous night's onslaught was even more shocking at the station. How anything was running I'll never know, but I was directed to the South Wales platform and told to get on the first train that got in. This I did, opening a compartment door, only to quickly slam it shut again. It was jam-packed with soldiers, some sitting, some standing, all of them sound asleep ! I managed to find a place in a corridor at the front of the train, sat on my case and dropped off myself. I leapt to my feet after a vague shout of 'Cardiff, Cardiff !' drifted into my subconscious but I needn't have worried. The train was carrying on westwards and the next stop would be Swansea. There, I was to see more damage than I had seen before. Buses were still running up the valley, however, and I eventually reached home and my overjoyed parents. My appearance caused them some concern and I was made to rest before giving them all the news.

They didn't like the idea of my returning to Bristol and were relieved when I explained that I would be sent to either Weston-super-Mare, Winford or St. Monica's Home of Rest on the Downs. Next day, Sunday, I slept very late, before visiting Mr Bisgrove who was pleased to hear about our visit to Huntspill. Then on to Marjorie, who was so weak that I didn't stay for long. Her smiling eyes followed me as I closed her door and Mrs Reeves thanked me for coming. There was nothing more to say.

The next day we were all up early. The Swansea to Bristol train was delayed and I arrived at one o'clock, two hours late for duty. However, some nurses returned later than me and others didn't show at all. A few had already been allocated places and Matron was deciding our fate, when a porter from the Eye Hospital arrived offering accommodation for two or three nurses. Matron had no hesitation and before long, several of us were sharing a taxi, being dropped off at various venues around the city. I dropped my case off at the Eye Hospital, before the driver kindly took me to the gates of Bethany. Vivien had by this time taken in a BBC evacuee but wouldn't hear of me staying anywhere else, and Matron was agreeable. Back then to the General to help with the cleaning up, with nothing to eat but Matron's legendary sweets. The cold was so piercing that working with our winter coats on top of our uniforms made little difference. At four o'clock we were given leave to go and I found that walking was much quicker than going by taxi. The recurrence of the awful pain in the side of my face stopped me from sleeping that night and in the morning Vivien wouldn't let me go to work. It was impossible to get a message through to the hospital until late afternoon, however, as only one phone line was working. The following day I was fine and to my amazement found that we were going to take patients again – to be nursed in the cellars – and that I would be on night duty !

We had finished all the routine work by about ten-thirty and with very little to do, I realised that I no longer had my knitting to turn to. The two pullovers I had left at home, my mother having promised to sew up the sides and sleeves and send Jack's back to me when it was finished. Down there in the cellars, it suddenly dawned on us that in ten days it would be Christmas ! Next morning, a few of us scoured Bristol for cards and I immediately sent one to Jack who was back in Kidderminster. The Baxter Young People's Group was intending to go carol singing around town to raise money for civilian victims. We in the General were doing the same sort of thing to help the homeless in the parish of St. Mary Redcliffe. Post was getting through despite the raids and that Christmas the most precious card received, enclosing a Postal Order, was from Marjorie, written in her own hand. I also heard from Muriel, Ronnie telling me all about Borneo and Jack, who sent me a beautiful brush and comb set 'to go with my long hair !'

Christmas 1940 – my Third Year Bows !

By that Christmas of 1940, many im-
provements had been made to the cellars
in terms of cooking, lighting and heating facilities and we were ready for any
eventuality. On the night of December
17th, Matron gave me the best Christmas
present I could have wished for, telling
me that I could put on my Third Year
Bows. The following Sunday Helen
came back from the Infirmary, over
the moon because she and Chris were
engaged to be married. The sad thing
was that her father was refusing to have
anything to do with him because he was
a Conscientious Objector.

That Christmas Day was the strangest
that any of us had experienced, opening
presents in the Nurses' Home, sleeping
in the recently patched-up Dental Depart-

Eileen's 'Third Year Bows'.

221

ment and working down in the cellars at night! However, from six o'clock on Boxing Day morning I was off on my two days' leave! The train took almost twelve hours to reach Kidderminster, poor Jack meeting train after train, until I eventually materialised. I received a right royal welcome in Ridgecroft, where amongst beautiful trimmings, we sat down to a tea of mince pies, trifle and Christmas cake. What I enjoyed most, however, was the plain bread and butter! After tea, Jack whisked me off to meet some of his friends who had congregated in Gwen and Frank's house in Blakedown. Watching their little sister soaking up the magic of Christmas helped me to forget work, air raids and the war in general. On the way home I could hardly keep my eyes open and resting my head on Jack's shoulder, I let him guide me as we whispered sweet nothings to one another.

The next evening I opened up to Jack, telling him that during those awful bombing raids I had felt that he and I should become engaged. In my heart, I knew that our lives were not just ours alone, but God's, and that in the dangerous times we were living through, we should make a deeper commitment. Jack felt the same way and facing one another under the stars, we underwent a spiritual betrothal and felt a heavenly peace. In the morning we left together before anyone was up, travelling to Birmingham where Jack had volunteered to do demolition work. In the early afternoon we said our goodbyes but this time it was different. Although sad to part, our eyes were shining and happiness

was bubbling up inside of me. When I handed in my ticket, I gave a sort of chuckle which prompted the ticket collector to smile back wickedly and say 'And don't look at me like that, either!' Then, at a crossing on the way back to the hospital, still thinking of Jack, I smiled at the policeman. He gently held me back, and with a smile and a slight bow said 'Now!' as he stopped the traffic for me to cross.

Two letters waiting for me from home shattered my happy little world. One sent on Boxing Day said that Marjorie was very ill, the other told me that she had died at mid-day on December 27th. I slumped into a chair in my chilly room and wept until my chattering teeth and shaking limbs forced me to move. I changed into my uniform, threw my

A precious photograph of Marjorie, sent to Eileen by Mr and Mrs Reeves.

mac around my shoulders, ventured into the bleak courtyard and on to Dental. With my fellow-nurses fast asleep, I felt for my bed and slid between the blankets in an effort to get warm. Just as I was beginning to do so, we were called for duty but passed a quiet night. I found it difficult penning a letter to Marjorie's family and had to put it to one side. Thinking about her short life, the pain and sorrow that she had suffered, overwhelmed me completely. Then it came to me that she wasn't really dead, that that ethereal spirit of hers was now with God and that she was at peace. Greatly comforted, I found that I could finish the letter. My parents next, giving them the news that Jack and I were officially engaged, but no ring yet ! Did they know when they'd be having the two little girls they'd agreed to foster ? A quick note to Ronnie, too, but a letter to Jack had to remain unfinished, for I was shattered.

Matron had stopped me that morning to say that she wanted me to do the rest of my night duty on the 'Gynae' wards, which would be re-opening on the Second Floor. I had no experience of Gynaecological nursing and Johnnie, who had, advised me to borrow some books from the hospital library. During a quiet period that night, I was able to browse through a couple of books that Sister Tutor had managed to secure for me. I was a little happier, therefore, when I was informed that I'd be starting straight away. That first night, there were only two patients and because no sirens sounded, I was able to study their notes and read up about their ailments.

The next morning, I changed into mufti and wandered off into the centre, my first visit since the devastating raid of November 24th. Going up Park Street, it seemed that every other building had been gutted. George's Bookshop at the top was thankfully still standing. A little further on, I saw demolition crews everywhere and thought of Jack doing similar work in Birmingham. One crew was working where the Coliseum and the Princes Theatre had, until recently, stood proud. It was so sad to think that no longer would we see ballet performed in that wonderful old theatre. Outside the University, I was told that the Great Hall had been completely destroyed, yet what I saw that morning was only a tiny fraction of the total damage. Shivering with cold, I returned to the warmth of Brights in Park Street.

There, with limited money and some coupons in my pocket, I scoured the store for any material that might catch my eye. At breakfast some of the nurses had discussed the shortage of 'undies' in the shops, others the difficulty of finding silk material to make them with. I decided it was high time to replenish my 'bottom drawer', which housed only a set of second-hand books by George Eliot ! It was in the furnishing department that I came across the prettiest curtain linen I had ever set eyes on, olive green sprinkled with dainty pink roses. I could only afford a couple of yards, but was purring with satisfaction by the time I got back.

Bomb damage to Park Street.
(Photograph courtesy Bristol Record Office).

Bombed out! Move to the Chesterfield

The New Year of 1941 came in quietly, but with a blast of cold weather. Jack wrote to say that he was waiting to hear from John Hoyland, a well-known Midland Quaker, about the kind of work available to Conscientious Objectors in the Friends Service Council. He also warned me that in 'taking him on', I might have a lot to put up with! I replied that it would be a labour of love, and I meant it. I knew we wouldn't be able to see each other for some time because our rota had gone back to the usual one night off a week. However, I was due for extra leave and together with my annual holiday, we could surely find a few days together.

My first evening off saw me heading for Bethany, where, after a lovely meal, I was looking forward to putting my head down. I had been up for twenty-four hours, after all! But then the sirens started, followed by nearby gunfire and all thoughts of an early night receded as we made for the shelter under the stairs. For three hours the bombs rained down and we dared not move, until we heard the 'all-clear' at about nine-thirty. We barely had time to draw breath, than another warning sounded, heralding a pulverising nine-hour assault on the city by a menacing plague of bombers. They came in five-minute waves, liberally sharing their deadly consignment with us. One bomb fell so near that we heard glass breaking and plaster falling. We hurriedly covered up the broken window to hide any light and had to wait until seven-thirty the next morning before we could eventually surface. There was no serious damage to the house but in the chill outside, we heard that Prince Street was ablaze. That wasn't far from the hospital !

I bid Vivien farewell and left hurriedly with Johnnie, who was on her way to the centre. We bumped into one of our probationer nurses, looking extremely distraught, her parents' home near Whiteladies Road having been destroyed. She was able to tell us that the top two floors of the General had been gutted but that all the patients had been transferred during the night to the Royal Hospital. We were loathe to leave her in such a state but had to get on. All around was devastation. The Homeopathic Hospital and Western College were both damaged. Then a strong smell of gas brought us to a massive crater from which water was gushing. We carefully negotiated it, before Johnnie showed me a hovel

A firefighter with his iced-up ladder.
(Photograph courtesy Bristol Record Office).

in which a family she knew was living. One of the little boys had been poorly and Johnnie was visiting him. The father told us that they had spent all night in a public shelter and that soldiers helping to put out the fires had been coming in at intervals because their uniforms were literally freezing on them as they became wet.

Leaving Johnnie there, I turned left along the quays to find buildings hitherto untouched completely gutted by blast or fire. The Germans must have used a combination of high explosives and incendiaries that night. On the right of the bridge I had to cross, a huge warehouse was still burning, one of its walls breaking away and hanging crazily over the water. On reaching the hospital, I stopped in my tracks. The dome had been severely damaged and the whole of the building had an unfamiliar look about it. Firemen still had their hoses playing on it. I rushed inside to find water and filth cascading down the lift shafts, staircases, through air-ducts and ceilings. There was neither gas nor electricity and I wondered how poor Matron was coping !

When I found her, little woman that she was, her bearing was that of a brave and practical General. Her first concern was that one of our firemen had been killed. High explosive bombs had gone off very near the hospital, followed by a

Icicles remain after firefighters had extinguished the fire in the Granary, Prince Street.
(Photograph courtesy Bristol Record Office).

'basket' of sixteen incendiaries right on the building. The fire had been so fierce and spread so quickly, that there was nothing anyone could do and it was almost inevitable that someone would die fighting it. She went on to suggest that for the moment I should return to stay with my friends, but that first I should pack my things. That did sound final !

After helping Matron to sort out and label the linen, curiosity got the better of me and I ran upstairs to the ground floor, then swiftly on to the first, to check the damage. In one of the wards I looked up to see two of my gynae beds dangling precariously over a jagged hole in the ceiling ! By this time the danger of smouldering timbers had passed and the hoses had been turned off. The weather was so cold that the last of the cascading water used to fight the fire, wherever it was, had frozen solid. In the lift shafts I saw the longest, most beautiful icicles I had ever seen.

My sight-seeing was interrupted by Matron, who buttonholed three of us, all third-year nurses, to help out in the Chesterfield Nursing Home. To soften the blow, she added that she was sure that we would be as good as any of the SRNs employed there ! I phoned Vivien, who had already arranged to pick up my luggage, to tell her of the change of plan and forlornly gathered together my uniform. We were given a lift to Clifton by one of the surgeons, who volunteered that the Chesterfield was one of Bristol's leading private nursing homes. Only the very rich dwelt there, paying as much as ten guineas a week. We were not impressed !

It was now early afternoon and we all hoped that we wouldn't have to make a start that day. No such luck ! Matron was short-staffed and I was sent to the first and Nurse Cobley to the ground floor, while our companion was dispatched to bed before beginning night duty. She impressed upon us that we were to consider ourselves 'State Registered' and that the patients were not to know that we had not yet taken our final exams. The work was hard and I was grateful when Vivien and Johnnie turned up a few hours later with my luggage, including my working shoes. Until then I had been teetering around in a pair of Matron's high-heels ! It was after nine o' clock before I went off duty, absolutely exhausted. I had had no sleep for forty-eight hours and very little to eat or drink. All I wanted was bed and even the sirens and furious anti-aircraft fire that night made no difference – the heavens could have fallen in as far as I was concerned ! The next morning I was told that I had slept through the most deafening air raids of the war. No bombs had dropped on Bristol itself, but the Germans had called at Weston-super-Mare, Clevedon and Portishead. The next letter from my parents told me that Swansea had also copped it that night.

My stint at the Chesterfield made me so miserable that I vowed never to do private nursing of my own volition. It wasn't all bad, one patient asking me to give a donation to Pastor Wallace for the demolition and rescue work his church was doing in the Blackboy Hill area. My day was brightened, too, by the occasional visit of a brilliant gynaecologist with whom I had worked in the General. He was one of a number of surgeons who visited and he would make a point of coming over, putting his arm around my shoulders and asking, "And how is my little nurse today ?" We continued with our Surgery lectures in the Royal Infirmary, something that would take eight weeks, provided that raids didn't interfere.

One weekend at the end of January, Jack and his mother arrived unexpectedly to visit Mrs Davies' elderly mother in Stapleton Road. Jack and I had little time together, but oh, what a lovely surprise ! As she left, his mother gave me half a dozen fresh eggs, which I took up to Vivien. Her cousin Leslie was there, all six foot three inches of him, and he insisted on walking me back to the Chesterfield. As we talked, I told him of our plans to go Youth Hostelling in the Lake District during the summer. I was taken aback when he asked immediately if he and a friend could make it a foursome but I promised to mention it to Jack. When I did, bless him, he said he didn't mind at all !

How I loved Jack and continued to miss him terribly. I wanted to tell him how my attitude to religion was changing, that I was breaking away from fundamentalism and that I needed his reassurance. I was being torn between the differing beliefs that Vivien, Johnnie and Jack held, three people that I loved dearly. Leslie didn't help, for he wasted no chance in trying to persuade me to apply to 'Emmanuel', an Evangelical Missionary College in Birkenhead, run by faith and a Mr Drysdale. Ruth was all for it but I knew it was not for me. I dreaded the day when things would come to a head !

News of a three-night bombardment of Swansea came through at the beginning of February, when the whole of the centre had been razed to the ground. However, things started to look up a fortnight later. I had just been told that I had two weeks' leave at the end of the month, when a letter came from home telling me that the two beautiful little foster girls had arrived. Also, at the end of my leave, I would be going to St. Monica's Home of Rest on the Downs, part of which had become an annexe of the General Hospital. This was a tremendous relief and may have been as a result of a chat I had had with Sister Marlowe, Deputy Matron at the General, expressing my feelings about the Chesterfield.

One afternoon, Vivien took a car-load of us to Clevedon, where an aunt of hers was living. It was a clear day and I was able to see barrage balloons above a Welsh town to the far west. Could it be Swansea ? I slept at Bethany that night and wished with all my heart that I didn't have to disagree with such a wonderful friend over her Pentecostal beliefs.

March 6th saw me heading for home, dashing for a train after a morning lecture. I was bowled over by the two little girls. Ray, aged four, had a head of golden curls and her two-year-old sister Vera dark brown curly hair. When they were safely tucked up in bed, my mother told me that they had arrived with matted hair, full of head-lice. They came from a large, happy-go-lucky family who lived in a filthy run-down shack. Both parents were irresponsible, the mother becoming pregnant time and time again and having aborted on her last pregnancy.

I had forgotten about my birthday and was delighted when I was awakened the next morning by two little voices singing 'Happy Birthday' outside the door ! They presented me with a beautiful little present and I responded by holding them in my arms one by one and

Ray on the left with little sister Vera.

*Notice the strips of plaster on the window that were supposed
to counter the force of a bomb blast.*

giving each a whopping kiss. For that day, the problems of the world were forgotten as I played with two delightful toddlers in my own home. A card arrived from Jack, enclosing a wonderful love letter and the news that I'd wanted to hear – he'd be down the following Saturday. I used that week to do as much studying as I could.

At High Street Station we hugged each other, oblivious to the world around us. The rucksack he was carrying was my present, a lovely Ladies' Bergen. The following day we learnt from Mrs Matthias that Vic's marriage was imminent and on the Monday we made for our 'Shangri-La' in the Giedd valley. Jack was keen to talk about the future, for soon he would be appearing in front of another Tribunal. He had been sent some Quaker literature, offering choices open to him should he leave the Post Office. I would have loved to have gone back with him for my last week's holiday but I was expecting an exam paper from the hospital. Annoyingly, it didn't arrive until the following Friday, the day before my return !

The day after Jack went back, I surprised myself by returning to Maesydder-wen, my old secondary school, now spanking new. I was slightly startled at the warm welcome I received, even from Miss Thomas (Llan). She asked me to her digs for an evening meal and arranged for the landlady's sixth-form son to escort me home ! I also bumped into Jackie White, who had been in the same class as me and was now studying Theology at Oxford. He had always been brainy but very pleasant. On the Thursday, a house-full of friends called, in-cluding Mrs Reeves. The crowd and chatter was too much for Ray, who dis-appeared with her little plate into the kitchen.

Back at the General I had a lovely chat with Matron, who told me that Nurse Jones (Big J) was getting married in June and wanted to know all about me and Jack. I explained that I planned to do both parts Midwifery, so that it would be at least three years before we tied the knot. She then gave me the next day and a half off before I started work in the Children's Ward at St. Monica's. On the way to Vivien's, I found Prince Street blocked off and had to go all the way back, through stricken streets, to Bridge Street. One of the places in ruins was my little wool shop ! From the centre, I went up Whiteladies Road, where demolition gangs were at work. It was good to be back in Bethany and familiar faces.

Whiteladies Road.
(Photograph courtesy Bristol Record Office).

St. Monica's

On Tuesday March 25th, I was among the first batch of nurses being greeted by Matron at St. Monica's. It was something of a miracle to find practically every one of our set there on the first floor and it felt as if we were back in PTS. We were told that on no account were we to wander about the ground floor or in the gardens, which were strictly for the residents. On Thursday there was a large intake of male patients, St. Monica's having agreed to consign one floor for the use of patients from the General. Only one of these was a boy, a little five-year-old, who was received into the Children's Ward, where Ruth and I were working. We decided to move him in with the men that night and they spoilt him rotten ! By the Saturday he had company of his own age but the two were as different as chalk and cheese. The first, Lindsay Dellacassa was quiet, rather shy and well-behaved, with a Spanish look about him. Ronald, on the other hand, was a talkative little scamp who kept telling us stories about his family. "My dad was standing on the step and a whistler came down and he died. Now we've bought a new one !" and "That Jerry knocked all our cups and saucers off the shelves and our milk jug !" Easter was approaching by the time both had been operated on and ready to go home.

On the evening of Good Friday, the sirens went at the usual time of about six o'clock and we spent the next ten hours in the shelter with the patients. The gunfire was deafening and continuous, the planes palpably low, though we didn't hear any bombs dropping. After getting the patients safely back into bed, we day nurses stole a few hours sleep ourselves. Not for long ! At eight o'clock the phone was ringing, ordering four of us back to the General to help out. We found out that bombs had rained down incessantly that night, some once again in the basin outside the hospital and there was a huge crater in Guinea Street. It took us well over an hour to find a way through the disfigured city to the hospital, where surgeons were still operating on the night's casualties. Two of us were assigned the job of putting up forty Army beds in a space on the ground floor designated as 'Blitz Wards', and with the lifts out of order, we had to carry them down two flights of stairs. Then to Casualty, packed with people carrying minor injuries. Just as numbers were beginning to thin out, two time-bombs which had not been spotted, exploded in nearby Bedminster and Knowle West, poor areas of the city. We were immediately inundated again, some people in a heart-breaking condition. At first there were no stretcher bearers, so the nurses had to carry the patients who could safely be moved, from Casualty to the wards. Conditions were appalling, the hospital having been damaged again and again, yet our Matron Robins continued in her quiet way to keep everything under control. She had already received the OBE for the work she had done during the January 3rd raid and most surely deserved another !

We stayed on at the General for a few days and Easter came and went without me even thinking about the Convention at the Mount of Olives. The return to St. Monica's was something of a respite from the chaos and horror of war, though the pain in the side of my face had returned. I remember one of Vivien's aunts praying over me up at Bethany. I felt much better the next morning, no doubt a combination of supplication and sleep !

One afternoon, returning from a trip to Westbury-on-Trym, two of us heard the lovely strains of music as we crossed the communal hall on the ground floor. Asking Sutton, the porter, what was happening, he took us to one side and asked conspiratorially if we had ever seen Sir Adrian Boult. We guessed then – the BBC Symphony Orchestra, now in Bristol, must be in the building – and the great man himself was conducting ! Risking the wrath of the authorities, we tip-toed over to the double doors dividing us from the concert hall. Very gently, we opened them enough to see the orchestra lit up by the sun pouring through the long, elegant windows. It was a privilege just to see the back of the famous conductor ! Sutton divulged that they were practising for a concert to be broadcast on the radio at four-fifteen that afternoon. Due to be on duty at half-past, I grabbed a sandwich, rushed to our sitting room and switched on the radio. I was in time to hear the delightful opening of *Fingal's Cave*, something I had last listened to cwtched up with Jack in Kidderminster. I was thrilled to hear the announcer say that the concert was coming from a Convalescent Home in the West of England and that the applause was that of the patients and Nursing Sisters !

We now had five babies to look after, ranging in age from five months to one and a half years. In the adjoining side wards were four adults. Sister-in-Charge at the time was our exceptional, if somewhat eccentric, General Hospital's Children's Ward Sister. Our newly arrived probationers from training school couldn't appreciate her qualities and she literally chased them around from the moment she came on duty to the time she went off. It was nothing for her to take each baby out of its cot, sit it on the floor, and tell the new nurses to make their cots up properly. She earned the nickname 'Day-Time Blitz', but I stuck up for her, knowing her for the good Sister she was, able to cope with anything thrown at her.

May 7th saw another heavy raid on Bristol, the Eye Hospital getting a direct hit and the Royal Infirmary 'cottage' and mortuary destroyed. Incendiaries also damaged the Chesterfield. That night I saw candelabra flares for the first time, unfolding like huge, brilliant fireworks and lighting up the sky like daylight. No wonder the Germans were making so many direct hits !

Just after Whitsun, Jack wrote to say he had been to Holt Youth Hostel with the Baxter Group and enclosed two books for me to read. Land mines had been dropped on Kidderminster for the first time but there had been no loss of life.

I was frightened. I could take any amount of danger to myself but the thought of Jack suffering was too much to bear ! I turned to God for strength and started a letter to Jack, pouring out my love and telling him how much I longed for him. It was such a desperate letter that I decided not to send it, at least for the time being. Which was just as well, for we were suddenly told that all holiday dates had been brought forward, giving us the period June 28th to July 12th. Halleluya, those were Jack's dates ! I immediately sent him a telegram and he rang me that night, telling me that the train fare to the Lake District would be his treat. Had he read my mind or what ? Only that day, we had been informed that the three guinea fee for sitting our State Finals in September was due immediately, more than I had managed to save since Christmas. This month's salary would cover the hostel fees and food, but no more. When he heard about my 'unsent' letter, he asked me to post it, saying he would love to know my innermost thoughts !

The thought of seeing him in five weeks' time gave me the impetus to revise for that last internal exam (Ear, Nose and Throat). I left all the holiday arrangements to him and for his twenty-second birthday sent a 5/- Postal Order towards a record of Beethoven's *Moonlight Sonata*. He tried phoning me that evening but I wasn't allowed to take his call, the porter, instead, delivering me a message. This caused uproar at first, until we were told that as there was only one line, it had to be kept open for hospital use only. Vivien suggested Jack phone me at her house on my day off, which he did only once – to confirm our travelling arrangements. Jack had written to Leslie, who replied that he'd be joining us after a few days, just for a short time, and on his own.

What a wonderful holiday that turned out to be ! Meeting up at Birmingham on the evening of June 28th 1941, we travelled up to Windermere by train. The first thing that hit us was the purity of the air and the incredible scenery, once the sun had shooed the early morning mist away. The terrific weight of our ruck-sacks, packed tight with tins of food, was a new experience. As were aching limbs, knees like jelly as we slithered down steep slopes, gnawing hunger and nutty rich farmhouse milk. But oh boy, was it enjoyable ! At Borrowdale Youth Hostel, we met up with two nurses from Barts' Hospital in London who were also taking their State Finals in September. We shared the same route with them for a couple of days, before being joined by Leslie. He was a great character, entering into all the fun, though we didn't realise that he had a slightly rocky heart condition. The night before we were due to climb Helvellyn, he confided in Jack and we took the climb slowly. We reached Striding Edge without trouble, where Leslie, shrouded in mist, decided to take a rest in the lee of a rock that resembled a fireside armchair. On the half-mile to the summit, we were buffeted by a gale-force wind and I could only laugh as Jack struggled to stop the wild swirling wind from snatching his oilskin cape and taking it to some foreign

Leslie joined in all the fun.

land. Soon we were both doubled up and in danger of falling off the ridge ! Jack gripped me firmly by the hand and guided me safely back.

Leslie was enjoying himself so much that he extended his time with us until we reached Grasmere, leaving on an early morning train. Only then were Jack and I able to talk properly. If he gave up his job with the Post Office he would drop from a good salary to subsistence money only, but I reassured him that I would be with him all the way. To me, the most important things were that we loved God, and loved one another. After thirteen blissful days, we returned south to Birmingham New Street. It was as much as I could do as my train drew out, not to fling open the carriage door and run back to his arms. I sank, broken-hearted, into the one and only seat in the compartment and gazed at the ruck-sack above me.

Back at St. Monica's that evening, Sister Marlowe told me that after a few nights on the Gynae ward I would be going to Weston to do theatre work, and remarked on how well and tanned I looked. As I went in search of Ruth, I bumped into another nurse who yelled out 'Baker's back !' They crowded round, wanting to know about the holiday and I felt tears welling up inside me, so great was their love. The next night, all I could think about was Jack, as from somewhere downstairs a song set to the tune of Chopin's *Tristesse* wafted up. (I think it was the theme tune for the film *Dangerous Moonlight*.) It wouldn't have taken much at that point to have given up nursing and join him, never more to part !

Weston

It was providential that I was sent so quickly down to Weston-super-Mare. Two things helped me pull myself together, the welcome I received from Mrs Harries with whom I was billeted, and the invaluable nursing experience I was being given. Theatre work at Weston was the very best available, with medical staff from many different hospitals utilising their skills. After four days of learning the ropes, I was suddenly thrown in at the deep end, as the regular theatre staff went off sick, one after the other. I not only had to 'lay up' for operations, but was also told to scrub up and assist.

We were so busy the next week that I didn't get the chance to write to Jack. However, one day an exquisite box of roses arrived from him and I proudly carried them back to my lodgings after work. I scribbled a note to him and ran out to post it; surely God knew how much we loved and longed for one another.

To my delight, two old friends arrived to work at the 'Old Sanatorium' at around the same time as me. One was Mary Gardiner from Royal Infirmary days, the other, Payne, my dear friend from the Eye Hospital! She was now working part-time with the Civil Nursing Reserve, having given up her general training in Southmead to be with her mother, who was very ill.

After some wheeling and dealing involving Theatre Sister and Matron, August Bank Holiday saw me meeting up with Jack at Cardiff station, from where we travelled to Swansea. Too late for a bus up the valley, we caught the 'Rodney train' from St. Thomas to Ystalyfera, getting home just before midnight. Home was heaven, my parents taking all the weight off our shoulders, allowing us to be relaxed and carefree. Vera and Ray were coming on beautifully and my parents looked truly contented. Jack eagerly shared the holiday photographs with everyone. I remember my father being surprised at how far we had trudged while my mother was more interested in how well we had fed ourselves! On the Monday Jack and I talked and talked, as we made our way along the Crynant Road. His application to Western College would depend on permission from the Ministry of Labour and there was still the small matter of another Tribunal awaiting him. We decided to go one step at a time.

After Bristol, work in Weston seemed strangely quiet, with the odd alert but no bombs. The shops were untouched and I was able to find a dainty piece of china for my mother's birthday. The hospital was in a beautiful location, right on the southern edge of the town's long beach. Not far away to the left was Bream Down, while the sea and Steep Holmes were directly ahead. The sunsets were beyond description and much of my swotting was done sitting in the solitude of the sands. At times I would don my swimming costume, wade into the water and relax. I still couldn't swim. The first Sunday after my little break, the tide was right out and I took the opportunity to walk up Bream Down to

Vera and Ray were coming on beautifully – in the back garden at Croesffyrdd.

pick a posy of sandy-soil flowers for Jack. I knew they wouldn't last long in the physical sense but they represented an everlasting spiritual love for the man I adored. A week later I wouldn't have been able to do it, for the area was commandeered and closed to the public.

Twice in the next few weeks I caught a train south to Highbridge to help Mary out. Poor girl, she had a kidney condition which affected her legs and work in the café was becoming increasingly difficult.

One day, I found myself on the carpet in Matron's office, apparently at the centre of a criminal investigation. It seemed that the police would be arriving any minute ! My eye caught sight of a letter on her desk in my father's distinctive handwriting and slowly I began to understand. He had written to both Matron and the Post Office, after a registered letter he had sent containing some money had gone missing. Post Office enquiries naturally led to the hospital, giving the Matron the hump. From that time on she never wasted an opportunity to show her dislike of me, but that didn't stop me from enjoying my stay. I had done nothing wrong and my parents could ill-afford to lose a single penny.

Jack, meanwhile, was having no luck either. The Principal at Western College didn't hold out much hope for him, simply advising him to continue with his Greek lessons. At the end of August, six letters from Ronnie arrived all at once, sent from Borneo during April, May and June ! He had joined the Brunei Volunteer Corps and though tension was high between the Japanese and Americans, I was not to worry. At the first sign of real trouble the Shell Oil Company would evacuate all its employees. My father reckoned that the oil fields would be destroyed before the Japanese could get their hands on them.

September arrived and our exams loomed large. Many of the General nurses were back in Bristol but after my time in theatre, I was simply transferred to the Male Medical Ward. The night before the first written exam on the 24th, I had a nightmare in which, try as I might, I found myself unable to get to the exam room in Southmead. The next morning I began to

Ronnie in the Brunei Volunteer Corps.

wonder if it had all been a terrible premonition, as the minutes ticked by and no taxi appeared. When it eventually arrived, our lady driver realised she needed petrol, but on reaching her usual garage, found it closed. In the boot she had a spare can and fed some of the petrol into the tank before setting off. Still on pins, we started to feel better as Bristol came in sight. However, on top of a hill outside the city, the taxi spluttered and came to a stop. The driver poured the rest of the petrol in but like a stubborn donkey, the engine refused to co-operate. She then took off the brake and allowed the vehicle to cruise silently down the hill, bringing about black looks from other motorists. Just as we neared the bottom, the engine decided the joke was over and suddenly came to life. Our young lady tore the rest of the way to Southmead Hospital, getting us there five minutes before our numbers were called ! Ruth and the rest of our set who had been on the look-out for us, almost fainted in relief.

A quick glance at the paper helped me relax, for the first two questions covered work I had done in the Eye Hospital and in which I was confident. The following Thursday morning, those taking their finals were summoned to the General to see Matron Robbins. For the two previous years her personal viva – a practical and oral exam – had been waived. This year she had decided to re-start it, apologising that as yet, neither gold or silver medals would be awarded.

237

She then asked those of us doing a fourth year to sign our contracts, adding that the only way these could be broken was by marriage or by payment. I was to start back on night duty at the General in a week's time and I took the opportunity to sound out Matron about holidays. I was delighted when, without hesitation, she gave me a weekend in October and two weeks over Christmas, something that in normal times would never be granted.

That afternoon I had arranged to go to see Vivien, wanting to discuss a few things that had lain heavily on my mind for some time. When I explained to her that I couldn't go along with all the beliefs as taught in the Pentecostal Church, she earnestly begged me 'not to go off the rails, not to waver and so trip others up'. The fact that she obviously thought Jack was influencing me for the worse was very hurtful. I felt obliged to tell her that listening to Jack was like breathing fresh air, whereas the Mount of Olives was stifling me spiritually. We parted as loving friends, though inevitably upset that we had to differ with one another.

A few days later I was put at ease by our Pastor, Mr Wallace, who was much more understanding and gave Jack and myself his blessing to 'find our wings and fly the nest'. I returned to hospital and Matron's exam walking on air, and still felt on a high the next day at Southmead when we did our State Practical. The custom was to go from booth to booth being questioned by surgeons, doctors and matrons on all aspects of nursing. I distinctly remember reaching one in which a matron was stationed and being shown a diagram on the wall. Strangely enough, it was of an apparatus for treatment rarely practised but I had had the good fortune to both see and use it. She informed me that her first question was whether I knew what the diagram was all about. When I replied that it was an 'ascending and descending pyleogram' she nearly fell off her chair and simply uttered, "No further questions, nurse!" Once the exam was over we all went a bit mad, dancing around and hugging one another until we dropped with exhaustion!

Before long, it was my weekend off to Kidderminster and Jack. He had wanted to see me wearing his ring and thrilled though I was, I begged him not to buy anything too expensive. He said that he'd leave the choosing to me and it's strange how things worked out. Waiting for me on my return was a letter from Mr and Mrs Harris, who I arranged to visit the next morning. On a shopping trip around Weston, she had once teased me about Jack as we passed a jeweller's shop. Knowing the owner well, she immediately took me back there, where I chose a dainty little ring of 22ct gold with a pretty cluster of diamonds, costing £5. He thoughtfully gave me a chamois leather bag to put the box into, which I could wear around my neck until such time as 'my fiancé' could put it on my finger. How proud I was of that little ring, embodying as it did the love that had grown since that weekend years ago when Jack had cycled down to Croesffyrdd.

Chapter Eighteen

THE 'EUGENE PERM'

Night duty at the General

Looking at the notice board that night, I was dismayed to find who would be working with me for the next two months. I felt ashamed of the way I felt, but it was the last name I wished to see, knowing from experience how rude, unkind and sarcastic this junior nurse could be. Authority regarded her as having a 'chip on her shoulder' but that didn't stop her from having a following of her own. Taking the report from the day staff in the dimmed light of the ward, I felt inadequate and silently prayed for help. As the dreaded moment arrived and she bounced jauntily into the ward, a miracle happened. It was as if God was telling me to let Him take over and as she approached me, a great surge of Christian love for her filled me. Before long, all barriers were down and I was hearing of her broken home, domineering mother and other painful details of her life. That stint of night duty turned out to be one of my happiest. Elizabeth, for that is what I will call her, remained a fun-loving scallywag, while becoming a fully committed Christian.

On December 1st 1941, our State Final results came out, but Matron didn't release them immediately. Apparently there had been a few failures. Later that morning, she handed us envelopes containing our individual results, by which time we knew which five had failed – all excellent nurses who didn't deserve such a fate. As I tore mine open, I felt tired and weepy. I was shaking so badly that I had to sit down and was soon overcome with a migraine that had been threatening for some time. After ringing Vivien and sending telegrams home and to Jack, I sought refuge in my bed for the rest of the day. These headaches were becoming more frequent, the only tablets that would touch them being Codeine. I began to wonder whether wearing my hair so long was partly responsible, something I had hitherto regarded as a Christian duty. Johnnie vehemently disagreed, of course, but my hair was becoming increasingly difficult to manage now that I was back in Bristol General, where facilities were now so limited.

My spirits were lifted by a letter from Jack telling me that he had time off over Christmas. I was a little surprised to hear that Muriel, his step-sister, was thinking of giving up her job in the Civil Service to do nursing. She wanted details of my own hospital and I couldn't help wondering why she would want to come to blitz-torn Bristol ! My parents had also written with news of Ronnie, who had been evacuated to Brisbane, Australia, and that they had, indeed, blown up all the oil-fields first. On December 7th, news reached us of the Japanese assault on Pearl Harbour and we wondered what would be the next twist in this cruel war. Hitler had turned his wrath on the Russian people, which meant that for the moment, at least, all was clear in the skies above us.

Jack and I had decided to buy the little girls at home a doll each for Christmas, but having no time to go down to Weston, I scoured the shops on the outskirts of Bristol. They were certainly not what I'd have chosen, but after knitting little garments for them, they looked very attractive. I travelled home five days before Christmas, my first at home for several years. Despite shortages, Croesffyrdd was better than ever, the presence of Ray and Vera adding to the joy of the occasion. On the Tuesday came a telegram from Jack saying that he would be with us on Christmas Eve and making me so happy that I was on the verge of tears again. My tendency to cry was concerning mammy and daddy, who had noticed how tired and thin I looked.

That Christmas, the first for Vera and Ray with my parents, was unforgettable. My misgivings about the dolls vanished as soon as we saw the look of rapture on their faces. They spent all day dressing and undressing them ! Our thoughts went out to Ronnie, our numerous friends in the Armed Forces or on duty in hospitals and the Friends Ambulance Units.

New Year's Eve 1941

My parents were not over-impressed to hear that Jack had arranged a romantic New Year's Eve for us in Llanmadoc Youth Hostel on the Gower. When we arrived, we found that Jack would have to sleep on the kitchen floor downstairs and I in the loft. He had to put up with people crossing crazily over him half the night, but at least he was warm. Upstairs, by the light of a candle, I slipped into my sleeping bag fully-clothed, grateful that I hadn't yet cut my hair which helped keep out the icy air. The next morning, we looked at one another ruefully and burst out laughing ! Things didn't seem so bad after the warden and his wife had cooked us a huge Welsh breakfast.

Hand in hand we walked happily along the coast and to the swishing of the sea below us in Broughton Bay, Jack gently, oh so gently, slipped our tiny ring on to my finger. From then on we were in dreamland, as we took in the wonderful sweep of Rhossili Bay before walking inland for about six miles to Fairwood Common. From here, a bus into Swansea and the train up the valley took us home, our excitement as we turned the corner to Croesffyrdd knowing no bounds. We began to race one another and fell, gasping, into the house. How happy my parents were for us as we proudly showed them the ring and how they enjoyed our tale of the previous night ! The little girls, looking on, wondered what all the fuss was about but lapped it up all the same. The remainder of New Year's Day was spent happily around the fireside, curtains drawn, blackout curtains up, secure in our own little world.

The next three days sped by. One morning, we met Glyn George, who was friendly with my friend Muriel. He looked very pale and although limping badly, having taken a nasty blow to the head when a bomb had fallen on New Street Station, Birmingham, was determined to get back to base. On our last night together, Jack and I stayed up late and I shall never forget the intensity of love that he showed as we at last whispered goodnight. It was as though he were trying to memorise every part of my face, just as I, too, wanted to memorise his. In the train to Newport the next day, we tried to envisage a future which was uncertain whichever way we looked at it. As before, we decided to leave our lives in God's hands. After we parted, I flopped back into my corner seat, feeling as if life itself had been taken away from me. Closing my eyes, I could see a triangle, God above with his two arms embracing Jack and me. I realised then that distance meant nothing and a voice seemed to say, "Let not your heart be troubled, neither let it be afraid." I prayed that Jack might be having a similar experience.

Bossy Moss

Back in hospital I came down to earth with a bump. As a fourth year nurse I could expect to be sent anywhere and everywhere. I had already done a stint in a new Casualty Receiving Station, staffed by well-trained auxiliaries such as Air Raid Wardens, Ambulance men and First Aid volunteers. We were rushed off our feet whenever there was a heavy raid, but in the slack periods in between we were considered 'fair game' by most of the men. This time I learnt that Matron was sending me, again on night duty, to St. Monica's, not in our annexe but downstairs on the ground floor with the residents. I knew that they were all retired gentlefolk of the Roman Catholic faith and gathered that I was replacing a nurse who had been seriously ill, but was otherwise given no brief.

From the outset, I realised that I had to be very careful with my senior. A most conscientious nurse, she was also a conscientious tell-tale-tit, crawling back to Matron every whip-stitch. Working there was like walking on thin ice and I very soon learnt not to trust anyone at all, glad to turn to Jack in my letters. He, in turn, was full of sanity and good humour, helping me put things into perspective. The Home's system of off-duty was its one saving grace, allowing us to save up our one night off a week until we had more than four. Then, at Matron's bidding, we were told when to take them.

On Saturday, January 10th 1942, I was able to go to Helen and Chris' beautiful wedding service. Her father was still refusing to have anything to do with his pacifist son-in-law and had already told Helen that any grandchildren would not be welcome in his house. This was the sort of prejudice Jack was experiencing from some of his colleagues in work.

The next letter from home brought me the sad news that Ray and Vera's mother had died in childbirth. Also, that Ronnie was on his way to Egypt, a country that seemed far nearer than Borneo or Australia. Jack, meanwhile, was keeping in touch with the Quakers in Birmingham and he had been so impressed with a book called *Christian Practice* that he sent me a copy. It was a challenging book and I found I could only digest a little bit of it at a time !

I had some respite from Nurse Moss when she took a week off, having accumulated the time by working solidly for eight weeks. Her replacement, 'Buggy', was a breath of fresh air. Despite being sixty, she was strong and hefty and although not as conscientious, I was far happier clearing up her muddles than being saddled with mournful, prim and strait-laced 'Mossy'. She was great with the patients and had the knack of lifting them in and out of bed easily. I missed her immediately Moss came back from her beloved Birmingham, which, she said, was colder than she'd ever known. I immediately thought of Jack shinning up and down telegraph posts. I would buy him a pair of wool mittens, the kind that left the fingers free for outside work.

At the end of the month I had a chance to see him, and was pleased to see that his mother was getting around again after a short illness. I was never as carefree in Kidderminster as I was in Croesffyrdd, mainly because unlike my parents, Mr and Mrs Davies didn't trust Jack and me. Their bedroom was directly above the sitting room and once eleven o'clock struck, we were subjected to thumps on the ceiling and shouts of 'Jack, do you know what time it is !' To give them peace of mind we always went to bed early . Jack was very busy, for besides work, he was now a lay-preacher as well as taking Greek lessons and doing A.R.P. work at night. I told him not to worry about writing 'proper' letters, that

Mr and Mrs Davies out the back at 'Ridgecroft'.

242

Jack in his Post Office van.

three little words posted once a week would do very nicely ! His engagement ring was giving me moral support, reminding Moss that somebody, somewhere, cared for me. At Baxter Church, it was good to see Mr Hooper again and I was tickled when he put his arm around Jack's shoulders and called him 'John' ! The next morning Jack surprised me by turning up at Ridgecroft in a green Post Office van to give me a lift to the station. This was against all the rules, but he wanted to reassure me that he no longer had to use a grotty old motorcycle.

Back on Wing 1 in St. Monica's, I was chuffed at the welcome the dear old ladies gave me. Even Moss seemed pleased, though I remained wary of her tongue at all times. Shopping in Bristol the next day, I noticed that household essentials were becoming scarcer and that there may well be nothing left by the time Jack and I got married. I determined that if I saw something I liked, I would buy it and send it home for safe-keeping. Then frivolity stepped in ! I noticed a 'Polyfolo' studio which could give you a set of quick snaps of yourself at a very reasonable price. Why not ? All the other nurses were trying it out and it was a bit of fun ! I was also able to buy a Greek testament for Jack at last, after George's Bookshop had directed me to their branch at Bishopston.

In mid-February I was home again, having just finished sewing a couple of dressing gowns for Ray and Vera. Nurse Moss had shown a real interest in my mother and father becoming foster parents and gave me two expensive-looking garments that she had finished with. Could they be cut down for the little girls ? Indeed they could ! The quality of the cast-offs was outstanding and were gratefully accepted by my mother. A letter arrived from Jack, asking sheepishly for some of my measurements, as my birthday present was to be a real Campbell kilt ! Realising the amount of material needed, my mother gave me lots of clothing coupons to send him. With the bounty I had brought home with me, she felt that she could spare them.

Back in St. Monica's, I found that Moss had gone on a three week holiday and that I was to do her duties. Nurse Westall, who would be working with me, had only just come back after three months on the sick with back pain, and one of the residents we would be nursing was critically ill with complicated pneumonia. All this initially made me feel weak at the knees, but I resolved to get on with it. Miss Payne needed constant attention and we took it in turns to stay with her until half-past five in the morning, when we had to wash and change the others. Nipping back frequently to check on her, we appeared to be managing. Then, having just finished lifting and changing the bed of the last – and heaviest – resident, poor Nurse Westall collapsed ! I helped her to a chair next to Miss Payne's bed and phoned upstairs for the young General Hospital Probationer. When the Day Sister came on duty, she was initially sympathetic to my suggestion that Miss Payne required a 'special'. However, when she heard about Nurse Westall, she unleashed such a scathing attack on her that I felt I was back in the air raid shelter. There was, indeed, a special for Miss Payne the following night. Nurse Westall was there too !

Miss Payne's condition had deteriorated, and though her life hung in the balance, she never complained. Her illness was affecting the other residents, for she had always pottered around doing little things for them. With everyone praying for her, she continued to be critically ill for three days and nights, before suffering a heart attack on the Saturday. Even so, she rallied. At night, it was I who was mainly responsible for her, but I couldn't have nursed her without God's help. On the following Friday she showed slight improvement and by the time Mossy arrived back, we were able to lift her out of bed. That was a real red-letter day !

Nurse Westall and I soon got to know each other. She was a committed Christian and a lovely girl but I began to realise that she had a terrible inferiority complex, which threatened to overwhelm her at times. One morning, I could hear some beautiful music coming from the ground floor and on investigation, found Westall at the piano. She told me that she had trained as a concert pianist but that her nerves had let her down. She had been playing her own composition. What a waste of talent !

For my birthday I had received some postal orders from home and wondered whether I should risk the new 'Eugene Perm' my friends had been talking about. Making enquiries at a reputable hairdresser, the new-fangled apparatus hanging down from the ceiling immediately unnerved me. I was reassured when shown photographs of some of the wonderful results and made an appointment for the next morning. I nearly backed out, but eventually entered the shop with the words of a friend ringing in my ears, "It's not like the dentist, you know !"

But it was, only far worse ! The hairdresser didn't help when, having noticed my engagement ring, she asked if 'he' knew I was having my lovely long hair cut. When I heard my beautiful plait fall heavily to the floor, my heart fell with it, and I fairly screamed at the girl to put it to one side it for me. Then started the painful process of mutilating my hair by encaging it in myriads of curlers, before stringing them up to the electric gadget on the ceiling. When the whole process was over, I looked in the mirror at a sorry stranger with a sore scalp and tight frizzy curls. What had I done ? I thought of Jack. Solid, sensible, adorable Jack, the man I was growing to love more and more every day. What would he think of me ? I had already mooted the idea of a hair cut but in his reply he hadn't even mentioned it. If he could see me now ! I rushed back to my room in St. Monica's and brushed and brushed my hair as if my life depended on it. 'Button' – one of my friends – gave me an almighty row, saying that I should have left it for at least twenty-four hours, and appalled that I had wasted my hard-earned pennies. I didn't mind. A lot of the frizziness had disappeared !

Jack had arranged for us to spend the last week of March youth-hostelling in the Ludlow area. I was very relieved that first evening to find that everyone at Ridgecroft liked my new hairstyle and things got even better when Jack presented me with my kilt. It was like having a second engagement ring and Jack jokingly told me that as his 'affianced' wife, I was entitled to wear the Campbell tartan ! Not only was I proud to don it, but it was like having a warm, snug blanket wrapped around me.

Fortunately the weather was kind to us, and by mid-day we were able to stack out, returning each evening to the magnificent Wilderhope Manor Youth Hostel and a lovely meal. In the main hall, where a huge fire spread its welcoming glow, Jack brought me up to date with Mr Hooper's endeavours with the Ministry of Labour. Unfortunately, its directive had mirrored that of the Tribunal – Jack was to unconditionally remain in the Post Office Engineering Department for the duration of the war. It seemed that all hope of entering Western College the following September had been dashed. Off his own bat, Jack continued to explore avenues of service with the Quakers, for he was now very concerned that his work was bringing him into direct contact with wartime technology. If he left, it would mean severe financial hardship, something that worried my father, but at least he could see that we were supremely happy together. With Easter only a week away, I could look forward to Jack coming down to Bristol.

Shortly after this, I bumped into Rev. Sutton, who had been a patient on Artisan Ward some years previously and was now an out-patient with suspected TB of the lungs. He was anxious to catch up on all my news and advised that whatever Jack and I decided to do, we must be certain about it. Jack, meanwhile, was getting stick off his stepfather, not only about giving up a good job,

Eileen in her 'Campbell' kilt.

but about the expense of coming down to see me. That made my blood boil, for I knew that Jack gave his mother a generous contribution towards board and lodge and did all the housework on the weekends. He neither smoked nor drank, whereas Mr Davies was a chain-smoker. I felt that he was entitled to spend a little of his money on me. Nevertheless, still feeling a little sore about it all, I suggested that the next time we met should be in Birmingham, and just for one day. This is what we did, despite me having three nights off, and apart from a mid-day snack, we simply walked and talked. My train left early but seemed to stop everywhere, and it was after midnight before I got back to St. Monica's. Of all the people I had to report to, it had to be Nurse Moss. Fixing me with eyes of stone she said icily, "You are very late Nurse Baker !" She didn't intimidate me. I returned her stare and threw down the challenge.

"I'm very sorry, but it wasn't me driving the train !" She could make of that whatever she wished.

The next morning we heard that there had been raids on Bath and Bristol. The General had taken casualties and some of those who had lost their homes were being housed upstairs, here in St. Monica's ! A letter arrived from home, enclosing one from Ronnie. He had left Effie behind in Adelaide, 'the young nurse', he had written to my parents, 'who might have become your daughter-in-law'. Poor Ronnie, how I felt for him. He was now in Ras Gharib, Egypt, working in the Anglo Egyptian oilfields.

In April I met a very gracious lady the Quakers had put me in touch with. Realising our predicament and after looking at all the options, she suggested that I go on to do Midwifery. By the time I finished (the training was in two parts and would take a year and a half), the way forward for Jack might have become clearer. I had, by this time, written both to Selly Oak Hospital and to the Birmingham Municipal Hospital for details of their courses, which were likely to start in December.

It was May 10th before Jack and I met up again. At short notice, Matron granted me time off for an interview Jack had arranged in Birmingham with Miss Backhouse, Missionary Secretary of the Society of Friends. She was a lovely woman, admiring Jack's stand and making us feel of worth. After a searching interview, she told us that as yet she didn't feel we knew enough about the principles of the Society of Friends. She begged us not to lose heart but Jack had now tried all avenues for serving God overseas. All had closed in his face. As a gesture of defiance, we decided that once I had finished my Midwifery course, we would get married. The world could throw anything it liked at us, we would meet it together !

The next morning, I accompanied Jack to a little Congregational church in the country outside Kidderminster, in which he was officiating. I was not to be disappointed. The service was well prepared and I felt his preaching, considering all he was going through, was inspired. After lunch we took a walk and discussed our marriage in an open and relaxed atmosphere.

On my return, I was greeted by the sad news that a Dutch nurse who had come to work with us on Wing 1 had attempted suicide the day before. One of my friends, who had asked her if she had wanted to go for a walk, felt that she had something heavy on her mind. When she didn't return that night, the staff became worried and alerted the police, who found her body in the river in the Bedminster area. Unconscious but still alive, she was taken to the Royal Infirmary and though very poorly, eventually came round. I didn't see her again, because I was suddenly put on district work for a month, visiting all known TB patients in the Knowle and Bedminster areas. It was a new experience which I thoroughly enjoyed, despite witnessing the obvious distress caused by the disease.

247

Patients in the 'TB' block at the General Hospital, pre-war.
Eileen's friend, Nurse Hesketh, is on the right.

My annual leave was now due, and on June 13th I was at Newport station, waiting for Jack. What a thrill, three quarters of an hour later, to see his train slowly chugging in and to be sitting hand in hand on the next train to Swansea. The first thing I wanted to tell him about was the night before, when, with my stint in St. Monica's over, I had bid a fond farewell to all the residents. Going round, dear Miss Biggs had told me to give my 'young man' her love, but the best had come at the very last, when I had entered roguish Miss Barridge's room. She would often listen to the radio with earphones on and shout out things such as 'Rubbish !' or 'I don't agree with that !' Slightly deaf, she always spoke loudly and as I was about to go, she piped up with, "Goodnight my dear, lucky man who gets you !" When I teasingly asked her why, she wagged her finger at me.

"Ah, now you're fishing for compliments – when are you two getting married ?" She couldn't understand why we had to wait another two years and as I left her and drew the screen across her door, I was slightly disconcerted to hear her repeating herself, like a demented parrot.

"Ah yes, lucky man who gets her. Ah yes, lucky man, lucky man !"

Relating this to Jack, I felt very self-conscious, but he enjoyed every moment. For his part, he had made a provisional timetable for our two weeks together, which included a few days camping. As we had discussed the idea many times, I had already bought a small lightweight tent for myself in Weston.

Chapter Nineteen

SUMMER 1942

Time with Jack

What excitement there was when we arrived home ! Ray and Vera climbed all over us and couldn't wait to tell Jack about his special birthday cake. Later, with the little ones in bed, we were able to discuss the future with my parents. Our health and happiness was their main concern and they accepted Jack's views on the war. I could now tell them that I would be leaving Bristol General in December and they were pleased that I'd taken their advice to do Midwifery. Their eyes sparkled when they heard that we had fixed a date for the wedding, which we hoped would take place in Ystalyfera Congregational Church. We spent most of Sunday at home, playing with Ray and Vera and listening to all my parents' news. It came as something of a shock to learn that Vic Mathias and his wife had had a baby girl, Marita, born six days earlier. In the evening we went down to congratulate the grandparents, only to find that Mrs Mathias was helping to look after mother and baby !

The next morning, Jack and I went to Pembrey to see my dear little grand-mother. We found her swilling her face with cold water in the backyard of Uncle Walter's cottage. Taken by surprise, at first she didn't know me, but when I introduced myself, she was overjoyed. From her tiny height, she scrutinised Jack and then gave her approval ! He was then introduced to Uncle Walter, daddy's brother, Gladys his wife, his sister, Auntie Fanny and her husband Dick Simcocks. I was so glad that Jack had met my grandmother, for she died shortly afterwards.

More fresh air the next day, when we climbed the Darren and stretched out for hours in the sun. Up there on our own, with only the soft breeze to keep us company, the troubles of the world couldn't touch us. We were back in time to put Ray and Vera in the bath, something they revelled in, for it meant that they had longer in the tub and could splash us to their hearts' content ! That night we told them lots of bedtime stories before teaching them the prayer 'Jesus, gentle shepherd hear me, bless thy little lamb tonight'. A goodnight kiss, then, before coming downstairs to pack for our next adventure.

Our plan was to camp for two nights high up in the Giedd valley, before moving on to Ty'n-y-cae Youth Hostel near Brecon. Feeling very fit and happy

*At Pembrey. From left to right – Grandpa Baker, Uncle Dick, Auntie Fanny, Auntie Emma,
Eileen's mother, Nanna Baker. Ray and Vera are standing at the front.*

and with the promise of fine weather for some days to come, we sought out Mr
Brown who owned the land through which the river Giedd flowed. He was
more than willing to let us camp and we made for our 'Shangri-La' to pitch
tents, before a leisurely six-mile hike to the river's bubbly source. We fell on to
the little fountain, eager to quench our thirst, before stretching out on the moor
land. It was eerily quiet and I was glad when, remembering the fiasco of our
first venture into camping, we started to laugh. It had been a few years back, on
a flat piece of ground near our little haven, where we had pitched our tents,
mine borrowed from Jack's step-sister Muriel. Sitting down to eat, we had been
joined by an army of ants and with storm clouds gathering, decided to move on.
I had a splitting headache and, of course, had forgotten to bring any tablets with
me. Suddenly startled by claps of thunder and flashes of lightning higher up the
valley, Jack had suggested that we move our tents to the top of the ridge. This
turned out to be a sensible move, for the little river soon became a raging torrent, but in hindsight we should have packed up there and then. Having decided
to stick it out, I felt the need to lay down in my tent, but no sooner had I done
so than the heavens opened, quickly finding scores of little leaks in the canvas.
The two of us then sheltered in Jack's tent until a lull in the storm had allowed
us to quickly pack up and trudge the four miles home !

This time it was different and that evening, comfortable in our little tents, we
were soon fast asleep. I woke next morning to the sound of Jack brewing up on
his tiny Primus stove. He had already been for a swim in the long pool and was

still in his swimming shorts. After a little banter, I scampered away for a wash and couldn't resist making for a beautiful flat stone in the middle of the stream. In no time at all, I was flat on my back, having somersaulted on its slippery surface, and was being carried rapidly downstream ! The strong current would soon deposit me in the deep pool and I screamed for Jack, knowing that I was already out of my depth. I somehow remembered Nurse Beynon's lessons at Hotwells and kept my mouth shut and arms by my side. Vivid scenes from my childhood with my loving parents and brother Ronnie flashed through my mind, before I felt my hair being clenched and strong arms lifting me out of the water. Jack planted me face downwards on the bank and once he knew I was all right, shepherded me back to our campsite. After digging out the lightweight woolly from my rucksack and wearing Jack's old shorts, I began to feel wonderfully cosy and warm. Jack thought that my plight was worthy of a photograph and snapped me with his camera.

Eileen smiles after her terrifying ordeal in the water.

After I had fully recovered, Jack tentatively asked me if I wanted to go on to Ty'n-y-cae as planned. He had warned me that his proposed route wouldn't be easy but I had no intention of giving up and had every confidence in his map reading. It was difficult, every inch of it, but the scenery was wonderful. Following a sheep track through Bwlch-y-Giedd, we could see the Giedd valley to the south, while below us to the north lay the shimmering Llyn-y-Fan Fawr, steeped in ancient Welsh legend. We picked our way very carefully down to it, past some standing stones, before crossing more rough terrain and eventually hitting the main Llandovery – Brecon road. When a bus came along, we stopped it, grateful to let it take us the six miles to Brecon. My feet had often ached when on duty in hospital, but never so much as that day, and I was glad when I could take my shoes off. The next day, we made our way home via bus and Shank's pony, past Cray Reservoir and the upper reaches of the Tawe valley.

The next morning we were off again, this time hoping to find the source of the Gwred river ! We followed it for miles, through the maze above the falls and across a bog at the top of Alltygrug hill, until we found a clear, twinkling little stream. Higher up again, it disappeared into the mountain called Penlle'r-fedwyn and we found ourselves in a veritable paradise, over 1,000 feet above sea level, opposite our very own Darren.

We had discussed a family trip to Mumbles and on the Saturday set off for Ystalyfera station, little Vera on Jack's shoulders. After a brief word with my father, who was working, we were on our way to Rutland Street, terminus for the Mumbles train. All tiredness disappeared as if by magic, as Ray and Vera excitedly clambered aboard. After exploring all the wonderful things Mumbles had to offer, including the pier, and buying a little present for my father – a family tradition – we made for Bracelet Bay. Here, Ray and Vera delighted in the little rock pools just as much as Ronnie and I had ever done. Back home, my father was wonderful with them, listening quietly as they presented him with shells and pebbles and babbled on about the big red train. No-one needed rocking to sleep that night !

Sunday was spent quietly, going to church and visiting neighbours. Mr Bisgrove was suffering with leg ulcers and had had another attack of recurrent malaise, but was determined to get well enough to join Mary in Highbridge. The next morning we set off for our 'Shangri-La' again. By the time my mother had insisted we take an extra blanket each and loaded us with tins of food, we looked like a pair of pack horses ! Words cannot describe those moments in the Giedd valley, three days of near perfection that will for ever be etched on my memory. The fact that we arrived home looking so tanned and fit made it easier for my parents to wave us off the next day. Parting at Newport station was a terrible wrench, nevertheless, and as I waited for the Bristol train I penned these words to Jack:

> "Jack darling – oh, how I miss you. Forgive me please for being such a baby, but oh, darling, when you've gone from me everything else seems to have too. My darling, I love you – but you must be feeling as bad. In everything but this body, which now feels like an empty shell, I am with you darling, right there by your side as you travel up home. God bless you and be with you, my darling, my Jack, my love – oh, it seems – my very life."

I quote those very intimate words because they illustrate the depths of love that we felt for one another.

The hustle and bustle of hospital life helped me cope with the anguish that I felt. I was now responsible for Sister's holiday duties, one of which gave me quite a jolt ! I had to write confidential reports on the nurses in my charge, each one having a little red book that was kept under lock and key. All kinds of information was collated, under such headings as 'prompt on duty ?', 'late on duty ?', or 'eager to get off duty ?'. It suddenly dawned on me that there was a book with my name on it and likely to be another one when I started Midwifery ! Off duty, in the quiet of my room, I could see again those Welsh hills, hear the bleating of sheep and the gushing river at our 'Shangri-La'. The overwhelming silence higher up the valley. See Jack swimming in the deep pool and as he dried, lying beside him in the sun, feel the hairs on his chest and arms. Most of all I could recall the intensity of his gaze as he lovingly wrapped his strong arms around me.

On the night of June 29th, Weston-super-Mare was bombed and fifteen of our nurses sent down to help with casualties. Leslie's mother, who up to that point had lived a quiet life in Weston, was hurriedly moved up to Bristol where she became another of Vivien's guests !

Jack's grandmother and Auntie Ada.

Later that summer I met Jack's grandmother for the first time, joining Jack's mother and Muriel who were visiting her at her home in Staple Hill. She was a very regal-looking lady, being looked after by Jack's Auntie Ada. Mrs Davies told me that Jack was putting a lot of time in at a Youth Club in the little church outside Kidderminster. I knew that he was hoping to take a few of them camping over the August Bank Holiday, but unfortunately I would be working. She also gave me the news that his close friend Chick, a Desert Rat, had been

Chick serving in the Army.

taken prisoner in Tobruk and that another friend was serving in the Far East. This would have a deep effect on Jack.

For the next few months, Ruth and I continued on day duty in the General, occupying rooms opposite one another in the Staff Nurses' and Sisters' Quarters. How different they were from the poky little boxes allocated to the nurses in training ! One day I was out on a shopping expedition with Vivien and her friend, when they turned into Jolly's at the top of Park Street, which was functioning despite bomb damage. I knew it as an expensive place and sheepishly followed at a safe distance, having never ventured inside this lovely shop before. Vivien needed sheets and made straight for the bedroom furnishings and this is where I noticed some beautiful open-weave all wool blankets for £3 9/6d each. I had no money on me, but with the end of the month upon us, asked one of the assistants how many they had in stock. Vivien, as alert as ever, heard what was going on.

"My darling, I have an account here. Get the blanket straight away and pay me back whenever you can !" She then took me to one side and quietly made me promise that if I saw anything Jack and I needed for our future home in either Jolly's or Bright's, to go ahead and buy it on her account and settle up later. She added that times were such that you had to try and buy essentials as soon as you saw them. I could have hugged her on the spot and with that lovely soft blanket under my arm, walked on air for the rest of the afternoon ! Need-less to say, I cleared my debt as soon as I was paid and also returned to the shop to buy a summer raincoat. It was the latest in fashion and I'd seen my mother admiring it in a store in Swansea. This would be her birthday present.

The weekend after Bank Holiday, I had arranged to go to Kidderminster. Friday arrived and I began to get excited. I was doing 'Sister's duties' on Artisan Ward at the time, where some of the patients, mainly TB cases, were nursed out on the balcony during the day. We had just pushed them out when the sirens sounded and with German planes pulsing over us, made a hasty retreat. We waited anxiously to see whether we had to move down to the shelters, but no message came, and we were serving lunches when the 'all-clear' was given. Once again we pushed our balcony patients outside into the sunshine, pulling down huge heavy blinds to protect their eyes. By the time that I went off duty, my back was aching so much that I wondered if I'd ever make it to Temple Meads. It became worse in the train and was so foreign to me that I wasn't sure how I was going to face Jack. Just seeing him on the station, however, made me feel better and he whisked me away to his Youth Club. There I met some real little characters, very curious to know all about their leader's girlfriend.

"Yer a nurse, then, Miss ?"

"Where do you work, Missus ?"

"Bristol ? Cor . . . have you ever been bombed Miss ?"

Soon, I was laughing so much that I forgot about my aches and pains. It was obvious that they were going to watch me very closely over the next two days – Jack had arranged a weekend in Abberley valley for us all, camping out for one night.

The next morning, Jack and I made for the Youth Club where the little 'tykes' had assembled. They greeted Jack by relieving him of his rucksack and slinging it into a large donkey cart, on top of a big pile of assorted clobber. It was sheer magic, as the boys took it in turns to pull the cart, chattering and joking all the time. They soon put pay to my jaded condition and somewhat recklessly, I volunteered to do the cooking. Having chosen their spot in the valley, they all worked like beavers, some pitching the tents, others gathering wood for the fire, which crackled merrily amidst the hurly-burly. The Billy can supplied us with a cup of tea and the cooking was easier than I had anticipated. There was no arguing, they all wanted their favourite sausage and beans ! Before long, we were squatting in a circle around the fire, wolfing down layer upon layer of bread, mopping up the meal. If there were any high jinks during the night, I was unaware of them, for I was out for the count as soon as my head hit the pillow. The next morning we were joined by Cliff and Muriel, but it was all too soon before I had to get back to Bristol, catching the last possible train. It had been a delightful weekend !

Jack and his little 'tykes'.

A letter was waiting for me from the Sorrento Maternity Home in Moseley, asking me to present myself for interview on September 2nd. Things were moving at last – and I was glad. After a most gruelling panel interview, the Matron told me that I had been accepted for training, pending a satisfactory medical report. In utter relief, I fell into Jack's arms, feeling certain that this would be the last lap before our wedding day. The letter of confirmation offered me a place on December 14th, two weeks before I officially completed my fourth year in the General. My request to leave early had to go in front of the Hospital's Committee and I later found out that a Mr Cox, who attended the Mount of Olives, had spoken up for me and swayed the result in my favour !

At the beginning of October that year, I experienced the rustlings of a wind of change. I was walking back through the Autumn black-out after a meeting at the Mount of Olives when I saw crowds of American troops pouring out of the

Colston Hall. Most were arm-in-arm with a girl and all were in high spirits. Laughing and smoking, they jostled their way casually through the traffic that was emerging out of the thickening fog. Turning right for my short cut through the docks, I wondered if things would ever be the same again and wished that Jack could have witnessed the sight.

Sad farewell to Matron Robins

Funnily enough, it coincided with our Matron Robins leaving. During the last few months, Ruth and I had been moved around like pieces on a chessboard and I was thankful when I was able to settle at last on the Skin Wards, to see out my time. One day, we were on our way to one of Canon Swann's Bible Study sessions in the hospital chapel, when we met Matron in one of the corridors. She conveyed to us her heartfelt gratitude for co-operating with her at all times, shrugging off our thanks for her kindness towards us. She told us that she would always be interested in us. It wasn't as if she was going to the other side of the world – in fact, she was planning a party for all her staff the minute the war ended ! Besides speaking to all of us personally, she left a letter – her wish was to leave unobtrusively – which was pinned up on the notice board, and it was then that we realised just how much she had meant to us. That was on October 8th and a few days later, one of our group, beautiful, bouncy Button, left for the Army. She would soon make an impact, I felt sure !

My next few days of leave was spent up in Kidderminster where, with Jack working part-time, I was able to read a couple of books. I was aware, however, that Mr and Mrs Davies were continually carping at one-another. Muriel was about to start in the Civil Nursing Reserve at the local cottage hospital before committing herself to full nursing training in Birmingham.

Back at the General, I met some very courageous people. Our skin specialists were doing all they could, but in 1942 the outlook for many patients was grim. That autumn there was a lot of sickness about, even hitting Vivien's normally bustling household. So much so, that on one visit Vivien was glad when I volunteered to help out. Instead of telling me to sit down and rest, I was given an apron, before washing dishes, preparing vegetables and laying the table ! When Leslie knew that I was soon to leave for the Midlands, he insisted on giving me the address of a Baptist church in Birmingham and offered his local knowledge if ever I needed it.

From home came the news that Vera had celebrated her fourth birthday (which I had forgotten !) and was about to start school and that Ray was on the waiting list at Swansea Hospital to have her tonsils and adenoids removed. I would have loved to have been able to get back home to be with her, for she had to endure the same barbaric treatment that we had practised until recently in the General. I had written to Ronnie in Egypt, explaining that Jack and I hoped to marry early in 1944 and asking if he could be our best man. Unfortunately, he couldn't get back until the end of the war and even then he'd have to sign another contract with his company. He added that by the time he next saw us, we may even have a little family !

With my date of leaving fast approaching, I began to realise how much stuff I had accumulated along the way. I sent all my textbooks on to Jack, confident that everything else would fit into one trunk. With a week to go, I was suddenly taken off Skin Wards and put on night duty in the ENT Children's Ward. With no warning, I found myself having to change rooms and forego time off. I wasn't able to sleep and felt wretched ! That all changed, however, when patients on the Skin Ward sent messages of love and best wishes for the future, together with a set of bolster and pillow cases of quality rarely seen in those days. I was overwhelmed when staff began to seek me out, some sisters and even doctors telling me how much they would miss me. Two patients gave me a present of their own, one hand-made, and before the week was out I rushed up to the ward to say goodbye individually to one and all.

At six o'clock on the morning of December 3rd 1942, filled with a mixture of emotions, I came off duty for the last time at Bristol General. I was catching the half-past seven train from Temple Meads and by the time that Vivien and Johnnie arrived to help with my bulging rucksack and dead-weight suitcase, I was finding it difficult to control my feelings. Ruth, too, came to wave me off. As the guard blew his whistle, Vivien, Johnnie and I hugged one-another as though we would never be able to let go. With tears in our eyes, we said our goodbyes. I can still recall that moment, the three of them waving on the platform, none of us knowing whether we'd see each other again. Oh, please God, I hoped so ! I felt so drained as I sank back into my seat, that I could only look to the loving support awaiting me at home for some crumb of comfort.

My parents were still waiting to hear from the Brecon County authorities regarding Vera and Ray's future, now that their mother had died. I knew what wonderful foster parents they were, as did the little innocents. I was a little sur-prised to hear that all four of them had received an invitation from Mr and Mrs Davies to spend Christmas in Kidderminster. They couldn't contemplate it that year because my father only had one day off (Christmas Day) and Ray was still washed-out after her operation. Although in the sanctuary of Croesffyrdd, I soon found myself missing Bristol and became restless. Unlike previous visits home, I looked for something to do all the time, washing dishes and grateful for any other jobs my mother could find me. Ray and Vera were home from school, so I spent a lot of time with them. At night I would put them to bed, read stories and say prayers with them. One evening, Vera made me laugh when, with eyes closed and hands clasped, she solemnly chanted, "Please God, make Ronnie and Jack good girls !"

Time was passing rapidly and my mind turned towards the evening of Saturday, December 12th, when I had been asked to report to the Sorrento Maternity Hospital. One day, I was relaxing with Jack's lovely letter, saying he was looking forward to seeing me on the 10th in Kidderminster, when a little question he posed sent me into the depths of despair. I'm sure he was only thinking aloud when asking whether he should stay with the Post Office and try to get into Western Theological College next year, or give up his job and join the Friends Service Council ! I thought that we'd discussed all these options several times. If he managed to go to Western, we wouldn't be able to get married for at least another four years, a prospect that nearly finished me. I felt dull in mind, absolutely despondent, more than a little fed up with Jack and unsure if I wanted to meet him ! I don't know quite what I wrote in reply, I hardly cared, yet as soon as I saw him waiting on the station, I knew everything would be all right. He assured me that I had nothing to be worried about, that come what may we would marry as soon as I had finished Midwifery. He made me promise never again to have any doubts about our marriage. I was in heaven again !

Chapter Twenty

SORRENTO MATERNITY HOSPITAL

Christmas with 'Mac'

And so to my next adventure, the Sorrento Maternity Hospital in Moseley, Birmingham, renowned for its 'Dr Cross Premature Baby Unit'. On that Sunday
morning (December 13th, 1942), I was amongst the latest intake starting duty at
half-past seven. 'Gynae' experience had already given me some insight into
Midwifery but didn't prepare me for the mind-blowing reality that I was suddenly exposed to ! By the middle of the first week I had witnessed three births,
including twins, though I was to feel the mystery and miracle of childbirth
every time. The extreme and unique pain that mothers went through was new to
me, a pain that seemed to disappear the moment the infant was born. Amazement and thrill on my part, unspeakable joy for them.

We were expected to learn quickly and were told that we would start delivering on our own, under the watchful eye of a trained midwife, once we had
witnessed eight births and assisted at two. In individual case books, we were to
write up thirty-six births we had attended and in another book, details of fifty
babies we had delivered or had witnessed coming into the world. The lectures –
more than I had expected – always took place in our off-duty time and I found
myself in an amphitheatre in Birmingham University on most Saturday mornings. Together with medical students and nurses from many other hospitals,
there was so much to learn.

I shared a room with McHugh, a beautiful Irish nurse with large blue eyes
and dark hair. I called her 'Mac' and she called me Baker. Her soft lilt was music
to the ears and she was always laughing. She, too, was engaged to be married
and we became good friends.

A week after leaving home, I received a parcel containing a small, but substantial Christmas cake. It didn't seem like Christmas at all, with a lecture
scheduled for Christmas Eve and another on Boxing Day. After that, if I was
lucky, I might get a half-day off, and in desperation slipped out to nearby
Moseley shopping centre to buy a few, very ordinary presents. I told Jack that
the balaclava would come in useful if he remained in the Post Office or ended
up in the wilds of Tibet ! For his mother I bought a green silk scarf and a
handkerchief for Mr Davies and Muriel. I didn't have a clue when I would get

260

'Mac'.

them over to Kidderminster. Our official Christmas dinner was on the 28th, when we were allowed to wear mufti, taking it in turns to relieve others on duty in the wards later on. I'm sure the patients were surprised to see us in our glad rags ! The night before that, however, four of us had organised a feast in our room. Jack had turned up on Boxing Day with a tuck box which he had had to leave with the porter. (I wasn't even allowed to see him which I thought was really mean !) Later that day an offering arrived from home, this time a large leg of cooked chicken, a portion of chicken breast with stuffing, as well as a quarter of a pound of butter ! After church, Elliott and I prepared everything, drawing both beds as near as possible to the gas fire with the food spread out on one, leaving the other free to sit on. By the time Mac and Leeson came off duty at eight-thirty, everything looked cosy and the kettle was boiling on the little gas ring. The feast was sealed with half a pear each and a piece of Jack's chocolate. Four replete, happy and very sleepy prospective midwives then spread out on their beds, incapable of delivering a word, let alone a baby !

Not until the first week of 1943 did I have a half day off, when I was able to pop over to see Jack. It had been two years since we had decided to get married, a year since he had put his ring on my finger. Would another year actually see us married ? By the time I saw him again two weeks later, I had delivered three babies on my own, on the first occasion having to stay up through the night.

After a few hours sleep I was delivering again, this time a much quicker period of labour. With only a couple of hours off in the afternoon, I reported for duty that Friday evening and just as I was about to finish, was told to stay on – another mother had started her labour. I delivered the baby at a quarter to two and later that morning I would be up again, this time for a lecture. By the time I met Jack in the afternoon, I was on my knees !

The training I had embarked upon was as complex and queer as any nursing could be. Matron had warned us that it would be tough, but I was enjoying it. The practical side was demanding but we also had to know the rules pertaining to Midwifery inside-out. I was abruptly put on night duty until the end of January, during which time I delivered seven more babies. In a little over a month I was well on the way to the required number for the first part of our training. I remember attending Carr's Lane Congregational Church one Sunday morning, having heard such a lot about it. During the sermon I kept nodding off, then suddenly jerking awake. I could hear the drone of the minister's voice while babies' heads kept appearing in front of me, all wet and beautiful. It was lucky I was sitting at the back !

I was not put on any more cases until May. We soon learnt that Matron was a local magistrate with a particular interest in 'fallen girls'. Mac and I were convinced that she eyed us with a certain amount of suspicion, having got ourselves near enough to a man to get ourselves engaged ! She was in our view a bit of a Martinet, but having to continually guide raw cadets, ten at a time, through a gruelling nine months of training, I suppose she had to be.

I celebrated my twenty-fourth birthday with Jack in Kidderminster. When he crept in, bright and early, with a hot cup of tea and a bunch of primroses, it was as much as I could do not to draw him down into the bed beside me. But it was not to be – in a year's time maybe, but not yet ! Back at Sorrento, the post had brought me lots of cards and presents. I had gradually been getting my 'bottom drawer' ready and Vivien, Johnnie and Doe always managed to get me something pretty in the underwear line, despite the scarcity. That evening I found Mac studying in the sitting room, looking fed up, so I told her to get changed and come for a walk. We set off in the direction of the Lickey Hills and felt better the minute we hit the countryside, with the crisp Spring air rustling through our hair. We were ravenous by the time we returned, the food in the Sorrento being good, but never enough. Matron must have been aware of the situation, for one of the first things she had told us was that there was always a cauldron of leftovers gently simmering away in the hospital kitchen. However, it was still my birthday and we decided to go to a good little eating-place in King's Heath. I treated Mac to whatever she wanted and I was glad to see that by this time she was her old self again. Back in our room we ate the nut chocolate bar Jack had given me. His box of chocolates could wait until I saw him next.

Eileen's favourite photograph of Jack.

That wasn't long in coming. The following Saturday I was back in King's Heath, this time with Jack, who had arrived late because he had been out on gale-damage repairs. As we relaxed over tea, I presented him with a surprise present for a change, a tough hard-wearing wristlet watch he had had his eye on for a while. In the cool of the evening, we strolled through parks in King's Heath and Canon Hill, arms clasped tightly around one another. He would only take one of the Black Magic chocolates – they were for me, not him !

Dr Cross' Premature Baby Ward

A letter from home, meanwhile, brought the news that Alfred Leyshon, my very dear first love, was missing in action. I felt so sorry, for now he had a little family. At the end of March I was sent to work on one of the Mother and Baby wards, witnessing the sad death of a young mother from post-partum haemorrhage. Jack attended a Quaker Missionary Conference in Selly Oak the following week and I was able to see him again four days later in Kidderminster. The weather was glorious and in the evening we cycled out to see some of his friends living in the country. Late again to bed, it was agony getting up at four o'clock the next morning and we both agreed that, with responsible jobs, we couldn't carry on as we were doing !

On April 19th, my parents, accompanied by Ray and Vera, arrived in Ridgecroft for two weeks' holiday. Muriel (still with the Civil Nursing Reserve but apparently unsettled) and I managed a few days off to greet them and then Cliff joined us, making ten altogether ! We all pitched in and after the evening meal, had a sing-song with Cliff at the piano. In looks he reminded me of Fred Astaire and was an accomplished pianist, able to play anything from classical to jazz. The next day, my family visited my father's brother at Belbroughton, the first time I had seen Uncle Mark for years !

In Baxter Church on Easter Sunday, Jack was to hear the terrible news that Stan Chadwick, son of one of the deacons and a great friend of all the young people, had been taken prisoner by the Japanese. Then Jack's grandmother died suddenly of a stroke. While taking Mrs Davies to the house, Jack and Cliff took the opportunity to look at my General Hospital – without its dome !

On the morning of May 18th, I was called to assist with a tragic case in which the poor mother had gone into labour during the thirty-sixth week of pregnancy. We all knew the baby was dead and when it was delivered, was found to have Spina Bifida. It was the couple's first baby and they were overwrought. Very soon after, I had my next case, a perfectly normal and healthy delivery. While my training continued, hard graft but absorbing, I began to feel sorry for Jack, who was becoming more and more frustrated. He was nearing his twenty-fourth birthday and in his seventh year of training with the Post Office Engineering Department. The Friends Service Council had been in touch with us and Jack was convinced that they were taking his convictions seriously, eager to help him find work overseas. However, another interview with Miss Backhouse was fairly fruitless, with her advising us to wait and go out with the London Missionary Society. She felt we were more in the 'Congregationalist' mould. I could tell that Jack was demoralised, depressed even, and I was glad when he and Cliff decided to cycle down to Croesffyrdd for a week's break in the calm of the Welsh hills.

In Sorrento, I had now been moved to Dr Cross' Premature Baby Ward. The Sister-in-Charge was a real gem, a large, bonny woman with a big heart. She told me that her treatment for 'prems' was love, and in her arms would 'love' them into sucking from a pipette, 'love' them to grow ! Most of the time, of course, they were in incubators, but I am certain that the little sessions in her tender arms went a long way to help them survive. I can see her now, sitting in a low chair, crooning and chatting softly to the tiny scrap of humanity lying in her ample lap. After a week on day duty I went onto nights, where I witnessed the birth of triplets, so tiny that we wondered whether they would make it. But

Mac and Eileen at the Sorrento.

live they did, and I was there on the day that their proud parents took them home, all three dressed in identical bright green outfits !

The week away did Jack a power of good. He had been threatening to throw in his job, but in calmer mood he could see that in wartime, the consequences could have been very dire indeed. He was prepared to press on, relying upon God to show him the next step. Pressure of work meant that I couldn't see him for his birthday, but at the end of June I was able to go camping with him and his boys' club again. The cart was in Bewdley, already packed for the short journey to Button Oak. Muriel, Gwen and a few other friends from the church joined us on the Saturday for the communal feast of sausage, beans and bread ! On the return journey the next day, the boys started to run with the much lighter cart. Full of high spirits, they failed to see the proverbial chicken trying to cross the road, and ran it over. Jack sought out the farmer to apologise but it couldn't dampen what had been a wonderful couple of days.

Meanwhile, application forms for second-part Midwifery had arrived from Heathfield Road Maternity Hospital in Handsworth. It wouldn't be long before I was provisionally offered a place. Ronnie had written, using an air-graph (the first type of air-mail) which had only taken four days from Egypt ! He was hoping for some leave during the early part of 1944, but with things so uncertain, we had considered asking Cliff to be our best man. It suddenly dawned on us that we could truly begin to plan for our wedding day ! Jack and I intended to camp again in the Giedd in July, though my parents had warned us that it might not be possible. A film called *The Silent Village*, about the Nazi massacre in Lidici, Czechoslovakia, was currently being shot there. In the event, we were able to go, though it was noticeable that the farmers were far more wary of visitors.

I spent the first weekend of my holiday visiting Vivien in Bristol, where we chatted like magpies. She recommended a little boarding house in Little Haven, Pembrokeshire, as a possibility for our honeymoon. If we did write to Mrs Owen-Davies we must be sure to mention Miss Vivien Armstrong's name !

Ruth joined us on the Saturday and having agreed to be my chief bridesmaid, we were able to discuss the pattern of her dress. I would send her the material and she would do the sewing. Her missionary course in Cambridge was going well and she would be returning to Kenya, to work in the village in which she had been brought up.

Wedding preparations !

When I arrived home, my parents told me that they had just had a visit from Cliff, who was evidently taking his best man duties seriously ! We all loved this slight, clever man, who had been a mentor and trusted friend to Jack for many years. Jack wasn't due home for another three days, so mammy and I busied ourselves working out a pattern for all four bridesmaid dresses. I had seen some pretty sateen lining in a shop in Birmingham and some dotted net in one of the arcades. My mother agreed that the netting would not only cover up the inexpensive sateen, but enhance it. We worked out a very simple, basic pattern, consisting of a high-waisted, darted square-necked bodice with puffed sleeves and wreathed skirts. After the cutting out, we could use what was left to make tiny 'Juliet' caps. If I sent my mother the material, I could leave the rest in her capable hands. I was pleased that plans for the wedding, which we hoped would be in March 1944, seemed to be going like clockwork.

Jack and I spent the weekend doing the rounds in the pouring rain ! The clouds were still low on the Monday when we set off for the Giedd valley, but it had stopped raining. The river was heavily swollen and we had to dispense with our shoes and socks for a couple of miles because even the path was waterlogged. It did not auger well, but on we pressed, choosing a high, well-drained spot on a slight slope to pitch tent. Presently, we were able to relax with a glorious mug of cocoa before reluctantly parting to our own tents. We slept on and on the next morning, Jack having had to get up during the night to deal with some nosey cows, intent on pushing our tents over ! We had a lazy day, enjoying one another's company in the peace of the valley. Then, in the afternoon, to our surprise and delight, who should turn up but mammy and daddy with Ray and Vera ! With their substantial knowledge of the area, they had been able to skirt the muddy path and knew that the river would recede as quickly as it had risen. The girls were in their element up there, as they tucked into the jam sandwiches we rustled up for them. My parents had been worried about us because of the weather, but were soon reassured that we were well-prepared for any eventuality. The love between my parents and the two girls was beautiful to behold as they made their way homeward down the hill.

The next day, Jack set out in the drizzle to look for some dry timber for the fire, while I *cwtshed* up with my Midwifery text book. On his return he decided

Jack in his hiking gear!

to test me, with hilarious results. His pronunciation of some of the medical terms was so comical that I fell about laughing ! My examination was interrupted by the appearance of the sun and Jack quickly made hay, fixing up a line to hang out our blankets and sleeping bags. Our hopes were dashed by an onslaught of the most atrocious weather we had ever experienced. There was nothing for it but to pack up, and as we began our retreat, we realised that the river was a dangerous torrent. Carrying a kitbag between us, we looked for an alternative route and followed a very uneven ridge for some time. We eventually came upon some workmen who had been building a new road, sheltering in their hut. Goodness knows what they thought when Jack and I suddenly appeared, looking like two exhausted drowned rats ! Kind men that they were, they relieved us of our load and accompanied us down to Cwmgiedd, where we were able to use the new bus service to Ystradgynlais. Before long, another bus was taking us into Glanrhyd and home, where my darling mother took over ! After a hot bath, we gratefully partook of a fresh pot of tea, sitting around the Croes-ffyrdd fire that burnt brightly summer or winter. Contrarily, the sun came out at about tea-time, hot enough to hang out all the camping gear on my mother's long garden line, which was propped in the middle for maximum effect.

Jack and I took the kiddies to Swansea the next day, buying a couple of presents in the market, before playing on the sands in the warm sun. We had hoped to visit the Mumbles on our last day, but Vera seemed to be coming down with a cold. Instead, we made our usual pilgrimage to the two signal boxes. Then we sunbathed at the back of the house, from where we could see our beloved hills – part of the Darren on the left and most of Alltygrug on the right. It didn't matter what we did when we were home, we were always happy. Such was the atmosphere !

We had to return the next day, Sunday, this time able to travel as far as Kidderminster together. I was on duty the following day, which was also the day when our set would be taking the written exam. When I read through Matron's questions, I had to stifle a gasp of surprise, for some were the very ones that Jack had stumblingly asked me in our little tent in the Giedd ! Remembering our laughter made it easy to recall the answers and I started to write furiously. At the end of the week, on July 23rd, we had our Oral exam which we knew would be a lot harder. Mac and I were pleased and relieved when we found we had passed. Our next big hurdle would be the State Finals in August .

Now that I knew the exact yardage I would need, I decided to spend the following week scouring Birmingham for wedding material. I made first for the shop in which I had seen the sky blue sateen, relieved to find that there was sufficient. When I went to the arcade for the dotted net, I began to wonder if my luck was beginning to run out. There was no sign of it and in a bit of a fluster, I approached the assistant. They had replaced the remaining bale with something else, as almost all of the material had been sold. How many yards was I looking for ? She wasn't very hopeful, but would bring it in from the back of the shop and measure it on the counter. I looked on, heart in mouth, as she rolled it out yard by yard. I could hardly believe it – there was just enough, not an inch to spare ! I happily returned to the Sorrento where I carefully packed it and sent it home to my mother. I determined to look for material for my own dress as soon as I could.

On the Bank Holiday Monday, Jack and Cliff had arranged to take myself, Mr and Mrs Davies and Muriel for a ride on the River Severn. In perfect weather we set off in two boats from Bewdley and I was able to catch up on all the news. Muriel had just started her training in Dudley Road General Hospital and Jack would be travelling down to the Vale of Evesham the next day, to start relief work. That Tuesday evening he phoned me, saying that he had found good 'digs' but was slightly puzzled because he was there to work as an extra, not as a relief. We arranged to meet the following evening in Birmingham and while I waited for him at the stop where the long-distance buses came in, I tried to do a bit of studying from a text book. Bus after bus arrived, all jam-packed, but no sign of Jack. I returned to the hospital to find a message waiting for me. So many people had been travelling that it had been impossible to get on a bus that evening. I knew that there would be a letter from him soon !

On August 10th, Mac and I attended interviews at Heathfield Road Hospital and were accepted for Second-Part Midwifery training. Next day, at Dudley Road General, we sat our written State examination and a week later, our practical, at Loveday Street Hospital. On Monday, 24th August, Matron sent for us individually to give us our results and we were surprised how pleasant she was. We had all been under the impression that she thought we were a dreadful set of nurses ! Mac and I were among the eight out of our ten who had passed and with only five days to get ready for Heathfield Road, neither of us bothered to go home.

That week, Jack travelled up after work and though we only had less than an hour together, I could tell that he was unhappy. He was contemplating taking the drastic step of leaving the Post Office and wanted me to know that he would be guided by his conscience. He couldn't go into detail, not even with me, but it didn't take much to work out that the nature of the work in that idyllic spot in Evesham was troubling him. He was worried about the financial implications, but surely he must know that whatever happened, I would remain at his side ? Taking his dear face into my hands, I made him promise to marry me at the end of my training. March 25th, 1944, had been decided on and March 25th it would be ! We clung together, then, as though we would never let one another go. All was well again and we parted feeling lighter in spirit.

Chapter Twenty-One

HEATHFIELD ROAD

Jack's pacifist stance

When Mac and I reported to the Matron of Heathfield Road Maternity Hospital to start the second part of our Midwifery training on September 5th, 1943, I knew that this was going to be the last lap. We would work first on the wards and annexe of the hospital, before going on to district. We continued delivering babies, of course, but with far less supervision, while our lectures at Birmingham University were much more advanced. The statistics and financial work often caused me real grief, though the sessions in the Child Welfare Clinics were a joy!

In October, Mac and I started night duty together in Bourne House (the annexe) and immediately took the opportunity to go into Birmingham to look for wedding rings. We had been given the name of a genuine jeweller who had second-hand rings among his stock, and soon found two of the 22ct gold variety that took our fancy. At eight guineas each, they were good value and having found everything in Evesham beyond his pocket, Jack was pleased with it. When we met up in Kidderminster, he was able to put me more in the picture regarding his work. When he first realised the nature of his new work, he had rung the Chief Inspector who had sent him there, but had been unable to speak to him. He then decided to write and had eventually been given an appointment. In the meantime, he had been helped by his minister at Baxter Church to pen another letter to the Tribunal Body. By servicing military telephone lines he had been made to take part in war organisation and felt that his conscience, therefore, had been violated. Jack was now convinced his dismissal was imminent, but his Inspector's attitude had been conciliatory. He tried to persuade him to stay, telling him that he had all but finished his seven year apprenticeship, paid for by the government. In his view, Jack was one of their best workers, having passed every examination with flying colours and didn't deserve to be dismissed. He could soon be in a well-paid, responsible post, with a good pension at the end of it. If Jack persisted in leaving, then he would allow him to 'resign', but if he stayed, Jack could be sent somewhere to the heart of the country, adding ironically 'somewhere like Evesham'!

However, once Jack had made the break and sent off his letter of resignation, he felt much more settled. Our parents, too, had accepted his stand and assured us of their total support . His last day with the Post Office was Friday, October 22nd, when he checked in his tools to his colleague Mr Wade, before driving the van back to Evesham. By the time I caught up with him the next day, he had already been out picking chestnuts with friends from the church and looked fine. He promptly whisked me off to the pictures to see a film called *Man in Grey*. The next day, we attended morning service before I returned for night duty at Bourne House.

It wasn't long before our Quaker friends sent us application forms for 'The Friends War Relief Service' and we were meeting David Cadbury and Leonard Bloomfield in Birmingham. In early November, Jack was interviewed at Friends House in London, and having found out what time his train was due back in Birmingham, I asked Sister for the evening off. When she heard that I would be meeting my young man for twenty minutes before he got his connection, she offered me two days' leave ! As the London train drew in, I could see Jack scanning the station and the look of relief on his face when he saw me made me realise what a strain he was under. He admitted to feeling depressed about the future and I felt for him, trying to imagine how I would react in his place. Deep down, we had known that such a situation might arise. A chat over a cup of tea on the platform bucked him up a little and when he realised that I could go home with him, he was over the moon !

He started work with the Friends Relief Service in London on Monday, 21st November. I spent the previous night unable to sleep, wondering what lay in store for him and hoping that he'd have a warm, comfortable bed. On the Thursday a letter arrived. The nurse who delivered it knew how much it meant to me and made me chase her for it, in between the cots ! As I tore it open, my eyes fell upon a sentence saying how kind and helpful everyone was. I might have known – all the Quaker folk we had met had been the same.

The next week we were able to see each other briefly, after he appeared in front of another Tribunal in Kidderminster, accompanied by Rev. Hooper. Jack felt that he'd been given a fair hearing, and smiled wryly as he told me that he'd been given 'exemption as long as he remained in social work'. Waiting for the London train over a cup of tea, I noticed that he had a cough and begged him to see to it. The weather was very, very cold.

It was not long after this that, while walking down Heathfield Road in uniform, I happened to pass the very shop in which I had worked on the cash register during the Christmas of 1936 – the shop owned by Mrs Hands' brother. As I approached it, he materialised at the door and gave a start of recognition ! Still full of antipathy towards anyone or anything to do with the woman, I simply went on my way, but it upset me for the rest of the day.

271

District work

At the beginning of December, Mac and I were sent to Wrethan Road, Handsworth, in the district of Hockley to finish our Midwifery training. In a large dwelling house, similar to many others in the area, we were to embark on the most challenging work of all, out on district. Sister Bradley, despite an obvious chest condition, was kind and helpful. A former colleague from Sorrento, Nurse John, was already installed there and it was she who would deal with any immediate cases, leaving us with the rest of that first day off. Mac rushed off to see Jock, while I decided to go looking for wedding dress material. I was grateful for the wrap-over winter coat I had bought in Bristol when on good money (we were once again on little more than 'probationer' wages) but even that could not deal with the Birmingham winter. I could not warm up and as the afternoon went by, began to feel shivery and decided to give up my mission. Back in Wrethan Road, I somehow finished the rest of my unpacking in the attic room Mac and I were sharing – the second reminder of the dreadful Mrs Hands in recent weeks ! That night, we nearly froze, in the end jumping into the same bed. I felt guilty because I spent the night sneezing but Mac was dead to the world, not even the 'call' phone at half-past five able to wake her !

A few hours later, with my head and body aching wretchedly, Sister Bradley packed me off to bed. I began to feel more and more miserable as my teeth chattered beneath the blankets, thinking how much I hated the cold, especially the cold that Birmingham could inflict on you. However was I going to be able to face it, especially out on district in the middle of the night ? The whole situation began to take on exaggerated proportions and I felt incapable of going on. Although I did feel a little better by evening, kind Sister Bradley suggested that I take my December and January weekend time off together and spend a week at home. Work would be 'slack' for a while and Nurse John was more than capable of dealing with any emergency. I sent a telegram home and wrote to Jack.

Finding myself home was almost unbelievable. On the Sunday I stayed in bed all day and slept – oh, how I slept – and by Monday morning felt fine. The next day, my mother and I tackled the bridesmaids dresses for Ray and Vera. I brought my parents up to date with Jack's news, though I was unable to discuss his 'hush-hush' work at Evesham, which I suspected involved the development of advanced aircraft technology. Jack's first letter to us all was cheerful. He was now an Orderly in the local hospital, something that interested my father, who had reason to think highly of the FAU (Friends Ambulance Unit) in the First World War.

While I returned to Birmingham in a much better condition, both physically and mentally, I found Miss Bradley very poorly with bronchitic asthma. Mac and I didn't mind doing the ante-natal and post-natal visits on our own, for we loved those rounds. Most of the families were very poor and you could never tell from the outside what condition you'd find the house in. The houses in the back-to-back streets were the most difficult to find, little streets teeming with children of all ages and dogs and cats of every shape and colour ! I couldn't help thinking about my father who could never pass a person in distress without giving them a penny or two. He would have ended up as poor as a church mouse had he done the rounds with us !

It remained quiet on the baby front for the next few days and Miss Bradley was soon back with us. She lent me her bike until such time that Cliff could put mine on the train at Kidderminster. I found some lovely material for my dress, just over three yards of it and again the end of the roll, but it was very wide. It was a creamy-white silk crêpe with a dainty all-over silk flower pattern and both Miss Bradley and Nurse John gave their approval. Then, about the middle of the month, things started getting busy. My first delivery was that of a darling little girl, 'Peccanini', who would be dearly loved by her parents and three siblings. The father was working when the baby arrived but the eldest boy, fifteen years old, turned up trumps. The mother had a retained placenta after the birth and after the given time, I sent the boy for the local doctor. He was out on a call, but the lad knew of an Indian doctor and returned with him in no time at all. Mother and baby were taken to Dudley Road Hospital, leaving the depend-able son to look after his younger brother and sister until their father arrived. That evening, I rang the hospital to find that all was well and Miss Bradley and I could breathe a sigh of relief !

The next morning, both Mac and I delivered babies with no complications. At 'home', letters from the Ministry of Labour were waiting for us, informing us that on qualification we would be expected to do a year's Midwifery nursing. Mac had something to say about that. After she and Jock had got married, the only Midwifery nursing she intended to do was her own ! Two months later I was at their wedding. I had never been in a Roman Catholic church, let alone attended a Nuptial Mass but despite having to stand during the entire service, I found it very moving. Mac looked radiant and I felt sure that they would be very happy.

Mac and I worked over the festive season, though we were allowed visitors when not out delivering babies. I had a day off just before Christmas and took the opportunity to go down to Kidderminster. I couldn't wait to feel Jack's arms around me again. Despite the London fogs, a bout of tonsillitis and a traumatic change in circumstances, he looked very fit. He couldn't speak too highly of his new workmates, whose company he found stimulating and he was enjoying communal life. People from all denominations were working there, including one from Swansea and another from Carmarthen. When we parted, I felt much happier about him.

We had no Christmas babies, but were kept busy with rounds, clinics and lectures. In the New Year, I attended an interview with Jack at the Friends War Service Council. Miss Bradley, interested in Jack's stance, gave me the whole weekend off and offered to look after my new arrivals herself. I caught the London train on Friday evening, January 14th. The next afternoon saw Jack and I cuddled in the warmth of a cinema watching *Snow White and the Seven Dwarfs* ! Afterwards, we visited Mr and Mrs Petche in Southall, before being taken for an evening meal by another of his friends. A full Sunday included morning and evening services, a concert and a swirling black fog, the like of which I had not seen since 1940 in Bristol. The interview took place on the Monday morning at Gordon House and was friendly and relaxed. I told them that although I was under an obligation to continue nursing, I wanted to take an active part in the work that Jack (or 'John' as they fetchingly referred to him) was doing. Within a week, Jack was interviewed again and subsequently asked to move to Bournemouth to work with a team dealing with 'unbilletable evacuees'. They wanted to know if I would like to join him there and Miss Bradley advised me to write immediately to the Matron of the Royal Victoria and West Hants Hospital in Boscombe. She would give me a reference. On the last day of January 1944, Jack moved down to Bournemouth. In seven weeks we would be getting married !

Meanwhile, I was called out to deliver twins to a young girl, not long married. She and her husband lived in one very tiny room, which she kept spotless, in the Hockley down-town area. I had seen a lot of her during her pregnancy and knew how difficult it was going to be for them all, in such a small space. The twins were born without any trouble within twenty minutes of one another and all three were moved to the Premature Baby Unit at Sorrento for a couple of weeks. In the meantime, Miss Bradley, true to her word, had found them a decent place to come back to.

Ronnie had mentioned in his Christmas letter that he might be able to get home in time for the wedding. One night I had a lovely dream about him, which recurred the following night and again on the third night, when I awoke with a shiver running down my spine. I mentioned the dreams to everyone at breakfast, as I had done the previous morning, then set out on my rounds. At dinner time Mac and I arrived back about the same time and met Miss Bradley on the doorstep. She beckoned Mac forward, telling me to stay where I was, and as they whispered conspiratorially, my Irish friend began to laugh heartily. Miss Bradley remained deadly serious, however, calling me in and announcing that she thought I might be 'psychic'. Smiling, treating her rather as I would a child, I asked how she had suddenly come to such a conclusion.

"Because," she said, "your brother is in Birmingham waiting to see you before he catches the South Wales train !" In a trice I was in my warm mufti coat, flying off to meet Ronnie. We had so little time and so much to tell each other. He hadn't changed at all and my thoughts immediately went to my parents and their joy at seeing him again !

During February, I was called out to a mother whose regular midwife was not available. I realised that the labour was not progressing as it should and that the baby was showing signs of distress, so I quickly scrubbed up. I discovered that the umbilical cord was tight around the baby's neck and must be cut as quickly as possible. Fortunately a neighbour was there, and she helped me sterilise the two clamping forceps and a pair of scissors. Clamping off the cord, I promptly snipped through it, causing one clamp to fly the length of the room. Released from its snake-like captor, the baby advanced normally and was born a little bit blue, but crying lustily. Never had I been so relieved to hear a baby cry, never had I seen such a long umbilical cord. Medical aid had to be sought to check whether there was any damage but the doctor pronounced him very healthy indeed ! Tea with plenty of sugar was now the order of the day and as we supped, I thanked that little neighbour for her invaluable help.

My last delivery, that of a bonny baby boy, took place on St. David's Day, and leaving mother and infant in Miss Bradley's tender care, I prepared to leave. Thanks to Miss Bradley, who had arranged for me to take my Final exams in Bristol, I was able to go straight home and plan for the wedding. The exams came and went, Vivien meeting me on both occasions and driving me to Southmead Hospital. Then she insisted on feeding me up before giving me a lift back to Temple Meads. It was a hectic time and I was grateful to have such lovely friends.

Chapter Twenty-Two

OUR SACRED VOWS

Arrangements for the wedding were well in hand. Jack had been home to see to all the legal details, the one hitch being that the only time the Registrar could fit us in was nine o'clock in the morning ! Some of our friends would be coming from afar, but I knew people would rally round. My parents had seen to everything else, helped for the past six weeks by Ronnie. He was a tower of strength to me, as indeed Cliff was to Jack. In less than two weeks, Eunice (my friend Muriel's sister), would have to cut out and sew my dress at home. A wonderful seamstress, only she would be able to do it in such a short time, working marvels with the small amount of material. She lent me her wedding veil, a truly beautiful one with a wide edging of embroidery. I planned to fix it very simply with a creamy white magnolia on either side of my head. I noticed that Eunice was looking a little 'seedy'. She smiled and told me that she was pregnant with their first child.

On Thursday, 23rd March 1944, two days before the big day, Jack gave me a beautiful necklace of tiny pearls. In the evening, Jack, Ronnie, Cliff, Will Morgan and Euryl were invited up to Eunice and Muriel's house for a meal and sing-song, while mammy and I put everything ready for the wedding. Muriel (Jack's sister) and Ruth arrived the next day, complete with their beautiful dresses and Juliet caps, again created from the minimum of material ! I had already seen Ray and Vera's dresses and had made floral coronets for them out of corded ribbon I had found in Kidderminster market. Ordinary satin ribbon had long disappeared from the stores. Muriel and Ruth were staying with us in Croesffyrdd, Jack and Cliff with Mr and Mrs Mathias.

Eunice and Muriel.

276

Left to himself, Jack would have turned up in sports jacket and corduroy trews but Mr Matthias had been a butler in his pre-railway days and I knew that he and Cliff would make sure that my husband-to-be would be turned out smartly.

Friday's post brought the results of my Final State Midwifery Examinations – I had passed ! No time for congratulations though, for guests were arriving all day, into the night and early on Saturday morning. Jack, Cliff and Ronnie met them and took them to their various hosts.

The next day I was able to see my four bridesmaids together in their outfits for the first time. How pretty they looked ! I stayed in my dressing gown until their bouquets arrived, my parents having ordered them from Maesydderwen Nursery, just around the corner. Used to austerity in everything for so many years, they took my breath away, made up as they were with a delicate mixture of fragrant Spring flowers, including different shades of freesias. Minutes later came mine, magnolias of every delicate shade imaginable, standing out magnificently against their deep green leaves. All were freshly cut, made up and held together cleverly by a variety of pale-coloured ribbons which hung down in cascades at the front. The two white magnolias to keep my veil in place completed the picture. My heart was beating fast !

There were so many neighbours outside the house that the taxi couldn't get anywhere near. Even out in the road, it seemed that the whole of the village had turned out. My mother, Ray, Vera, Ruth and Muriel made the first trip and it soon returned to pick up my father and me. He was such a darling, concerned for my every move. As I was about to enter the taxi, a woman from the crowd took my face in her hands and kissed me, wishing me every happiness. Unfor-

After the ceremony. From left to right: Kenny Cornelius, Muriel, Mr Davies, Rev. Melville Philips, Mrs Davies, Ray, Cliff, Jack and Eileen with Ronnie standing behind, Mammy, Daddy, Vera and Ruth.

Married at last !

tunately, she dislodged one of the flowers holding my veil ! I tried to remedy it, but my hands were shaking too much.

As daddy took me up the slope into Ystalyfera Congregational Church, I could hear the strains of *I Know That My Redeemer Liveth*, the music Jack and I had chosen, gently floating out into the crisp, morning air. Ronnie was at the porch with the bridesmaids to greet us, and I asked him to give me a few minutes while Ruth fixed my veil. That done, he gave the organist the sign to begin Mendelssohn's *Wedding March*. Trembling on my father's arm, with my bridesmaids in support, I walked down the aisle of the crowded church. As I approached Jack, Cliff at his side, I was flabbergasted to see that he was wearing tails. I had had no idea ! He looked most elegant and when he turned round to smile at me, our spirits soared. All was well with our Heaven again, only this time it was for good ! 'Thank you Lord, oh thank you !' At last, in front of Rev. Melville Philips and all our family and friends, Jack and I made our sacred vows, one to the other, in the sight of God.

POSTSCRIPT

Jack went on to obtain a combined English and Theological degree, having studied for four years in Bristol University and Western College, the Congregational Theological College. At the beginning of December 1950, the Rev. John and Eileen Campbell with their two little children, Ruth Myfanwy (born April 4th, 1945) and David John (born 4th April, 1948), sailed for Madagascar to serve as Missionaries with the London Missionary Society.

In the next five years, John and Eileen had three more children, Gwyn Richard (1952), Robin Stuart (1953) and Huw Philip (1955), all born in Fianarantsoa, Madagascar.

Eileen and Jack with Ruth and David.

Eileen and Jack with Gwyn (standing), Huw and Robin.